ULTIMATE SPA

ASIA'S BEST SPAS AND SPA TREATMENTS

by Judy Chapman   photography by Luca Invernizzi Tettoni

PERIPLUS

Published by Periplus Editions, with editorial offices at
130 Joo Seng Road #06-01, Singapore 368357.

Printed in Singapore

The recipes and techniques outlined in this book are
intended for cosmetic and relaxation use only and are
not meant to replace diagnosis and treatment by a
medical practitioner. Before using any of these recipes,
author and publisher recommend consulting a physician. All the recipes have been tested and are considered safe, but since some people have more sensitive
skin than others and since the user's actual recipe
preparation is beyond the control of the author or
publisher, we can accept no liability with regard to the
use of recipes or techniques contained here.

Distributed by:
North America, Latin America and Europe
Tuttle Publishing, 364 Innovation Drive,
North Clarendon, VT 05759-9436 U.S.A.
Tel: 1 (802) 773-8930; Fax: 1 (802) 773-6993
info@tuttlepublishing.com
www.tuttlepublishing.com

Asia Pacific Berkeley Books Pte Ltd, 130 Joo Seng Road
#06-01, Singapore 368357
Tel: (65) 6280-1330; Fax: (65) 6280-6290
inquiries@periplus.com.sg
www.periplus.com

Indonesia PT Java Books Indonesia,
Jl. Rawa Gelam IV No. 9, Jakarta 13930, Indonesia
Tel: 62 (21) 4682 1088; Fax: 62 (21) 461 0206
Email: cs@javabooks.co.id

Page 1 Morning yoga on the beach at Park Hyatt Goa
Resort, India.

Previous page Enjoying the view across the Ayung River
Valley at Kirana Spa in Sayan, Bali.

Right The invigorating barefoot *shiatsu* treatment at
Prana Spa at The Villas, Bali.

Overleaf The Island Spa at Four Seasons Resort
Maldives at Kuda Huraa is located on a private atoll in
the Indian Ocean.

10 09 08 07
8 7 6 5 4 3 2

contents

The Ultimate Spa Experience *Asia's Best Spas*

Asia's Best Spa Treatments *The World is Our Spa*

the ultimate spa
experience

FROM THE SURROUNDING SPLENDOR OF RICE FIELDS AND INDIGENOUS PLANTS TO THE ELEGANCE OF THEIR ARCHITECTURE AND INTERIORS, THE EXQUISITENESS OF THE ASIAN SPA IS UNSURPASSED.

Nature is an integral part of the Asian spa. Imagine bathing in a rock pool on the edge of a riverbank with the sounds of the river rushing by and the cool mountain air caressing your face. Time melts away and the sheer luxury and space makes you feel as if you're the only person on earth.

The spa phenomenon in Asia is so much more than a massage or a scrub—it's a way of life. The daily rituals and ceremonies are all part of the spa experience and are designed to restore your body and soul. Treatment rooms, relaxation spaces and outdoor pavilions are fitted out with handcrafted furnishings and textiles; every bowl, cup and flower is deliberately selected for its visual appeal and significance—don't be surprised to find delicate offerings made for the gods placed outside your treatment room by the spa staff.

"Grace is what separates the Asian spa from any other in the world," says David Haughton of Bagus Jati Wellbeing Resort in Bali. "That, and the staggering variety of treatments on offer."

Where else in the world can you immerse yourself, at the very source, in the treatments, philosophies and wisdom of the Asian ancients that have been refined over centuries? Influences from the Orient can increasingly be seen and felt in all the most beautiful spas around the globe. But only in Asia itself can one experience the real thing first-hand.

Just consider the following options. Trekking through the mountains in Yunnan province in China, renowned for being a center for the finest traditional Chinese physicians, herbal medicines and treatments. Stay in a traditional Tibetan lodge and experience the *tui na* massage in the country of its origin.

Or travel to the Himalayas where you can revitalize your body against a backdrop of majestic mountains, overlooking the birthplace of yoga and the ancient wisdom of ayurvedic medicine. Elsewhere in India, select spas are situated in restored Moghul palaces or in Maharaja–style luxury canvas tents in the wild.

Opposite Spas are places to reflect and restore one's inner balance—the royal spa suite at Four Seasons Bali Jimbaran Bay is alluring, private and peaceful.

The divine Asian foot ritual at the Kirana Spa, Ubud, Bali. Here the Japanese know-how of beauty company Shiseido is combined with celestial surrounds.

Alternatively, take a trip to Northern Thailand where spas resemble Buddhist monasteries and offer treatments that were originally only performed by saffron-robed monks. These have been revived, adapted and reintroduced into tranquil destination spas near Chiang Mai.

Water babies can dive off a boat into the translucent waters of the Maldives and feel what it must have been like to live upon a pristine earth. Afterwards, a traditional Maldivian wooden *dhoni* boat transports you to an island spa for a soothing massage while watching marine life swim by. Observe how the tropical weather provides inspiration for treatments such as the Maldivian Monsoon Ritual where a gentle rain of rosewater rinses you for rejuvenation.

In Indonesia, spas are located in bamboo forests where frangipani gardens, outdoor *balés* (pavilions) and sunken baths strewn with flower petals and fragrant with aromatic oils are the norm. In a similar fashion, spas in Thailand merge indoor and outdoor in an innovative way. Expect a massage on a sarong-clad table in an open-sided *sala* overlooking a shimmering sea. Fresh ingredients are hand blended to make the most of treatments and the approach to service is absolutely divine.

Both India and Sri Lanka offer ayurvedic journeys that can be life transforming. Ayurvedic spas appear more "earthy" than other Asian spas—the treatment rooms are often built out of clay, with wooden slats for massage tables and perhaps a little camping cooker nearby to heat up medicated herbal oils. Drying herbs hang nearby, ready to be picked and placed inside one of the intriguing-looking steam boxes. Plants and flowers are close at hand for therapists to cast into copper bowls to bathe your feet. Choose from a seven- to 28-day package monitored by therapists, doctors and yoga teachers. Holistic treatments merge with yoga, meditation and herbal therapy to bring the guest back to balance.

Modern Asian cities like Singapore are steaming with spa potential. Interesting day spas are perfect for a self-indulgent treat, and, for the more adventurous, traditional Chinese healers and herbalists practice their ancient arts in small shophouses and medical centers.

New spa concepts are born in Asia daily. Here, spas are so much more than treatments—perhaps this is why people are intuitively drawn to the East. Certainly the influences from this region can be seen and felt at spas all over the globe.

The quality of care and service is legendary. Thailand is renowned for a people who have elevated grace to an art form, so expect to be greeted with a prayer-like bow before treatments. Many therapists in Malaysia and Indonesia come from a lineage of healers: channeling thousands of years of knowledge, they are renowned for a strong sense of community and this energy transports effortlessly into the spa environment. It is the goodness that flows from the therapist's hands that matters. Caring is in their blood.

This nurturing feeling distinguishes spas in Asia from others elsewhere in the world. It is also revealed in the way that treatments are shaped. An example is the difference in heat therapies. In the West,

Opposite This Tibetan *thangka* painting is one of a set of 79 illustrations of the Tibetan medical system demonstrating the diagnosis, treatments and cure of various ailments.

Below Yoga is originally from India but is now offered in almost all spas throughout Asia—including Martha Tilaar Eastern Rejuvenating Center.

sauna and steam are the usual healing via heat practices. In Asia, there are herbal poultices, hot packs, warm wraps and even reiki, all of which are performed through the warmth of a therapist's hands.

The feeling is far more intimate. Personal contact is one of the consoling ways towards healing—and this is emphasised in Asian spas. In cultures like Bali and India ,for example, bathing and anointing the body with oils and giving massages to others or self are regular daily rituals. These centuries-old practices continue in today's spas.

A life force flows throughout Asia that is so alive that once you've had a taste of it you will be ravenous for more. It permeates into the Asian spa in many ways. Be it the deep resonating sounds of a Tibetan bell, the colors that shimmer from crystals and stones or the ingredients used in herbal teas, medicines or treatments—all is exotic, all so appealing.

Another reason to travel to the East is that there are a handful of spas and wellness destinations that are easier on the pocket. Unlike in the West, spas here cater to all budgets and styles. In Bali and Thailand, for example, a number of affordable retreat destinations with excellent reputations offer detox, fasting, yoga and spa therapy programs. Observe where the locals go . . . and follow.

As there is beauty in diversity, Asian spa menus are a melting pot of enticing treatments and therapies. Because the countries that gave birth to ayurveda, traditional Chinese medicine (TCM) and the healing systems of Malaysia and the Philippines are virtually neighbors, it isn't uncommon to find spa menus that combine a number of different influences.

The Spa Village in Kuala Lumpur honors Malay, Indonesian and Chinese cultures with treatments that combine unusual ingredients like warmed herbal eggs with jade rollers and bamboo stick tapping. Their resident TCM doctor is also a *tui na* massage specialist. Not far away, the sister property at the Spa Village on Pangkor Laut offers traditional Malay and Chinese therapies—and also Indian ones. There can be few places in the world where a yoga and *tai chi* teacher is also a physician and therapist.

While there are definite differences between spas in Europe and the US and those in Asia, there are also similarities. Certainly the word "spa" came from the original European town where people went to take the waters or bathe for health, but many Eastern cultures have their own wellness through water traditions too. Japan, Taiwan and Korea are just a few of the countries where hot spring bathing is celebrated on a regular basis. And, today, many Asian spa operators are offering guests the finest in both Eastern and Western therapies. A new breed or hybrid is being born.

A beautiful example is the Ayurvedic Ceremony ritual at the spa at the Mandarin Oriental in Chiang Mai. Here, guests are given an ayurvedic *ubtan* scrub while they lie on a warm marble slab inspired by the traditional *hamam* or Turkish bath found in Eastern Europe. Another example is at the Ritz-Carlton in Bali where you can bathe with friends in the French inspired thalassotherapy pool and follow a session here with a Balinese massage or hot sand pouch treatment and a Japanese *shiatsu* massage.

The graceful architecture and interiors of Asian spas also give them great beauty and individuality. When you enter Kirana spa in Bali, for example, it's like walking through a temple of living spirit. There is a sense that something special is about to transpire. It is as if the creators have succeeded in capturing the quintessential soul of Bali within the spa's walled gardens.

Other creations have a distinctly royal aura. From India to Indonesia and China, ancient temples, monasteries and palaces provide the template for contemporary spas. Ingo R. Schweder, group director of spa for the Mandarin Oriental hotel group, explains why he seeks spiritually influenced locations for unique spa developments: "There is an energy that is manifested where prayers and worshiping have been practiced and when you walk through ancient sites such as those in Angkor and India, you can feel sacredness emanating from the grounds—devotion, friendship, love and spirituality. It makes good sense to create spas upon them." Special things happen in sacred spaces. There is a rich energy to tap into—and spas in ancient healing places vibrate with mystery and sensuality.

Asian spas are also blessed with the luxury of space. Treatment rooms are often enormous luxury suites with private steam rooms, saunas, changing areas and relaxation spaces with outdoor baths and tropical showers. Visualize a holiday where your villa accommodation includes a private spa and gymnasium—and you get an inkling of the potential of the rituals on offer.

But before you sink into the bath and disappear into bliss, remember that the Asian spa is not only about grandeur. Beneath the aesthetics, there is much more to uncover—and this is what makes these pockets of paradise so appealing. Treatments are far more than mere pampering and pots of dripping oil. Whatever their derivation, they help balance the senses and work deeply to restore equilibrium. Their aim is to stimulate the body's own natural healing system. In the same way that modern medicine is integrating Asian systems like acupuncture into its practices, the Asian spa movement is introducing other traditional therapies to the modern world.

What resonates with many is that the philosophy behind Asia's medical systems is based on the mind-body connection. Guests find it reassuring to be diagnosed and given treatments by qualified practioners and practice yoga and *tai chi* with those who understand that the mind and body are one. In fact, all Asian treatments advocate that it is only when the entire mind, body and soul are rested that true healing can begin.

As the marriage between traditional, allopathic and alternative medicine deepens and health becomes the new wealth, the world is looking towards Asia for knowledge. The Asian spa is part of this global movement that is encouraging all of us to value not only our earth's natural elements, but also our own inner glory. Through the treatments of the East we learn to trust our body's inner wisdom. No longer do we need to put our health and wellbeing in the power of a select few. The current renaissance of Asia's spas is intended for all.

The spas and treatments celebrated in the following pages have been selected for their individual atmosphere as well as for their variety. Each one is unique. Through these pages, discover what treatments and places appeal to you most—there is a perfect spa experience waiting for everyone. Whatever your choice, the simple joy of bathing outdoors in a petal-strewn bath with fragrant tropical air filling your being will remind you there is still so much beauty in the world. It isn't hard then to realize that it is our earth, in its entirety, that is the ultimate spa.

asia's best spas

Previous page The experience of a dramatic tropical sunset in an exquisite luxury setting accompanied by tea light candles provides the experience of a lifetime at the Anantara Spa in Hua Hin in Thailand.

Left and below Bagus Jati focuses on the natural in both therapies and architecture: Galangal, turmeric root, lemongrass, cinnamon and vanilla seedpods are just some of the local ingredients that are handpicked and ground for preparations here. The resort's hand-hewn ochre sandstone jacuzzi filled with warmed spring water is a wonderful spot to take in the exquisite natural beauty of Bali.

Right A therapist prepares the traditional Banana Leaf Body Wrap that utilizes a green pandanus leaf scrub.

SEJATI SPA
AT BAGUS JATI WELLBEING RESORT

TEGALLALANG, UBUD, BALI

Bagus Jati Wellbeing Resort is a small destination spa located in the tropical mountains of Bali, about an hour's drive from Ubud. Its eight luxury spa villas, all featuring a private treatment room and whirlpool, are designed to integrate the spa with the lush natural surroundings.

Bagus Jati (translated literally as "good teakwood" with the meaning in Balinese of "strength of character") was founded to preserve the timeless wisdom of traditional Indonesian and Balinese healing and offer educational programs through adventure tours, jungle or garden walks, and cooking classes. All products used in the spa are based on the healing properties of Indonesian *jamu* and use indigenous ingredients to refresh and rejuvenate. Therapists from surrounding villages are trained to guide guests on a journey that may well include ayurveda, acupuncture, hydrotherapy, life enhancement and detoxification programs. Throughout the year a variety of retreats is offered to give guests an opportunity to reflect and transform.

Innovative spa rituals merge Vichy rain showers with pure volcanic mud from nearby Lombok Island together with mind-soothing ayurvedic *shirodhara* (oil therapy). One of the signature treatments is the three-hour Sejati ("Real Self"), inspired by an ancient Balinese royal court beauty recipe. It was traditionally used to warm the body during the monsoon season or at the first sign of cold, flu, rheumatism or fever. The treatment, which takes place in a room overlooking the jungle, begins with a full body massage to ease you into a lingering state of

calm. You are then immersed in a warm bath of Madura Island rock salt before being cocooned in a herbal conditioning body mask of aromatic tropical spices like ginger and cloves, ground together with brown rice, all enclosed by an outer banana leaf body wrap. A soothing scalp and face massage completes this journey, bringing you into a state of blissful contentment.

Other treatments include traditional Balinese village massage and the Jati Alami, a nutritious body polish and cell renewal treatment combined with acupressure massage. Ground indigenous spices from around the archipelago, including sandalwood, turmeric and rice, are used for skin exfoliation. The finale is a protein-rich papaya and yoghurt body mask and a flower and milk bath. Bliss—or as expressed in Balinese—*kebahagiaan*.

Bagus Jati is a recommended destination for those who wish to experience natural surroundings, bathe under a waterfall in a pristine spring water gorge, give nutrition to the body via a high protein diet and organic juices with fresh ingredients hand-picked from the nearby garden—and then return in the evenings to a reassuring luxury villa. You can rest knowing that you have the space and time to be intimate with lover, friends and self.

Above Bagus Jati is the ultimate spiritual retreat offering total privacy and quiet moments with oneself.

Below A small selection of the many natural herbal products used at Bagus Jati, most of which are grown on the premises.

Opposite top and bottom Nature is all encompassing at Bagus Jati: A natural spring-fed pool is close to a holy waterfall and the yoga and meditation pavilion is set in a bamboo grove.

MANDARA SPA
AT ALILA UBUD

MELINGGIH, UBUD, BALI

Something mysterious happens when you spend time in the Balinese village of Ubud. With ceremonies and temples, leisurely cafés and art galleries, emerald-colored rice fields and dance and music performances to enjoy, life here appears to be one big celebration. Once you've tuned into the essence of this place, you'll probably return, as, for many, Ubud becomes a second home.

The Alila Ubud is perhaps best known for its dramatic infinity pool that is one of the most photographed resort pools in the world and an inspiration for many others. This luxury 56-room and 8-villa resort is positioned high up on a ridge with views of lush green river valleys leading to the sacred river Ayung below. It's also home to the very first Mandara Spa that remains one of the most exquisite.

Who can forget the classic image of the girl in the frangipani flower bath that has defined the image of the Asian spa for many years now? Mandara Spas are known in the region for their appreciation of Asian traditions. Even the name has Asian origins: derived from the Sanskrit word that variously refers to a sacred mountain from a Balinese legend about eternal youth, a chain of pearls, and one of the five Hindu trees of paradise—it embraces the company's vision for health and relaxation.

A morning offering welcomes you as you enter the spa. Made from banana leaves and filled with rice, sweet cakes and flowers, these are placed in temples and shrines in the early mornings. Three final splashes of holy water create a positive mood for the day ahead.

Comprising one double spa pavilion and a double spa suite, a Thai massage suite and two single spa suites, the feel here is all about open spaces inviting the natural world of Bali into the treatments. Think outdoor tropical waterfalls and bathtubs set in lotus ponds and inhale the mountainside fragrance of Bali.

Mandara Spas are well known for their classical Asian menu of treatments, for Mandara was one of the companies who pioneered many of the spa "standards" that are now offered all over the world. Start by plunging your two feet in a traditional foot wash before being escorted to your villa for a

choice of Balinese massage, reflexology, Thai massage, Warm Stone Massage, a facial ritual or the ayurvedic oil *shirodhara*. Javanese *lulurs* and Balinese *borehs*, staples on the menu, always delight first time visitors to Bali.

In the early evening, when you are feeling quite rested, that memorable fragrance returns, and may well linger for hours. There is a reason we are called "human beings" not "human doings" and in destinations like the Mandara Spa at Alila Ubud in Bali you're bound to find out why.

Above and opposite top The emerald green infinity pool at the Alila Ubud seems to hover between heaven and earth, giving spectacular views over the Ayung River valley below.

Opposite bottom The classic tropical frangipani flower bath was pioneered by Mandara Spas in Bali.

KIRANA SPA

UBUD, BALI

Kirana Spa is one of the largest day spas in Bali, and one of the island's most exclusive. Its calm and sophistication blend to create an almost ashram-like ambience. The design of the spa subtly echoes a traditional Japanese temple, evoking a spiritual feeling of peace and tranquility. A meandering entry-way is filled with aromatic white jasmine trees, while walk-ways beneath trellises of scarlet passion flowers connect private villas. Humorous artworks and sculptures are placed around the bougainvillea gardens and lily ponds.

Kirana means "light" or "aura" in Sanskrit, and Kirana Spa is an open-air sanctuary situated above Bali's sacred Ayung River. Occupying 5 acres (2 hectares) of lush forest, it is a collaboration between the royal Sukawati family of Ubud and Japanese beauty company Shiseido. There are 15 villas in total (suite, treatment and presidential), all set in a garden filled with a variety of relaxation options. Nine of the villas have their own private plunge pool and herbal mist sauna, while outdoor showers, relaxation arbors and daybeds are the norm.

The philosophy at Kirana is simple and zen-like. There are just four special treatments: Relaxing Body Treatment, Revitalizing Body Treatment, Foot and Leg Treatment and Facial Treatment.

During the preliminary consultation, treatments are chosen to best suit the guest's requirements. "We believe that the flow of *ch'i* or energy keeps us healthy," explains a spokesperson from the Shiseido Institute of Beauty Sciences. "So, all our treatments are focused on keeping the body and mind well balanced so our energy circulates."

Each treatment focuses on *tokumyaku* and *nimyaku*, processes believed to govern the flow of *ch'i* and keep energy circulating. The art of *shoku* (touch) and *atsu* (pressure) is also applied throughout each treatment to help reduce tension or stress held within the body. The combination of these two techniques helps to relieve any stiffness and instils new energy into both the body and mind. In addition, the "art of breath" is taught during treatments. Therapists encourage each guest to return to their own natural rhythm of breathing.

The Relaxing Body Treatment is a meditative rejuvenation experience, where the rhythm of the treatment is synchronized with the rhythm of the guest's respiration. The aim is to bring the guest into a state of sublime relaxation. Another soothing ritual is the Foot and Leg Treatment (see page 139).

Opposite A yoga session in the relaxation pavilion of the Presidential Villa. This is also where one would normally relax after a treatment and sip calming tea.

Above top and left The design of Kirana's private villas draws its inspiration from traditional Balinese art and architecture, while the interior of the female dressing room in the Spa Garden area uses local woods and white river pebbles imported from Java for vernacular effect.

Above This amenities box is one example of the attention to detail that makes the Kirana experience so unique.

Opposite top and bottom The lower pool in the Spa Garden overlooks the Ayung River, while the Villa Suite is like a private spa fitted out with a personal herbal mist sauna and jacuzzi. Guests may order extended treatment time here.

Right One of the many paintings and sculptures found around the spa resort.

Below Kirana Spa was designed by architect Lek Bunnag and landscape designer Bill Bensley. The energy of the nearby area of central Bali seems to filter into the Spa Garden area creating a magic all of its own.

Left The view from the jacuzzi pool in the Spa Garden is one of pure natural beauty and serenity.

Right Ceramic sculptures showing the simple daily life of Balinese girls playing a traditional game. The idea behind this is to remind us of the benefits of being playful and to enjoy the simplicity of life that in turn encourages relaxation.

Below left A stairway in local stone leading from the upper level down to the lower area of the Spa Garden, where pools of water and relaxing pavilions beckon.

Below right Ceramic goddesses frolic in a fountain at the Spa Garden plaza entrance.

Left and below The Balinese Hindu deity Dewi Sri, the beloved goddess of rice and fertility, is a decorative element, as are these fragrant offerings of jasmine and rose petals.

Right A scene from the Hindu Ramayama epic is depicted on the walls of the shower area in traditional Balinese temple relief style.

MARTHA TILAAR EASTERN
REJUVENATING CENTER

SAYAN, UBUD, BALI

Dr Martha Tilaar is highly regarded all over the world as an ambassador for Indonesian beauty treatments, and deservedly so. Considered one of the leaders in reviving and preserving ancient *jamu* recipes and remedies, Dr Tilaar creates products using local aromatic essences, herbs and traditional medicines. Merging ancient *jamu* knowledge with modern-day research, they appeal to the contemporary market. Currently she owns and operates a number of spas throughout Indonesia and sells her products in literally thousands of outlets throughout the country. One of her newest spas is the Eastern Rejuvenating Center, a 15-room neocolonial-style property near Ubud in Bali. A private resort and spa, it is ideal for weddings and corporate retreats—in a location with a strong Indonesian flavor.

Most treatments are *jamu*-inspired, but Dr Tilaar borrows freely from other cultures too. The Chinese accusage facial and Indian *marma* facial, as well as the traditional Indonesian rebirth facial, are good examples of how her work crosses all national boundaries. Special treatments, such as the traditional Indonesian post-natal treatment given to new mothers to quicken the healing process after birth, are also offered. Here, ingredients including galangal, lime, turmeric, betel nut and rice starch are mixed into a warm paste and placed on the abdomen to relieve pains and colic after delivery, as well as to improve blood circulation and firm the abdomen to its former contours. Other ingredients are then placed over various parts of the body to relieve any discomfort. Another beautiful creation is the Grecian Ritual, where flowers wrapped in muslin cloth are placed on different parts of the body including the solar plexus, heart and third eye to harmonize the *chakras*.

Dr Tilaar also offers a series of unique Eastern Body Events that include the Chinese Empress Ritual and Eastern Princess Retreat: the former honors Chinese traditions with a pressure point massage and a herbal-rich, toning facial, while the latter is inspired by a 7th-century Javanese treatment dating from Majapahit times that includes a cleansing body smoking, a *lulur* scrub, a steam bath, a hot oil massage and a herbal bath. Other treatments, such as the signature Cooling Mask, are given by exceptionally well-trained traditional therapists.

Opposite top Tirta Puspa is the name of this private indoor bath area where guests are bathed in a variety of natural Indonesian herbs and botanicals.

Opposite bottom and below The open-air bathing pavilion is known as the Tirta Amarta. This is a wonderful environment in which to receive the golden *lulur*, a spice-filled scrub based on a royal treatment from the Indonesian courts.

Left Martha Tilaar's signature massage oils are made from exotic ingredients like rice extract, ylang ylang, jasmine, rose, nutmeg, neroli and sandalwood.

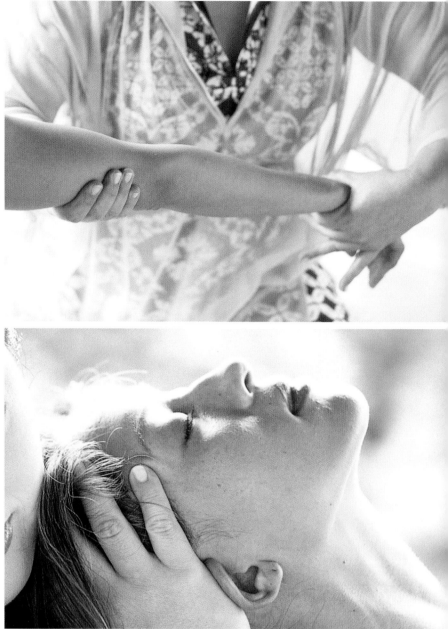

One of the most interesting aspects of Asian spa culture is that many of the therapists come from backgrounds where expressions such as "energy" and "healing" are a part of their daily existence. Healing hands are an integral feature of Asian cultures—and those with healing abilities often receive them from parents or teachers. Perhaps this is why many revered Western therapists have trained with Eastern masters in a variety of modalities—and continue to do so today.

Many of the therapists at Dr Tilaar's spas come from generations of such healers—and many subscribe to the Javanese philosophy that sees beauty as a whole: known in Javanese as "*Rupasampat Wahyabiantara*," it means "living in harmony with the natural cycles of life." In fact, all Dr Tilaar's products and therapies are based on this premise.

When visiting Asia's best spas, every now and then you come across a unique treatment such as the Bio-Energy Massage exclusively offered at the Martha Tilaar Eastern Rejuvenating Center. Developed by Dr Martha Tilaar and

incorporating old Indonesian and Chinese traditions, it offers a profound healing experience. "One can fulfill life's desires through Bio-Energy Massage," says Dr Martha Tilaar. She describes it as a massage of "radiant beauty" utilizing *daya putih* or "white energy."

The massage looks like a dramatic combination of yoga, dance and Thai massage. It begins with deep breathing in unison. Then the therapist performs stretches and uses various methods to move energy and stimulate circulation within the guest's body. The movements work to unlock and release blockages along the body's meridian lines, creating overall inner harmony and flow of *ch'i*. The intention is to re-energize and re-vitalize.

During the exercise, Dr Tilaar assures that *bakti* will occur: this is "a self-submission to God vertically and to human beings horizontally." She says some of the benefits may include stress-relief, a rebalancing of mind and spirit, improved intuition and strengthened memory as well as vitality in the body.

Above and left Healing hands at work. In this "white energy" or *daya putih* treatment, the body is pulled and stretched into balance. A variety of techniques are used in this "laying of hands" healing session. Dr Martha Tilaar describes the Bio-Energy Massage as one that produces "radiant beauty from within." The intention is to re-energize the body and create overall harmony and flow of *ch'i*. The rubbing of hands to generate energy for healing is common in many traditional Asian massage treatments.

Opposite top The bathing pool area is a quiet, relaxing place for contemplation.

Opposite bottom, anti-clockwise from top left
Ingredients used in the signature Cooling Mask treatment are pressed into small pill-like beads. They are then blended with rosewater and rose petals for added sensuality before being applied to the face. Other facial treatments at the Eastern Rejuvenating Center include Indonesian Rebirth and Chinese Acupressure Facials.

Above Couple's treatments are formulated to promote a connection between people. In the Rama-Sinta Room, couples are offered a retreat-like experience, with a shower, steam bath and aromatic body massage for two.

Right The Indonesian post-natal treatment known as *bengkung* is an external therapy believed to help flush out bacteria that gathers in the body after childbirth. Heat and herbs help to cleanse and stimulate the lymphatic system as well as reawaken the body's organs.

The Four Seasons Resort Bali at Sayan drops down vertically to the Ayung River valley. There are 18 suites and 42 villas with views across the ravine and the entrance is via a dramatic catwalk leading to a lotus pond on the roof of the hotel.

THE SPA
AT FOUR SEASONS RESORT BALI SAYAN

SAYAN, UBUD, BALI

With the scent of frangipani infusing the warm tropical air and a lotus pool floating above the treetops, the Four Seasons Resort at Sayan overlooks Bali's sacred Ayung River. It is a place of extraordinary natural beauty with rice fields and volcanic vistas—and a philosophy of living in harmony with the natural world. Accommodation is in the main block or in garden villas down below. The latter have outdoor bathing pavilions and private garden courtyards and are ideal for ayurvedic, herbal and couple's treatments. The villas beautifully reflect Bali-style architecture and are constructed with thatched roofs, hand-crafted Sulawesi textiles and hand-blown local glass.

The spa is located in a secluded environment and consists of four treatment rooms and three luxury spa villas. The village-like atmosphere reflects perfectly the communal spirit of the Balinese. The spa is surrounded by beautiful rice fields and vegetable gardens scented with lemongrass and features hot and cold plunge pools.

As Bali is predominantly Hindu, ayurveda resonates well here. Classic ayurvedic inspired treatments, adapted and refined to suit the Balinese temperature and lifestyle, are the first choice for many. One example is the Chakra Dhara Ritual designed to restore *dosha* (an individual's constitution) and *chakra* (energy point) imbalances: it begins with a back, scalp, hand and foot massage performed by two therapists to clear any toxic blockages, and is followed by herbal oil dripping on

Left Healing bath treatments with local spices and clays can be taken in the privacy of one's own suite or villa or in one of the large soaking tubs in the spa area.

Below left and right Herbal oil continually dripping on all four key energy points along the central nervous system comprises the signature Chakra Dhara ayurvedic treatment. Taken in one of the three spa villas, exquisitely designed with natural materials including hand-blown glass, Sulawesi silk and smooth terrazzo massage tables, it is truly relaxing.

Opposite top and bottom The hotel's rooms are accessed by open walkways and running water is an ever-present feature. Daily treks, cycling, a fitness center and yoga and meditation classes feature strongly on the menu here.

four key energy points along the central nervous system. It is a wonderful experience especially given the beautiful natural environment in which it is performed. Other treats include the *shirolepa* which is a soothing herbal head and scalp treatment with a back massage, and some Balinese-inspired bathing rituals where guests bathe in ingredients like mineral clays, local herbs, spices and mountain wild flowers.

More recent rituals include Sole to Sole—a five-hour health course that incorporates a steam shower, hot stone therapy, exfoliation, hot oil body wrap, massage and soak, finishing with an elixir tonic. If this were not enough, there is the Red Ginger Body Polish using organic red rice and ginger root to stimulate circulation, and the spicy, exotic Basil and Rosemary Mud Wrap.

Asia's largest aquatonic seawater therapy pool with temperate water drawn from the Indian Ocean is the place to immerse oneself for complete rejuvenation.

THE RITZ-CARLTON
BALI THALASSO & SPA

JIMBARAN, BALI

Inspired by traditional thalassotherapy spas in France, the thalasso and spa at the Ritz-Carlton Bali is Asia's largest and most rejuvenating seawater spa. Founded on the premise that seawater heals, it hosts one of the world's largest aquatonic pools. The sea is full of negative ions, now known to keep our atmosphere clean and help clear out pollutants, toxins and viruses. These same ions, when applied to the body, enhance our mental and physical wellbeing. This spa merges the many curative benefits of seawater, seaweed and sea-based minerals with holistic treatments designed to create a rejuvenating spa experience.

The 7,000-square-foot (650-square-meter) aquatonic pool contains filtered and heated Indian Ocean seawater. Its blend of cleansing minerals possesses natural antibacterial properties, while a temperature set at 31–34 degrees Celsius promotes relaxation and rebalances the body's mineral deficiencies. A dip in the pool is similar to an underwater circuit gym. Jet massages boost circulation, strengthen muscles, improve the respiratory system and increase red blood cell count, while the rich waters invigorate and detox. Surrounding the pool are six thalassotherapy rooms featuring hydrotherapy facilities, jet baths and circulatory showers where seawater and seaweed combo treatments are offered. There are underwater massages, seaweed body wraps and dynamic affusions, to name a few.

Above The spa treatment rooms are contained within their own separate complex that features a lovely private courtyard garden.

Right The warmed seawater pools form the heart of the spa here.

Opposite The unisex jacuzzi is a large freshwater pool set in a Balinese cavern. Nearby are the sauna and steam rooms that together form a striking hot and cold water therapies area.

In addition, there are 20 violet-themed treatment rooms with subtle Balinese accents and the newer Spa on the Rocks where two luxurious villas perch on natural rocks stretching out to the Indian Ocean. Ingeniously created so as to give the illusion of being suspended above the ocean, they are as unique for their lavish treatments as for their exclusive use of the fabulous Crème de la Mer products.

As is expected, the menu reflects a sensual summer affair, with names like Aromatic Petal Massage or the energizing Kubu Beach Full Body Treatment. The latter is named after the Ritz-Carlton's own secluded private beach enclave, and

appropriately uses sand, lime, mint, sea salt, sea kelp, sea mud, shells and minerals. Particularly noteworthy is the two-and-a-half hour *Cinta Abadi* (Eternal Love) treatment. Perfect for lovers, it begins with a flower petal foot wash and hot towel wrap, followed by an aromatic petal massage, a choice of body scrub, body mask or mineral scrub, and an intimate outdoor flower bath. Alternatively, the couple's massage in the Taman Asoka Suite, followed by a bath in a traditional coconut wood bathtub, is a lovely experience. Be it a three-hour walk-in treatment or a seven-day package, The Ritz-Carlton offers a caring environment in which your love may deepen and grow.

Left Elaborately landscaped terraces step down from the reception area of the resort to the edge of the Indian Ocean.

Right A bowl of tropical frangipani petals—a vital element in any Balinese spa experience.

Below The Marine Wave Deluxe treatment is a sensual sea-inspired treatment for detoxification and rejuvenation. This package is a combination of seaweed wrap, circulatory shower, herb balm massage and a 10-minute dynamic affusion where warm seawater is gently drizzled over your skin to ease you into a welcome state of total bliss.

The Marine Wave Deluxe (pictured above) is another innovative creation that draws on the benefits of sea mud to nourish the body. This sensual, sea-inspired wrap-style treatment works to deeply cleanse and detoxify the body. The session starts with a 20-minute seaweed wrap, during which the therapist also administers a herbal balm facial. Afterwards, a shower spills warmed seawater over the guest for 15 minutes to stimulate circulation. Therapists then administer a Hawaiian *lomi lomi* massage while pouring warm seawater over the body to moisturize and induce relaxation. The finale is a 10-minute dynamic affusion—a warm seawater spray over the entire body that both relaxes and tones the muscles.

The highlight of the treatment is a herbal balm massage using a blend of detoxifying blue kaolin clay, kelp (seaweed) powder, nourishing apricot kernel oil, pure beeswax, rosemary, geranium and grapefruit essential oil, and vitamin E oil. Kelp powder is renowned for its mineralizing and detoxifying properties; kaolin tightens and purifies; vitamin E oil is an antioxidant that nourishes and repairs the skin. The essential oils also perform several distinctive functions: geranium invigorates, heals and calms, grapefruit is considered a diuretic that stimulates the lymphatic system and rosemary is great for toning and stimulating blood circulation. Overall, it is a wonderfully invigorating experience.

Left and below The baroque design of the Prana Spa is all about fantasy and escape from worldly cares. Prana Spa manufactures its own line of spa products so guests have the pleasure of soaking in the fragrances of the East with exotic oils and herbs.

Right Many of the treatments at Prana Spa integrate traditional ayurvedic practices—including yoga.

PRANA SPA
AT THE VILLAS

SEMINYAK, BALI

Some of the newer boutique spas in Asia offer authentic treatments flavored with the unusual and unexpected. Situated in The Villas, a group of 50 luxurious Bali-style villas in trendy Seminyak, is the Prana Spa and the clean, smooth massage venue called Chill. The former, with a cloistered retreat ambience, is designed along the lines of a 16th-century Indian palace, while the latter offers reflexology sessions only. Both are very private.

"Create your own retreat" is the motto of Prana (whose name is not just based on the Sanskrit word for "vital force" but was also the name of owner Jim Elliott's great friend). Some guests have been known to book a morning helicopter ride to have breakfast on a remote island followed by horse riding along the Indian Ocean followed by three hours of solid pampering in the evening. Others simply kick back and relax in the quiet compound.

Within the theatrical spa enclave are complimentary hot and cold plunge pools to dip in before, during or after your treatments. Signature treatments reflect an ayurvedic approach with Prana Rebalance being one of the most popular. This is a therapeutic ayurvedic treatment from Southern India that appeals to those seeking more than mere pampering. The philosophy is to restore the body's natural balance by first cleansing the circulatory system and then nurturing it with concoctions to heal and nourish.

The session takes place in the Ayurveda Room where you are welcomed by two therapists with an Indian-style *namaste* greeting. A synchronized massage known as *pizichil* is performed with warm medicated oils, then the *udgharshana* takes place. This involves healing powders and herbs being massaged over oiled skin to help stimulate circulation. Next is *mavarakizhi*, in

Left Barefoot *shiatsu* massages are given in daybeds set in alcoves facing a central courtyard.

Above left Indian silk and gold-painted archways are just some of the fantastic details that make Prana Spa so memorable.

Above right and below Indian inspiration can be seen in the herbal-infused steam room, where warm aromatic essences ease away tension, and this bathroom with elaborate mosaics.

which steaming hot poultices filled with curative herbs and powders are rubbed in circular motions over the body to help alleviate fatigue, improve digestion and relax any stiffness within the body. The final *pina sweda* session involves steaming hot towels infused with herbs that are draped over the body. An all-over detoxifier, this has a warming effect, so expect to depart feeling grounded and nurtured.

One of the best treatments for your day of departure is the three-and-a-half hour Divine Renewal ritual that starts with a sea salt body exfoliation followed by a shower rain massage to cleanse and stimulate. Your choice of either creamy clay or pure seaweed mud is then massaged into the skin and further detoxification takes place in the steam room. The middle section consists of an hour-long soothing full body massage and a hydrating seaweed facial, while the traditional Indonesian crème bath to nourish the hair and scalp is given at the end.

For those who love a stronger massage, the Prana barefoot *shiatsu* comes highly recommended. It especially caters to those who are physically strong and require treatments that work deeply on the body tissues and muscles.

Reflecting the water element that is so sacred in Bali, a variety of pools are dotted throughout the resort. Particularly striking is an infinity-edge pool where water cascades over a 22-foot (7-meter) waterfall into another soaking pool below.

THE SPA
AT FOUR SEASONS
RESORT BALI
JIMBARAN BAY

JIMBARAN, BALI

The Four Seasons Resort Bali at Jimbaran Bay perches elegantly above the Indian Ocean and draws up cool energy from the waters that flow throughout its confines. Built to resemble a traditional Balinese village, it is lushly planted; accommodation is in an extensive complex of private villas, each with its own private compound and oversized outdoor soaking tubs. The experience is an exclusive one, with all amenities thoughtfully provided.

The spa at the Four Seasons embraces the natural beauty of Bali and is intended to be "mystical, tropical and spiritual." Treatments employ local spices, flowers and herbs and, combined with the healing touch of experienced therapists' hands, epitomize the essence of Bali. The spa includes spacious relaxation lounges with juices and magazines on hand. In the Royal Spa Suite you are treated like a goddess (or god): this is the perfect place to experience the Four Seasons signature Rainshower Ritual. This begins with a sea salt scrub, and is followed by a gentle Vichy shower, a soothing lavender bath and ends with a lavender lotion moisturizer.

Many treatments at Jimbaran are inspired by the nearby ocean and use water, sea crystals and plants found and grown locally. One signature treatment that reflects the oceanic beauty

Opposite Four Seasons Resort at Jimbaran Bay comprises 147 thatched-roof villas all with private compounds and plunge pools overlooking the Indian Ocean.

Below It is the small things that count: these aromatherapy diffusers sweeten the spa's air with essential fragrances from Bali and the surrounding area.

Bottom The Coconilla Skin Scrub is an exfoliating treatment that uses shredded coconut, vanilla beans and coconut milk—all geared to cooling down and nourishing the body.

of Bali is the Sea Mint Detoxifying Ritual, where sand, sea salt and minerals are used as exfoliants before an icy mint purifying mousse is applied. This is finished with a scalp massage using a blend of mint, tangerine and rosemary. A peppermint rose milk bath with a refreshing cup of herbal petal tea serves as both a tonic and elixir. Detoxified and refreshed, the balance of the skin is restored with a lemongrass and mint body lotion, plus a hydrating facial gel of lavender and geranium.

Many facials include a hand or foot massage during the mask portion, and whoever created the Four Seasons' Island Fruit Ritual was certainly in a joyous mood! This delicious sequence encourages the shedding of skin layers and is also a beautiful mood-lifter. It begins with a papaya and hibiscus scrub followed by a papaya and passion fruit body mask and then a wild fruit bath where fresh fruit tea is served. Passion fruit, papaya, blackberries, raspberries and strawberries are all used in abundance. And in keeping with the Balinese philosophy of living in balance, many treatments incorporate a beautiful hand massage—firm, yet soothing, which brings the guest back to center.

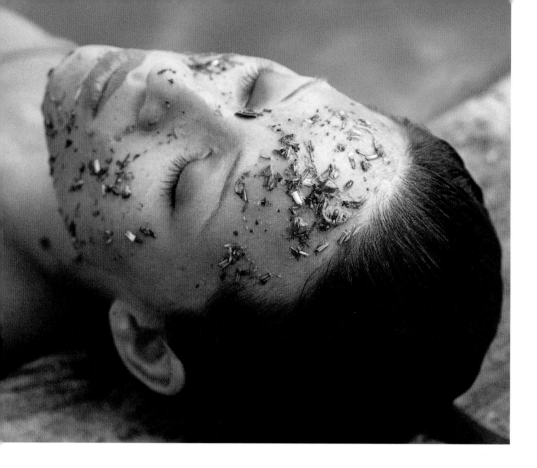

Left and below middle The Sari Jimbaran Facial is one of four facial treatments on the menu here. Part of the sequence is a mask that uses local herbs and flowers.

Below and bottom left Spas are all about connecting with others, and bonding with friends can be deepened when in beautiful surroundings. The spirit here is all about blending a human touch with natural tropical spices and flowers to create a profound sense of peace and wellbeing.

Above One of many grotto-like pools found in the grounds of the resort.

Right Whimsical drawings of Balinese dancers enliven the walls of the Bali-style compounds.

SPA BOTANICA
AT THE SENTOSA RESORT

SENTOSA, SINGAPORE

Located on Sentosa Island just a few minutes' drive from the city center, Spa Botanica is a lush tropical retreat far removed from bustling Singapore. The spa space covers an area of 6,000 square feet (550 square meters) and is set in a renovated colonial building with extensive gardens. Cool and inviting, water and nature are the main features here. Man-made waterfalls, a swimming pool, rock pools, and therapeutic mud pools sit amidst a profusion of ornamental flowers and shrubs. There is also a meditation labyrinth with a spiral walkway, which is a metaphor for self-discovery, and a relaxing tea pavilion.

Each of the treatment rooms, suites, villas and pavilions is named after a local spice or flower. There are 14 indoor treatment rooms, nine beauty rooms, wet rooms and suites, as well as six outdoor massage pavilions with their own private baths and gardens.

Unsurprisingly, the philosophy here is all about growth, regeneration and Mother Nature. Treatments feature an East-West blend of massage, acupressure and hot stone massage together with hydrotherapy, aromatherapy and treatments for new mothers. Bathing rituals are celebrated with a selection of tea tub baths, mud, aromatherapy and milk baths. One innovation is the Galaxy Steam Bath, designed as a Turkish-style steam chamber. Before entering this exotic room where the roof is a blanket of stars, you are invited to smother your body in a selection of medicinal clays and muds. Once inside, you are encouraged to relax and allow the muds to thoroughly

Above The spa garden features waterfalls, mud pools, bathing pools and outdoor showers where one can relax before or after a treatment.

Left Frequent afternoon rain showers are a tropical experience to be enjoyed at the spa's lap pool, where a large frangipani tree scents the equatorial atmosphere.

cleanse the body whilst a purifying herbal steam infuses the skin. The session is completed with a gentle rain shower.

Other alluring treatments include the Jungle Rain which consists of a herbal-infused mud wrap using Colombian clay, aloe vera and manuka and kanuka essential oils, followed by a Vichy shower and a one-hour chlorophyll butter massage. There is also the Golfers' Tonic that tees off with a relaxing back massage and treatments to relieve aches and pains, as well as the Flight Reviver designed to soothe and rebalance the body after traveling. Men's spa treatments are increasingly popular and the 90-minute Men's Aromatherapy Facial includes a stimulating scalp massage combined with foot reflexology.

In addition, Spa Botanica offers treatments in the wellness realm with a view towards becoming more "results orientated." The focus here is on detox, so there are treatments influenced by the five-elements theory and herbal traditions of Tibet and China created with exciting ingredients such as lotus blossom, ginseng and wild ginger.

Right The royal bath has a tub made of solid copper that weighs more than a ton. Treatments including the Frangipani Flower Bath and Coconut Bath are given here.

Below, clockwise from top left Mimosa and hibiscus balms are applied to moisturize and rejuvenate the skin. Handmade paper-wrapped soap is part of Spa Botanica's natural retail spa range. Loofah sponges are used to exfoliate the skin. A natural leaf fan is perfect for hot Singapore days.

AMRITA SPA
AT RAFFLES

SINGAPORE

the relaxation lounge before being led to one of the 35 treatment rooms. For a romantic treat, indulge in the VIP Couple's Treatment Suite, equipped with its own private jacuzzi and aromatherapy steam room.

Without a doubt, hotel spas are ideal for relaxation during business trips or to celebrate the end of a holiday with friends and loved ones; the RafflesAmrita Spa Ritual packages are specially created for this purpose. The half-hour Anti-Stress Massage that focuses on releasing tension from the back, shoulders and scalp is perfect to experience on arrival or before an important meeting.

Apart from Bridal Spa Retreats for her and Gentleman's Executive Rescue for him, also recommended is the Day Spa Escape for couples. This includes a soothing back, neck and scalp massage and facial. Or opt for the three-and-a-half hour Total Body Wellness that's all about the sea—think salt scrub, sea mud wrap, sea mud hair treatment, acupressure body massage and aromatherapy facial, and you're probably feeling a whole lot better already.

Amrita's name refers to the legendary Indian "elixir of eternal youth" and reflects the essence of these spas. When you incorporate treatments as part of your daily travel routine, you take the best route towards maintaining on-going health and longevity.

Urban spa retreats set in city hotels are now an integral part of hotel life and most luxury hotels offer a spa sanctuary within their premises. The philosophy behind hotel spas is straightforward: arrive at your hotel jet-lagged and fatigued and depart refreshed and transformed. RafflesAmrita is a top-of-the-range brand offered exclusively at Raffles Hotel and Raffles The Plaza in Singapore, Raffles Grand Hotel d'Angkor and Raffles Hotel Le Royal in Cambodia, as well as at other properties within the group around the world.

Most of us have dreamed of staying at the original Raffles. With its expansive colonial architecture, lush gardens, promises of romantic high teas and afternoon tropical rain showers, it oozes old-world glamour. Inside, the spa is completely private and caters only to hotel residents. Treatments range from luxury European facials to an ayurvedic *pancha karma*—an hour-and-a-half program of ayurvedic body massage with sesame and herbal oils for your *dosha*, with a sumptuous *shirodhara* that is affectionately called "heaven in a cup." Afterwards, as you recline on a lounge chair on one of the expansive verandahs, you can imagine what it must have been like to stay here during the bygone days of the Exotic East.

Across the road is RafflesAmrita Spa at Raffles The Plaza, a perennial favorite among hotel residents and Singapore locals alike. Before your treatment, take a soak in the steam, jacuzzi and sauna baths, preparing your mental and physical self in

THE SPA VILLAGE
AT PANGKOR LAUT
RESORT

PANGKOR LAUT ISLAND, PERAK, MALAYSIA

Pangkor Laut, a small private island off the west coast of Malaysia, is home to an exclusive resort of exceptional beauty. Part of this resort is given over to a Spa Village, an entity that offers an excellent array of spa treatments. It comprises a series of pools and water features, "healing huts" offering Chinese herbal, ayurvedic and Malay treatments, as well as Thai and Balinese massages, bath houses and nap gazebos, a *jamu* bar and a herb garden. This is one of Asia's most unusual and exciting destination spas.

The Spa Village is exceptionally quiet and secluded, with dense rainforest as a backdrop and a sandy beach in the foreground, not to mention Malay village-style wooden guest houses on stilts over the water and first-rate facilities. Spiritual health is the focus at the Spa Village: one can participate in programs that enliven physical and spiritual wellbeing based on the themes of rejuvenation and longevity, relaxation and stress reduction as well as detox-ification and romance—all necessary elements in leading a balanced life.

Not to be missed is the unique Bath House Ritual, a seven-part celebration of Asia's varied bathing traditions (see page 219).

The range of other treatments offered here is vast. If ayurveda is your preference, your journey begins with a diagnosis to determine your body constitution or *prakruthi* via pulse diagnosis and body checking. The ayurvedic physician (who is also a qualified yoga teacher) dispenses advice on how to achieve a harmonious lifestyle and may prescribe a course of treatments. A consultation with the Chinese doctor gauges how well *ch'i* is flowing through your body and meridian points; treatments may include cupping, moxibustion and *tui na an mo* massage. In addition, daily *tai ch'i chuan* classes are held to improve one's breathing, posture and energy. Inside the Malay Hut, there is a whole world of traditional health disciplines to discover: many have been passed down through generations, and treatments are designed to bring back equilibrium using indigenous plants and herbs. *Ukup Wangi*, a scented body steaming ritual, and the traditional body rejuvenation treatment known as *Sesegar Bayu* are highly recommended.

Alternatively, if you simply need some time just to be by yourself, you can head to the private beach at Emerald Bay. Here the waters shimmer like a thousand green jewels and a nap in a hammock is sublime.

Opposite top and middle Chinese herbs are brewed into a tea in the Chinese Healing Hut, while a Malay consultation employs a large array of locally-grown leaves and roots.

Left Serenity and total privacy are two of the great advantages of staying on a private island resort like Pangkor Laut.

Above In the Malay Healing Hut one is given insight into the traditional healing culture of Malaysia.

Right Private bungalows suspended on stilts and surrounded by an endless sea are only a stone's throw away from the spa.

Below A steaming poultice of herbs is pressed upon the body.

Left and below The Spa Village, with its tranquil reception area on left, comprises a cluster of villas and treatment pavilions set amidst a herbal garden and lotus ponds.

Opposite The Malay Bath area, created to recapture the essence of ancient royal water palaces, is where you can experience the different bathing traditions of Asia.

Above A stunning recreation of a Japanese *onsen* at the Japanese Bath House: guests are invited to take a traditional *goshi goshi* scrub, dip into the heated *rotenburo* pool and experience a Japanese green tea ceremony here.

Right Shimmering seclusion where forest meets the sea. Emerald Bay is a small cove that offers private swimming, candlelight dinners, a sandy beach and memorable sunsets.

ANANTARA SPA
AT ANANTARA RESORT HUA HIN

HUA HIN, THAILAND

Warm sesame compresses, *dosha*-balancing color therapy steam baths, and Thai healing massages—this is a spa that offers a unique blend of Indian and Thai treatments in a stunning setting on the Gulf of Thailand. Here you can roam through garden pavilions (*salas*) and courtyards intermingled with reflecting pools and tropical gardens filled with orchids.

The Anantara Spa is run by MSpa International, an international spa operating company well known in the region for an approach deeply rooted in the traditional healing philosophies of Asia. The Anantara name derives from a Sanskrit word reflecting the flow of water without borders, supporting the company's vision for health and relaxation in an extremely peaceful setting.

At the Anantara Spa, we suggest surrendering to signature Anantara packages that last a full or half day, such as the Soul Revival and Body Symphony, in which face and body rejuvenation treatments are combined with traditional beauty elixirs made with indigenous herbs and spices. Or, for the serious spa enthusiast, embark upon Anantara Journeys of three, five and seven days that can be individually tailored to provide the ultimate in rejuvenation and calming of the spirit. Traditional Thai treatments include the 200-year-old Thai herbal compress that contains five locally-grown herbs known

to heal and rejuvenate. Given to war-weary soldiers during the Ayutthaya period, this treatment is great for anyone with aching muscles.

Another Thai favorite is the Thai Herbal Steam Bath which uses herbs and spices combined with heat and steam to detox and revitalize the body. The treatment is inspired by the herbal steam baths that Thai women use to regain skin tone after childbirth. Other treatments include a traditional Thai facial and a stress recovery facial made with local herbs and spices. The Enzymatic Sea Mud Wrap is a sequence consisting of footbath, wrap, shower and body lotion. Lasting 60 minutes, it is redolent of the ocean with ingredients like seaweed, botanicals and plant enzymes in a mineral clay base. Fruits including papaya and pineapple containing the enzyme bromelin are blended with essential oils of lemon, lime, lavender and petitgrain.

This is a spa founded on the Buddhist philosophy that the inner and outer worlds are connected. The beauty we see outside of ourselves reflects the beauty within. Treatments at the Anantara offer a window into Thai healing traditions and provide an opportunity to experience tropical Thai culture in sensual surroundings. Bathing in the sweetness of these offerings is all part of the Asian spa journey.

The Anantara Spa was designed by award-winning landscape architect Bill Bensley whose intention was to create a space where guests feel "at one" with nature.

Opposite bottom left Inside the spa suites are dual al fresco rain showers suspended in cast-bronze cages inspired by traditional Thai fish traps. Bill Bensley is regarded as a master of little decorative touches like these: along with stone figurines, antique birdhouses and ceramic vases, they are all a tribute to the ancient Thai and Khmer heritage of this region.

Opposite bottom right Two therapists work in rhythmic harmony to deliver the signature Anantara Four-Hand Massage, which is a blend of five massage techniques including traditional Thai, Japanese *shiatsu, lomi lomi,* Swedish and Balinese.

Right A treatment room set up for a Thai massage, one of the most popular items on the menu here.

Below Many activities, including horse riding along Hua Hin beach, are offered at the spa.

CHIVA-SOM INTERNATIONAL
HEALTH RESORT

HUA HIN, THAILAND

Integrative medicine combining the best of East and West is the basis of the spa of the future—and no other spa currently combines traditional Asian therapies with the best of rejuvenating Western medicine as well as Chiva-Som.

With a name that means "the haven of life," Chiva-Som is set within seven acres (three hectares) of lush Thai gardens on the beach at Hua Hin. With world class facilities and 57 pavilions and oceanview suites, it's a luxurious antidote for any physical or emotional challenges you may be experiencing. It is also a place where you can relax easily either alone or with friends.

Recognizing that "whole" and "healing" derive from the same root, every treatment program and session is geared towards encouraging you to fulfill your potential. From the excellent food that includes detox juices, wheatgrass juices, organic produce and raw food options, to the quality fitness, yoga, martial arts and dance classes that run from 7 am until dusk, wellness here is very much about enjoying life's offerings.

Upon arrival at the spa, each guest is given a health and wellness consultation that sets the pace for the time ahead. In addition, there is a consultation with a spa professional that helps the guest design an individual program for treatments. The packages range from overnight one–day, two–day and three–day stays to 10– to 28–day retreats.

What sets this destination apart is the pre-treatment diagnostic therapies that are offered at the start of your stay.

Whether you decide to embark on the popular detox program or simply want to treat the time as a relaxing but healthy holiday, there are a host of medical services such as blood testing nutritional anaylsis, physiotherapy, live blood analysis, echocardiography examination and bio-terrain—designed to give a complete picture of the internal workings of your body.

Preventative health is a passion and, if it's a transformation in your lifestyle and self that you seek, then rest assured that the quality of healers, health practitioners and therapists here is very high. There are over 130 therapies including reiki, weight management programs, colonic irrigation, ayurveda, TCM therapies and craniosacral therapy, together with skin rejuvenation treatments such as meseotherapy. The Niranlada Medical Spa Rejuvenation Center also offers Botox (Botulinium Toxin Type A), laser skin rejuvenation and restylane, to name but a few. Water therapies abound. Every guest is encouraged to take a steam, sauna or hot and cold water therapy prior to treatments to keep their bodies fully cleansed and energized. Massages are also plentiful, or if you want to lie about the pool and observe the day go by with a good book, that's fine too.

Many guests depart with a deeper understanding of their own health—and many return. Be prepared to emerge from Chiva-Som feeling inspired to continue taking care of yourself. By integrating the very best of Eastern and Western modalities, Chiva-Som gives you the potential to really rejuvenate.

The pool area facing Hua Hin beach features a bar where wheatgrass and other healthy juices are served. Chiva-Som is renowned for its detox, yoga, spa, weight-loss and fitness retreats that are held all year round.

Right The stunning Floatation Chamber offers treatments designed to relieve jet-lag, hypertension and insomnia.

Below The Emotional Freedom Technique (EFT) is based on 5,000-year-old ayurvedic principles and can be loosely described as a "psychological version of acupressure." Here, therapist Paul Emery performs a "tapping" technique to help release blockages within the body's meridian energy system, that in turn releases submerged emotions and memories that may prevent you from living to your full potential.

Above Thai-style villas located near a banyan tree and koi pond—the place to rest after spa therapies.

Left A nurturing and therapeutic aquatic *watsu* therapy is given in the *watsu sala*. Like an underwater dance, guests are gracefully swirled and stretched for 90 minutes to a place of profound peace and deep relaxation.

SIX SENSES SPA
AT EVASON HUA HIN RESORT

HUA HIN, THAILAND

The Evason Hua Hin Resort sits along the peaceful Gulf of Thailand near the seaside market town of Hua Hin. Its clean-lined, pure white architecture, delicate lotus ponds and tropical gardens all face the sea and induce a sense of calm.

The spa itself is designed to complement the resort experience and offers pampering and healing therapies centered around health, de-stressing, relaxation and beauty. Blending indoor and outdoor life, it comprises five thatched *salas* (outdoor pavilions) set amongst tranquil reflecting ponds. Inside is the Cocoon Room where therapies are performed. Next door in the Evason Hideaway at Hua Hin is one of the most eco-friendly spas in the region—the Earth Spa by Six Senses. Here, Eco-cocoons (five *salas* in the northern Thai style constructed out of a local clay) rely on the surrounding lotus ponds and sea breezes for natural air cooling. Nearby spa suites each come with their own private pool, treatment room and steam room.

As the name suggests, the range of treatments is intended to "balance the senses" through a holistic approach. To experience the best that Six Senses Spas has to offer, it's suggested you book ahead for the Sensory Spa Journey, a treatment tailored personally for you by the spa staff. It starts with a luxurious footbath filled with fresh aromatic flowers and a skin renewing exfoliation followed by a comprehensive massage. A unique variation on the traditional four hands massage performed by two skilled therapists working in tandem follows to "take you on a journey of the five senses and beyond." This aromatic body massage is performed together with a cleansing facial and a stress-soothing scalp massage.

Left A close-up view of one of the five thatch-roof treatment salas surrounded by lotus ponds.

Below Specially-prepared outdoor baths can be taken in your own room. Shown here is the Cleopatra Milk Bath made with fresh milk, bananas, honey, yoghurt and rose petals.

Right One of the greatest luxuries at the Evason Hua Hin Resort is time spent alone relaxing and contemplating—for example in the two-level open-air bar area that overlooks the Gulf of Siam.

Opposite below It's the little things that count—stylish offerings of water, soaps, juices and healthy snacks at Six Senses Spas are all as pure and simple as possible.

Six Senses Spas are highly regarded for delivering innovative therapies in a harmonious environment with minimal impact on the environment. They specialize in experiences that are designed to shift and transform your mind space, as well as relax your body. If you have been experiencing stress and your mind feels overworked, the Indian Head Massage soothes away worrying thoughts and tension. For the terminally tight, a hot stone treatment softens muscles and melts away stress. The Harmony face, scalp and body massage treatment offers a combination of therapies: designed to relax the entire body, it is a great stress buster too.

Six Senses Spas lead the way with their innovative "spa within a spa" concept. At most of their properties, from Thailand to the Maldives, guests can book into a suite that includes accommodation and private spa facilities. An outdoor bath, private steam room, gymnasium and a dedicated treatment area means you can enjoy an entire course of spa treatments without ever having to leave your hotel room. Bliss!

THE SPA
AT MANDARIN ORIENTAL DHARA DHEVI

CHIANG MAI, THAILAND

The Mandarin Oriental's spa jewel in Chiang Mai, northern Thailand, manifests the Asian spa in one of its most authentic forms—embodying beautifully the understanding that all Eastern therapies evolved over time in palaces and temples across Asia. Housed in a golden teakwood structure modelled on the ancient palace of Mandalay in Myanmar, it sports carved wooden interiors, white marble floors and Lanna scrolls and antiques. Individual spa suites are all equipped with their own steam room, heated marble scrub table, private whirlpool and relaxation area. Treatments are based around traditional "life-enhancing rituals" that originate from Burma, Laos, northern Thailand and India. It would not be an exaggeration to say that this is the world's most luxurious and advanced destination spa.

The resort is composed of a myriad of temples, wooden rice barns, prayer halls and colonial-style villas set amidst 60 acres (24 hectares) of rice fields, lakes and tropical gardens with sacred Bo trees. Accommodation is provided in 144 villas and all spa treatment rooms are actually spa suites; there are luxury six-bedroom villas with private gardens and pools creating private spas-within-a-palace. Spa penthouse suites where a private spa is attached to the villa are perfect for those who want to experience treatments in total seclusion.

Signature treatments are appropriately referred to as "ceremonies," and some are over 5,000 years old. The Mandalay Ceremony is inspired by ancient Burmese beauty rituals and the Ayurvedic Ceremony includes traditional *ubtan* body scrubs and wraps, and Indian foot massages. Western treatments— from lymphatic drainage massages to vitamin C glow booster facials—are also offered. The Turkish *hamam*, Lebanese *rhassoul*, and ice fountain are innovative features for Asia, but it's the *watsu* pool set in a Buddhist-like temple with antique rooftops and golden walls that makes the spa experience so special. There is also a sophisticated fitness center with yoga masters, Pilates instructors, naturopaths and Western medical doctors to complement the traditional Thai, Chinese and Indian therapists.

One feature that takes this holistic spa to a whole new level in the region, if not in the world, is the Ayurvedic Center. These 15 villas are a luxurious setting in which to experience detoxifying and rejuvenating ayurvedic treatments. The center is designed according to the principles of *vastu* (a kind of Indian *feng shui*), and has an ayurvedic restaurant and meditation/yoga center too.

Above This central cluster of teak buildings in the spa grounds house 25 treatment rooms and suites.

Below The *tok sen* Lanna massage is part of the Lanna Ceremony inspired by ancient beauty rituals from northern Thai royal culture. Here the therapist taps the body with a stick from the bark of a tamarind tree to increase circulation before applying a warm herbal oil massage and compress.

Opposite top Colonial-style villas with Lanna or northern Thai decorative flourishes hark back to an earlier period of luxury and grace.

Opposite bottom Inspired by Wat Umong, a 500-year-old cave monastery near Chiang Mai, this tunnel is positioned at the entrance to the health and fitness center.

One of the exciting elements at Dhara Devi is the use of advanced technology to support ayurvedic and traditional Chinese medicine (TCM) diagnoses. A Computerized Meridian Diagostics (CMD) machine offers guests a revolutionary new health-check system to measure the body's vital energy points and get an immediate indication of wellbeing. Says ayurvedic practitioner Dr Suchada Marwah: "The TCM physicians were aware of this thousands of years ago and understood that any illness could be traced to an imbalance in the body's energy systems. Correct the imbalance and you cure the illness."

At this Mandarin Oriental Spa, expect to hear the sound of Tibetan cymbals, inhale fragrances of essential oils, transform your emotions with mood-enhancing color and light therapy, and imbibe a sense of calm via healing teas. Chiang Mai is already a spiritual destination and certainly this palatial spa is as near to the celestial as possible on this earth.

Left Many rituals begin with a foot bath.

Right The *ubtan* body scrub is given upon heated marble tables.

Below Preparations of natural ingredients for the Royal Lanna Time Ritual treatment.

Bottom and opposite bottom The spa's philosophy is about engaging each of the five senses in an atmosphere of calm and serenity.

THE SPA
AT FOUR SEASONS RESORT CHIANG MAI

CHIANG MAI, THAILAND

A visit to Four Seasons Resort in northern Thailand offers guests a luxurious spa experience coupled with adventure travel. Where else can one go on an elephant or rice field trek, visit a hill-tribe village and be pampered at a spa, all in one celebrated day? This mountain region is one of the most beautiful areas in the whole of Asia.

There's nothing more divine than waking up beneath pure cotton sheets in a spacious pavilion overlooking the Doi Suthep Mountains. The views are magnificent, the air is fresh and clear, and the sounds of birdsong fill the air. When walking to the spa you can absorb the richness of the natural surroundings—working rice fields, waterfalls, lily ponds and gardens containing over 300 species of plants and flowers on the 20-acre (8-hectare) property. It's a tiny kingdom all its own, and the Buddhist philosophy of northern Thailand permeates throughout the grounds.

The spa itself is a three-story villa with magnificent views designed in the ancient Lanna style. There are seven private suites, including a palatial penthouse suite, and stepped terraces equipped with deep tubs for body soaking. A vigorous day at the spa might include *ashtanga* and *iyengar* yoga classes, Thai boxercise, body toning workouts, Pilates and stretching classes, not to mention meditation and *qi gong*. In the evening, a fireplace and fresh ginger tea offer warmth, as do a range of herbal aromatherapy steam rooms and rain shower massage beds.

Treatments are inspired by indigenous northern Thai healing practices combined with ayurvedic oil massages, natural body wraps and scrubs enriched with clays, spices and ground rice. The *samunprai*, a Thai herbal heat energizer, is a signature treatment. A hot pack filled with rejuvenating freshly-picked local herbs is steamed and placed on the body to remove toxins and tension. Another beautiful treatment is the Herbal Blend Ritual, a four-hour indulgence focusing on the use of rejuvenating Thai herbs in various applications including herbal steam, herbal body polish, herbal wrap, herbal bath and a herbal oil body massage.

Recently added to the menu is the *ch'i nei tsang* internal massage that works to unblock unresolved energy and emotions in the abdominal area. Another interesting addition is the Ancient Arts Awakener that begins with a *chakra*-balancing sea salt foot bath followed by a reiki treatment and an ayurvedic *shirodhara*, not to mention a head massage, Thai stretches and a private herbal steam bath.

Above The stunning Lan Chang Room has the feeling of a Thai temple and is the place to rinse off your scrubs, herbs and oils.

Opposite top left Private deep-soaking bathtubs are set within semi-enclosed sala terraces.

Opposite top right and right A time to relax amidst the trappings of a traditional Thai palace. The three-level spa is designed in the ancient Lanna style of northern Thai temples.

SALUS PER AQUA SPA
AT THE FARM AT SAN BENITO

LIPA CITY, THE PHILIPPINES

Previous page A moment of quiet meditation in the Lagoon Lounge is an integral part of the wellness experience at The Farm.

Left The Stone Massage treatment uses crystals and stones demonstrating The Farm's unique holistic approach.

Below and bottom right Therapists add to the evening's radiance by decorating the infinity pool area with small candles.

Opposite top and middle Outdoor bathing in natural surrounds: An outdoor bath in a treatment room and rock pools and a small waterfall in the Secret Garden surrounded by lush greenery.

Farm. The result of thousands of years of cultural influences, it is given by a traditional massage therapist known as a *hilotsa pilay*. Warmed strips of banana leaves dipped in coconut are applied to various parts of the body to reveal which areas may be blocked or need more attention. According to Dr Ronnie Royo, president of the Natural Health Foundation of the Philippines, this traditional massage was learned from the ancient Chinese and is similar to acupressure and chiropractic methods with Swedish massage strokes. We also suggest the *hilot hapolos*, a scrub made from powdered cacao and fresh coconut cream with a warm coconut milk bath and massage under the stars.

The Philippines is an Asian spa destination with its own indigenous treatments that have developed organically from traditional healing methodologies. Their introduction to the spa treatment room has been relatively recent, and The Farm at San Benito has been instrumental in taking this heritage and setting new trends for the future. Realizing the importance of nourishing body and mind to sustain overall wellness, their philosophy is simple: stay in tune and in balance with natural laws, and emotional wellbeing and good health will be yours.

Set in tranquil gardens overlooking a delightful panorama of forest and mountain, The Farm is rich in natural abundance with a slight native vibe. Accommodation ranges from villas to rustic *sulu* terrace suites, modeled after traditional rice barns in the southern Philippines, so there are options for all budgets and styles. The restaurant (named 85/15 to reflect the ratio of raw to cooked foods) serves up exceptional vegetarian and other dishes—and is considered an integral part of any stay.

Detoxification and rejuvenation are at the heart of The Farm's Salus Per Aqua spa. On hand is a team of experts including Western-trained medical doctors, chiropractors, fitness experts, living food chefs, colonic therapists, meditation gurus and organic gardeners. Live blood analysis and iridology are just some of the diagnostics practiced, while holistic medicine, naturopathy, colon detoxification, ayurveda, traditional Chinese medicine (TCM) and other alternative therapies are fundamental to most of the treatments. A number of individually tailored programs—from detox and cleansing, to courses to quit smoking or eliminate disease or stress—are also offered. Recent additions are facial enhancement and Botox procedures.

One can't travel to the Philippines without trying the locally inspired *hilot* (a sensual Filipino massage) to get you into the swing of things. It is the most popular healing practice at The

Discover the mysterious beauty of the nearby Songzanling Temple that is home to over 700 monks and lamas. Inside, incense and yak butter oil lamps set the mood for prayer and meditation amongst ancient Buddhist scriptures.

BANYAN TREE
SPA RINGHA

YUNNAN PROVINCE, CHINA

Take a spa sojourn through China, the new frontier for spas in the 21st century, and experience a surge of new treatments originating from the Himalayan region. Banyan Tree Spas, well loved throughout Asia for their romantic experiences, have created one of their most tempting spa concepts yet—the Tibetan-inspired Banyan Tree Ringha resort in Yunnan Province.

At 12,000 feet (3,600 meters) above sea level, ancient life is recaptured in the architecture of the resort, which comprises reconstructed old timber Tibetan farmhouses, featuring 15 beautiful one-bedroom Tibetan suites and 11 rustic two-bed-room Tibetan lodges. In fact, one may well wonder why one needs a spa treatment at all when pristine lakes, streams and snow-capped mountains frame your view whilst you luxuriate in one of the handcarved wooden Tibetan bathtubs.

Yunnan is renowned as a source for traditional Chinese medicine (TCM) practices, so the spa takes its inspiration from its milieu. Two signature warming treatments to counter the coolish weather are offered in six exquisite Spa Suites. Choose

Below Accommodation here ranges from the Ringha Lodge to the rustic traditional charm of Tibetan lodges and a Tibetan Spa Suite that is a spa within a spa concept.

Opposite Capturing a sense of place, the Tibetan lodges are built in the tradition of old Tibetan farmhouses.

from the Tibetan hot stone massage therapy combined with *tui na* techniques in the Ringha package and the Himalayan Harmony treatment with *gui shi* hot stone massage designed for complete nurturing. The massages here are based on the five-element principles of traditional Chinese medicine.

The *gui shi* hot stone massage has its roots in Himalayan healing techniques described in the ancient *Gui Shi* text, Tibet's medical bible, and incorporates the use of smooth heated river stones. The stones are used for a slow but deep massage. Warm stones are left on specific points to move *ch'i* throughout the body. What makes these stones precious is that each one has been handcarved by monks from the nearby Kopan Monastery. Different healing mantras and Buddhist symbols are crafted on to the stones in the belief that the therapist will pass these qualities to the guests via the massage.

For natural warmth, the Himalayan Harmony package combines the *gui shi* hot stone massage with a black sesame scrub and a rice wine bath, so be prepared to experience a sensation of clearness whilst you bathe in warmth. Another sensation is the Tibetan Tiptoe package for feet—perfect after a day spent trekking in the nearby mountains. It starts with a herbal foot soak, then employs foot reflexology and conditioning to relieve sore muscles and improve energy flow. As evening descends upon your intimate world, take a moment to breathe in the mystery of mountain life and express gratitude for the life and experiences that you've been given.

THE SPA AT THE LALU

SUN MOON LAKE, TAIWAN

Previous page In ancient times, the area around Sun Moon Lake was known as *shuishalian* meaning "where water and sand meet."

Left The leisure center spa area features warming fireplaces and views across the lake, not to mention a host of alluring water therapies.

Left below The Lalu was designed by world-renowned architect Kerry Hill. Each of the resort's rooms overlooks the largest freshwater lake in Taiwan and teakwood, glass and stone are the main materials used. Tempting ingredients used for the beauty rituals range from green tea and rice wine to ginger and rice bran.

Below and bottom Water is a meaningful element here: generous soaking tubs, Japanese-style hot, warm and icy whirlpools, scented steam rooms, dry saunas and wet rooms are all surrounded by the endless calm of Sun Moon Lake. Each of the spa suites has fabulous airy views across the lake.

Positioned in the abundant countryside of Nantou County, central Taiwan, the Lalu is a peaceful retreat for relaxation and rejuvenation. Situated beside the tranquil waters of pristine Sun Moon Lake, the hotel, accentuated by Oriental elegance and contemporary style, is a haven for body, mind and spirit.

The spa offers a seamless blend of professional service and natural luxury. It is among the most beautiful spas in all of Asia. State of the art facilities include a spacious yoga/aerobics/dance studio, gym, beauty salon and spa lounge complete with a fireplace and juice bar, separate male and female spa areas with dry Swedish sauna, aromatic steam, cold plunge and hot whirlpools—all facing the gorgeous Sun Moon Lake. Private, modern spa suites feature open fireplaces, steam showers and enormous terrazzo baths.

The philosophy is that of a 21st-century spa combined with a restorative destination for mind, body and spirit. Inspired by the five elements theory of traditional Chinese medicine, there are five areas of expertise: fitness, treatments, nutrition and counseling, beauty and health, and meditation.

Many treatments are designed to activate the Chinese energy meridian points. This is a good place for reflexology or a traditional Taiwanese acupressure massage, an oil-free treatment that releases tension in tight muscles and other stressed areas. What's also special is the Lalu's own signature style of long stroke massage with essential oils to heal the mental and emotional needs of the guest.

The Japanese tradition of hot spring bathing in Taiwan is honored via a range of water therapies. There's a hot whirlpool and chilled plunge pools to stimulate muscles and increase circulation; a body-tranquilizing cold plunge pool; a sauna in a *hinoki*-paneled room; and a ceramic-tiled herbal steam room to refresh the respiratory passages, detoxify the whole body and soothe muscles. And for pampering, the menu offers a choice of Chinese-inspired body elixirs and beauty rituals. Try a jade massage with two therapists working in harmony, or the two-hour Orient Body Elixir Ritual consisting of a ginger scrub, honey body mask, ginger bath and acupressure massage. The strong ancient healing arts of the East are combined at the Lalu with a touch of aromatherapy, green tea body scrubs, slimming treatments, and marine rejuvenation.

ANANDA
IN THE HIMALAYAS

TEHRI GARHWAL, INDIA

Ananda in the Himalayas is regarded as one of the world's top destination spas. Combining a beautiful natural environment with a plethora of treatments, healthy food and ample time and space, it offers an extremely nurturing experience. Situated in the foothills of the mighty Himalayas where ayurveda and yoga were born thousands of years earlier, it is set in the grounds of a 19th-century palace.

Getting there is a journey in itself. The property is a four-hour train ride from New Delhi to Haridwar, followed by a pleasant one-hour car journey up into the mountains. Along the way you pass through the pilgrimage town of Rishikesh, where millions travel each year to bathe in the sacred waters of the Ganges. On arrival at the Ananda, you are led into the palace annexe that houses the reception area, suites, library, yoga and meditation rooms, and conference halls. Separate and more modern wings nearby house the accommodation, restaurant and spa.

At the Ananda, the focus is on innovative organic ayurvedic-macrobiotic food, yoga sessions supervised by highly qualified instructors, and plenty of spa treatments. There is a resident nurse, ayurvedic physician and physio-therapist, and both ayurvedic and Western therapies are offered. Treatment rooms are decked out in rich red and saffron colors which represent spirituality in India's far north.

Capture the essence of the Himalayas with treatments beginning with a foot bath in a copper bowl containing rocks collected from the Ganges that give a reflexology-like effect. The ayurvedic wing is extremely thorough and an ayurvedic session always begins with the customary consultation by the physician. It offers a comprehensive range of treatments such as *abyanga* (synchronized massage therapy), *chakra-dhara* (oils poured over the *chakras*), *takradhara* (like *shiro-dhara* but with buttermilk) and *mukh lepa* (an ancient Indian facial beauty ritual). In addition, there is an abundance of other treatments, including a full range of massage styles, reiki, hydrotherapies and body therapies.

However, it's not all health-focused, holy and ashram-like. Ananda is fun too! Wine and coffee are served, there is a

small golf course, an outdoor squash court, tennis courts and swimming pool—and treks in the surrounding area are offered. But most people find that, after a couple of days at the Ananda, they slow down and begin to find their inner stillness. The Vedic texts say that "what surrounds us is simply a reflection of what resides within"—and surrounded by the peaceful beauty of the Himalayan foothills and the expansive grounds, many guests take time out to contemplate, reflect and give thanks.

Above The restored Viceregal Palace provides a dramatic entrance to this destination resort.

Opposite top and bottom Offerings of flowers to beautify the soul. Ananda houses India's only Aveda Beauty Institute—a collaboration with Estée Lauder.

Right A marine facial is one of many treatments on the menu at Sereno Spa at the Park Hyatt. Shimmering with memorable ayurvedic and European traditions, it is regarded as a complete wellness destination.

Below A sunset stroll along Arossim Beach. Goa has long been known as a soulful place with graceful palms and white beaches, festive celebrations, and a vibrant fusion culture.

Opposite top and bottom An evening ritual where a therapist lights *diyas* or "little lamps" around the spa lobby. The *shirodhara* treatment is like "heaven in a cup" for anyone in search of inner calm.

SERENO SPA
AT PARK HYATT
GOA RESORT

SOUTH GOA, INDIA

If you want to explore the true essence of ayurveda, yoga, meditation and sacred body treatments in their original forms, a visit to India is definitely your karma! India is the birthplace of yoga, meditation, ritual bathing and *tantra* not to mention dozens of massage styles (the Thai massage style originates from here), so it's little wonder that the country sparkles like a thousand candles on the fast-expanding international spa scene.

Sereno Spa at Park Hyatt Goa combines a five-star luxury hotel experience with a holistic spa. There's something nurturing about knowing you can laze on a lounger by the biggest swimming pool in India, then wander up to the spa and receive a quality treatment where the benefits will linger for days. Communing with nature is the philosophy here: Goa itself wraps around the Arabian Sea and the Park Hyatt is situated on a very long, crisp white sand beach fringed with coconut palms. It offers plenty of solitude, even though there are many facilities. The spa takes its design inspiration from Goa's Portuguese heritage: cool mosaic-tiled Iberian court-yards with fountains and tranquil treatment rooms and an outdoor meditation enclave set in a casuarina grove.

The list of treatments is extensive and authentic. Ayurvedic options include the *abhyanga* synchronized massage, *pizhichil*, *shirodhara* and *thakradhara*, as well as some less well-known treatments that are not normally found in the West. The *choorna swedam* is a full body massage: practised with a bolus of herbs and grains, it helps relieve neurological disorders, rheumatism and arthritis. The *udwarthanamis* is a therapeutic form of dry herbal powder massage that is given with firm pressure and promises to help slim the body, impart mobility to the joints, strengthen muscles and refresh the body. Another unusual therapy is *nasyam*—based on the theory that stimulation of the limbic system via the olfactory nerves can have a profound effect on mood, emotions, desires, appetite and memories, it involves

the application of medicated oils to the nose. During the process the area around the nose, neck, and shoulders is massaged to clear impurities from the head and sinus, reducing tension and promoting relaxation.

For those serious about detoxification and rebalancing of the body, the five-pronged *pancha karma* is offered in comforting surrounds. This therapy helps body tissues to release their wastes and toxins and restores the natural function of both tissue and *dosha*. It is only recommended after consultation with a physician and takes a minimum of seven days. On a more lighthearted note, there is yoga massage, Indian head massage, *shiatsu*, a crystal energy healing treatment (see page 133) and a comprehensive range of holistic facial treatments—all given within view of the magnificent beach.

THE ISLAND SPA
AT FOUR SEASONS RESORT MALDIVES

KUDA HURAA, NORTH MALE ATOLL, MALDIVES

There is only one way to reach this tropical island spa, and that's by *dhoni* (a traditional Maldivian wooden boat). Situated on a small sandbar just across the lagoon from Four Seasons Resort Maldives at Kuda Huraa, the water element flows generously throughout this stunning facility. Each of the seven spacious free-standing spa pavilions has massage beds positioned above translucent floors allowing you to observe colorful marine life during treatments. The gentle *dhoni* trip across tranquil waters helps to relax you before you reach the spa.

The Island Spa menu features a comprehensive range of ayurvedic, Thai and Indonesian treatments as well as skin scrubs inspired by various Asian traditions. The Oceanic Ritual reflects beautifully the essence of this spa resort: blending aromatherapy with a blue ocean sea salt scrub as well as a mineralizing body mask and ocean bath enriched with salt and citrus blends, it finishes with a coconut milk and vanilla bean elixir.

Another alluring treatment is the Maldivian Monsoon Ritual. Here you are invited to lie on a wooden bed as jets of warm water caress your skin. A ground mix of *kela gana*, a sandalwood exfoliant, starts your journey and is followed by a soothing rain shower and rosewater rinse. Next, you are treated to a full-body herbal oil massage and a steam bath featuring frankincense. A sandalwood body lotion completes the ritual.

For many, the atolls of the Maldives represent the ultimate tropical seaside holiday. Sun-drenched sensual days, pristine tranquil waters, empty white sand beaches—these are the images we all have in mind. And for once, the dreamy picture-postcard brochure isn't a myth: this resort has powdery white beaches, clear turquoise waters and a divine thatched roof spa in the midst of it all. It is a true celebration of the beauty of the Asian spa.

Previous page What better way to arrive at the Island Spa than by traditional wooden *dhoni* native boat?

Above Streams of water flowing from Vichy shower jets represent a gentle monsoon rain during the signature Maldivian Monsoon Ritual.

Right top left Cardamom seeds are one of the stimulating Indian spices used to create the spa's almond *marsala* skin scrub. Blended with clove leaves, black pepper, nutmeg and raw almonds, this preparation is given in combination with a soothing neck and back massage.

Right and above right Inhale a whiff of the exotic as you meander amidst villas with Indian, Arabian and Moroccon influences. At the spa, each of the treatment pavilions is positioned directly over the lagoon with a port hole in the floor allowing views of water and marine life.

asia's best
spa treatments

the world
is our spa

OPEN YOUR EYES AND LOOK AROUND. BENEATH YOU LIES THE EARTH, OXYGEN SURROUNDS YOU, BEYOND IS THE OCEAN AND

EVERYWHERE THERE IS SPIRIT.

In the past the word "spa" was synonymous with European destinations, but today it has far wider connotations. As our appreciation of the need for health, beauty and rejuvenation grows, so too has the interpretation of the spa evolved.

This is especially true in Asia where many of the best spas and retreats now offer a variety of treatments drawn from many parts of the globe, albeit with an emphasis on those culled from the East. The huge storehouse of Asian wellness therapies blends life force, nature, water and kind healing hands with disciplines that have developed over the centuries. In the past we cleansed and bathed ourselves in natural sources of water; now, with the advent of spas, the ocean has become the thalasso pool, natural hot springs are *onsen*, and a variety of heat and cold therapies deriving from ancient steam bath practices have developed.

Returning the body to equilibrium—through ancient botanical recipes and time-honored rituals—is the prime focus of most Asian spas. Some treatments pay tribute to ancient bathing practices, others revisit beautifying treatments once administered in royal palaces, while others have been passed on by monks or local village healers. Disciplines such as martial arts, meditation and yoga practiced for centuries in monasteries and temples, are currently experiencing a renaissance. Most treatments originate from Asia's holistic medical systems, as in the past doctors were often healers, philosophers, shamans, monks and priests all in one.

An understanding of "life force," also known as body energy, *prana*, *ch'i* or *ki* that flows through all life forms and through the earth itself, is a vital element of the Asian spa. In Asian medicine, therapists and physicians work to free up stagnated energy to return the body to balance. Yoga, pranic breathing, massages, scrubs, acupuncture and more are all geared to stimulate this life force. Awareness of how energy flows through a nourished body is believed to be the key to health and longevity.

Previous page The hot stone therapy at Six Senses Spas works deeply into muscles and tissues with extremely rejuvenating results.

Opposite Water is the soul of spa and reflects our inner beauty.

Asia's two oldest medical systems—ayurveda and traditional Chinese medicine (TCM) and the therapeutic treatments given by traditional healers in Indonesia, Malaysia, the Philippines, Thailand and Tibet—advocate that the world is an expression of our inner self. What goes on around us also resides within. Texts on ayurvedic medicine and yoga explain this in detail. Similarly, TCM is based on the belief that external appearances are not separate from inner organs and body functions; rather the outside manifestation is a mirror of that within. When eyes are radiant, complexion clear and body functions regular, it is thought that a person is in good health. Realigning our emotional and spiritual wellbeing is also a key factor in achieving a balanced body.

Exploring the origins of Asian's healing systems is a pilgrimage in itself, a tapestry that weaves together centuries of philosophies, practices and rituals. Since so many spas in Asia base their treatments on past modalities, it is important to consider how and why they evolved —as well as how they are offered in a modern-day environment.

The rebirth of ayurveda

Research suggests that the ayurvedic system of medicine was one of the first scientific methodologies to exist. Ancient texts, written some 5,000 years ago, are still being refined with many scholars sure that certain aspects of ayurvedic practice are at least 20,000 years old.

Translated from *ayur* meaning "life" and *veda* meaning "knowledge," ayurveda or the "science of life" is currently experiencing a global renaissance in spas and wellness centers. Legend has it that 52 scholars and *rishis* (sages) traveled to the Himalayas to gather life knowledge from the Vedic gods. Their intention was to find a solution that would give every person the tools to maintain his or her own health. Knowledge of health (which incorporated the physical, mental, spiritual and emotional) was never meant to be for the select few—and thus the philosophy behind ayurveda was born.

Regarded by many as the "medicine of the gods," ayurveda is laid out in the ancient Vedic texts. Although there are three Sanskrit

ayurvedic texts containing the secrets of health and longevity, the most recent is the *Ashtanga Hridayam* by Vagbhata (600 BC). This divides ayurveda into eight limbs or branches: *kaya chikitsa* or general medicine; *shalya tantra* or major surgery; *shalakya tantra* or treatments for ears, nose, throat, eyes and mouth; *bhuta vidhya* or psychiatry; *bala tantra* or gynecology and pediatrics; *agada tantra* or toxicology; *rasayana tantra* or rejuvenation; and *vajikarana tantra* or aphrodisiacs.

Dr Rajeev Marwah at the Mandarin Oriental Dhara Devi Spa near Chiang Mai explains that ayurveda is "like a large river or an ocean with so much knowledge yet to be rediscovered." He says that the essence of ayurveda is to give people the inspiration to take care of their own health. The World Health Organization now recognizes ayurveda as a proven health system, and its ancient treatments, herbs and oils are continually being researched and refined.

Dr Suchada Marwah, an ayurvedic doctor and practitioner at the same spa, says that prevention lies at the heart of ayurveda. "When we are healthy then we are empowered," she says. "This was the underlying principle of ayurveda in the first place—to empower the people." Ayurvedic physicians do not perceive sickness or disease as something to be feared, but rather as a phase and a timely opportunity to improve lifestyle habits. Prescriptions range from oil massage, herbal preparations and medicinal baths to diet and lifestyle recommendations in order to regulate the function of the body's organs, improve circulation and balance the nervous system. On another level, you may receive advice to alter your approach to life or do something radically different for 20 minutes each week, or be offered a deep luxurious face massage to give you a fresher outlook.

In essence, ayurveda aims to increase *ojas*, the substance that nourishes and connects our mind, body and spirit. The mind is seen as a tool for intention, for how we want to live our life; the body is a tool to become what we want to be; and the spirit, the omnipresent energy that fills our being with vibration, gives us the power to lead the life we want. The renaissance of this ancient science—and its present-day applications in Asian spas—is encouraging indeed.

Traditions of balance and healing

Most Asian healing systems emphasize that a balanced, healthy person is nourished, detoxified and has free, unfettered circulation of energy flowing throughout the body. Traditional Chinese medicine (TCM) advocates this in all its therapies. It says that when an area of the body is blocked or blood flow stagnates, then imbalance or disease may occur. Its main goal is to unblock channels and allow *ch'i* to flow harmoniously. Disturbances in *ch'i* flow can derive from many factors: emotional instability or lack of a balanced perception,

extreme environmental changes such as cold and hot weather, as well as a deficiency or excess in *yin* or *yang* diet and lifestyle.

The ancient Chinese medical text *The Yellow Emperor's Medicine Classic* (*Huang Di Nei Ching*) believed to have been written around 2,000 years ago, contains the roots of TCM within its pages, and the work of many scholars and practitioners has helped to continually evolve it. This medical system blends Taoist, Buddhist and Confucian beliefs, all of which have contributed to its current form.

Many Asian spas have TCM therapies on their menus, and some even have on-site Chinese doctors. In TCM, a consultation with a TCM doctor or practitioner takes place before any treatment, prescription, medication or remedy is given. Dr Li Hongke from Pangkor Laut Spa Village explains that the Chinese method of diagnosis involves four principles: the study of the body, particularly the facial area; listening to the sound of the patient's voice and breathing; asking questions; and taking the patient's pulse. What is important is how well the blood is flowing through the body, as well as the quality and quantity of the blood, if the body is excessive or deficient in heat or cold, and how well *ch'i* is flowing through body. A careful study of tongue, face, skin texture and eyes is usual, and many questions on diet and lifestyle history are posed. Prescriptions are normally in the form of acupuncture, massage and herbal remedies—all geared to rebalance the body's energies.

In traditional Malaysian healing, diagnostic approaches vary from healer to healer. However, all agree that no one food or herb actually cures a physical ailment, but rather, the body has its own healing mechanism. Malay healers advocate the maintenance of balance in the human constitution. If all constituents are balanced, then one will have a long and fulfilling life. The main constituents used for diagnosis are the Four Body Elements—earth, water, fire and air. The others are the Four Humors that include blood, phlegm, bile and spleen, and the fundamental body organs, spirit, faculties (natural, vital or psychic) and functions (attraction or repulsion). In traditional Malay medicine, it is believed that an imbalanced constituent either individually or in combination with another constituent leads to disease in people.

Treatments vary according to diagnosis but most use a holistic approach: Naturopathy (herbal concoctions for internal cleansing and blood purification), physiotherapy (exercise, massage or other external methods to reduce or eliminate toxins in the body) and diet suggestions (advice to regulate the quality and quantity of food and water intake or fasting), are all used to achieve a physical and spiritual balance.

Another health system that centers around balancing the body's energies with the rhythms of nature, internal nutrients and the flow of circulation is the ancient one that developed in Tibet. Tibetan medicine

the world is our spa

Below Ayurvedic herbs and medicinal products ready for a consultation by a traditional physician.

Right In ancient Thailand, Buddhist monks were responsible for transcribing and maintaining the ancient medicinal systems of ayurveda and Thailand's own healing knowledge.

is thought to have Persian, Chinese and Indian-ayurvedic influences as well as incorporating some Mongolian practices. Ian Baker, author of *The Tibetan Art of Healing* and co-founder of Kamalaya Spa in Koh Samui, explains: "The Tibetan *sowa rigpa* or "science of healing" developed in tandem with Tibet's tantric form of Buddhism. Their medical tantras —the *Gyushi*—categorize various types of *ch'i* that circulate through-out the 72,000 body meridians and affect both one's physiological functions, as well as one's mental and emotional wellbeing. Treatments focus on restoring optimal flow to the body's vital energies and often lead to profound physical and psychological transformation."

He says the flow of life force or energy essential to health is known as *tsok loong*. "It is believed that if *tsok loong* is balanced, it will spread harmoniously through the meridians bringing integration, clarity and bliss to mind and body." However, it needs to be stressed that Tibetan doctors maintain that the ultimate goal of healing is not just physical and mental wellbeing; rather it includes "the flowering of wisdom, compassion and generosity in full awareness of our interconnectedness with all life."

Tibetan diagnostic techniques are called *ngozen*, which means literally to "identify" or "see through," and treatments include dietary changes, massages, mineral baths and moxibustion. Tibetan doctors take pulse readings and study the patient carefully, checking skin color and listening to the tone of the voice to gauge how well energy is circulating in the body and where rebalancing is needed. There are reportedly over 1,500 herbs used in Tibetan medicine and today Tibetan healers are working to preserve and sustain their practices. Even though genuinely authentic Tibetan ther-apies are rare in spas, many thera-pists incorporate certain Tibetan aspects in their rituals nowadays.

Thailand, today, has an out-standing spa and wellness industry—with many Thai treat-ments having their roots in TCM and ayurveda. Buddhism was introduced from India to Thailand some 23 centuries ago and most of Thailand's monasteries house ancient texts on astrology and healing. One of a monk's tasks was to spend several years rigorously studying meditation, medicine, massage and the use of herbs before educat-ing, teaching or healing others. In Thailand, diagnosis involves taking the pulse and temperature and checking skin texture and color. Doctors may prescribe special herbs and medicines to take internally or apply externally, give advice on diet, recommend meditation or prayer, or suggest some form of massage.

Similar to Tibetan medicine, traditional Thai medical texts indicate that the body contains a network of 72,000 acupressure points known as *sen*. Thais believe that energy flows through these points: if it is flowing unchecked and blood circulation and lymphatic flow are also healthy, then wellbeing is the result.

The classic Thai massage is probably the most well known Thai treatment—and is given in spas worldwide. The Thai word for massage derives from a Sanskrit word meaning "ancient and sacred," —and the essence of *nuat bo'rarn* or Thai massage is to heal through touch. Other Thai traditions that help to rejuvenate are Buddhist-inspired prayer and meditation, as well as herbal and dietary prac-tices. The delivery of Thai treatments varies from region to region with therapies from the northern Thai Lanna and Burmese cultures now being rediscovered.

The cluster of atolls that make up the Maldives has a fascinating history of healing that is being adapted by local spas. Sand poultices steamed in salt water, ancient bathing rituals known as *lonu veyu* and sand massages are some examples. The influences here are mainly ayurvedic introduced from nearby Sri Lanka and India, together with Arabic and traces of Chinese practices passed on by early traders.

According to the creators of Per Aquum Resorts & Spas, who spent several months tracking down one elderly Maldivian healer to help them develop treatments, a traditional Maldivian diagnosis involves checking the quality of one's circulation and body condition to understand whether one is a hot or cold monsoon person. Once this is ascertained, herbs and oil massages are prescribed. A herbal apothecary of cooling and warm-ing barks, shrubs, flowers and resins are all used to infuse massage oils.

In Japan, traditional medicine is known as *kanpo* or "the Chinese method," and, unsurprisingly, it is also based on the regular flow of *ch'i* or *ki* as it is known in Japanese. With the exception of their signature bathing rituals, most of Japan's medical practices come from China and Europe. Like the ancient Chinese and indeed many Asian cultures, the Japanese believed that illness was a result of spirits' actions. Hence, rituals were performed to purify and prevent sickness. In the 5th century, TCM was introduced to Japan along with Buddhism, and in 560 AD, moxibustion and acupuncture started to be practiced.

Today, the Japanese integrate TCM ideas with other systems to re-energize and stimulate *ki* in order to restore equilibrium. A Japanese diagnosis to determine one's *ki* includes a concentrated study of face,

skin, hair, nails and body proportions. This is called *bo shin*. *Setsu shin* or the "taking of the pulse" is said to reveal the state of internal organs. Remedies are usually herbal, and also include acupuncture and massage. One example is *shiatsu* massage, which is performed on the points that move *ki* through the body. Another is through reiki: introduced to the west via Japan, it is a healing with hands therapy system that is performed without touching the client, but rather by channeling energy through the hands from a distance to heal. It is also regarded as a powerful self-healing tool that anyone can learn.

Filipino traditional medicine is an eclectic mix of healing knowledge, attitudes, skills and methods. Dr Jaime Galvez Tan, Vice Chancellor for Research at the University of the Philippines in Manila, reports that it dates back thousands of years. As in Malaysia and Indonesia, many practices were introduced by traders, including 11th-century Arabian traders who brought the Greek-Persian *Unani-Tibb* practices, as well as Chinese and Indian travellers.

He explains that traditional medicine is based on the theory of macrocosm and microcosm (or the *kalawakan* and *sangkatauhan*). "The indigenous thinking here is that everything is interlinked and intertwined and that whatever happens in the universe has an effect on humankind and vice versa," says Dr Tan Living in harmony and respecting nature is essential to good health.

According to Dr Tan there are seven traditional healing treatments: bathing (*paligo*) with concoctions of indigenous roots and aromatic leaves and flowers; herbal steam inhalation (*oslob*) using a cotton cloth to increase a hot infusion into the body system; the renowned *hilot* (Filipino massage) to move excess wind out of the body; decoctions made from medicinal herbs to restore balance (*dinalisay*); a kind of reiki with the healer using their hands to transfer healing energy into the guest known as *kisig galing*; the use of *unang lana*, a highly nutritious, fresh coconut oil applied in massage, hair tonics and masks and drunk as a rejuvenating elixir; and the use of long bamboo sticks (*kawayan*) to tap certain areas of the body to unblock unwanted energy and release wind or cold out of the system.

Ultimately, what binds these Asian medical practices together is the understanding of how nature works and that, given the proper conditions, the body has the ability to heal itself. With this knowledge, practitioners work to treat the root of a problem rather than the symptom, knowing that in the long term this is the most effective way to heal. Increasingly, more Asian spas are offering preventative therapies, as well as treatments geared to specific problems and purely pampering ones.

From temples and palaces to the spa

Now that Asian spa therapies have been embraced by wellness experts worldwide, the effort to understand the true nature of these treatments has begun. So many of the alluring therapies we experience today were developed in temples, palaces and monasteries in areas as far apart as the Himalayas, China, Japan and the countries of southeast Asia.

In India, beautifying rituals were offered in ancient palaces and forts. Dating back some 5,000 years, they comprised three- to four-hour rituals whereby women celebrated their femininity prior to their wedding ceremonies. Foot baths, *ubtan* scrubs, wraps and massages used exquisite essences of pure rose and sandalwood and rosewater. The focus was not entirely on the physical, and much attention was given to beautifying the spiritual self through dance, sensory and meditative rituals and decoration with gems and pearls to balance circulation. Many ancient temples sport carvings of women admiring their bodies and receiving beauty rituals.

In Thailand and Indonesia, temples were and still are significant in storing and recording many of the most valued recipes. Some of the

pampering Indonesian treatments like the *mandi lulur* were developed from the 16th century onwards in the royal palaces of Java, while the traditional Thai "yoga massage" was originally only practiced and given by monks in the *wat* (temple). We now know that the origin of Thai massage may be traced back 3,000 years, when an Indian doctor, Shivago Karmapaj, traveled to this region and introduced ayurveda, massage, herbal remedies, meditation and yoga to the Khmers.

In China, Buddhism entered China during the 1st century AD and became popular in the 3rd century. Buddhist (and earlier Taoist) monasteries specialized in different aspects of TCM. At the Shaolin monastery in Henan Province, treatments such as trauma and injury massage, moxibustion and acupuncture, as well as external applications of herbal oils to combat swelling, bleeding and trauma, reached their peak in the Tang dynasty (618–907 AD). Another

Below Bottles filled with *jamu* plants and herbs from the gardens at Bagus Jati Wellbeing Resort.

Opposite From the forest to the spa—plants, flowers, roots, barks and leaves are ground, blended and boiled before they are bottled as *jamu* elixirs for internal and external applications.

important monastery that had a strong healing tradition is where *tai chi* was founded in the Sung dynasty (960–1279 AD), at the Taoist monastery on Wudang Mountain. Here, even until today, practices dealing with self-cultivation and meditational enhancement are encouraged, and calligraphy as a healing technique was also developed here.

In Japan, both Zen Buddhist temples (from the 6th century onwards) and much earlier Shinto shrines were built adjacent to cleansing *onsen* or volcanic hot springs. The monks had specific bathing facilities built and utilized them in order to purify both mind and body. Early collections of Japanese religious thought and practice —*Kojiki* or *Records of Ancient Matters* (712 AD) and the *Nihon Shoki* or *Chronicles of Japan* (720 AD) are mainly about mythology, Shinto rituals and culture, but also include descriptions of healing plants and *shiatsu*'s predecessor *jin shi jyustu*, a massage style that worked to unlock blockages of life force within the body.

Current spa practices in Asia pay tribute to the ancient practices originally formulated in these spiritual centers. All over southeast Asia, healing methods and recipes were formulated and passed on by Buddhist monks and sages who traveled throughout the region exploring, discovering and sharing. Now, inspirational spa directors continue their work. Just as the temples of the past sought to illuminate, so too the spas of today are creating a culture of healing and holistic wellness.

From the forest to the spa

Nature plays a vital role in the development of treatments and therapies in Asia. Squeeze the healing essences from indigenous plants, flowers, trees and barks and you have one of the most effective apothecaries in the world. Recent research into traditional Asian ingredients is revealing just how important they are. The Japanese propensity for drinking green tea has resulted in the discovery that it contains many antioxidants. It is now accepted that ginger purifies, lime is an energizing tonic, and ginkgo and ginseng have very powerful properties for both mental and physical health. Increasingly, innovative spa therapists are utilizing the healing properties of Asian plants in new and enticing spa treatments.

A reliance on local plants is integral to ayurvedic remedies, while according to the precepts of TCM, the choice of plant is dependent on its cooling or warming properties. Puan Sairani Mohd Sa'ad, the Malay specialist at Pangkor Laut Resort who comes from a long line of Malaysian healers, explains that many recipes and products were (and still are) kept secret within the family. "The properties of turmeric, Kaffir lime, rice powder, sandalwood, nutmeg and clove are commonly known," she says, "but it is the traditional Malaysian healers known as *bomoh* or *pawang ku kuan* who know the other secret ingredients for healing."

Malaysian treatments primarily revolve around healthcare in the family. External treatments include deep massage, and various techniques to beautify the female and strengthen the male as well as improve the digestive health of small children. Ground rice mixed with a touch of turmeric was used to heal the complexion, while smearing the face with fresh egg white is common. Lemongrass, ginger, galangal and coconut were (and still are) used extensively in cooking, treatments and offerings.

Observe one of the oldest continuous cultures in the world, Japan, and see how the Japanese sustain themselves internally and externally. Mineral-rich hot spring bathing, green tea ceremonies and eating seaweed are valued age-old health practices here. Local produce like bamboo, *nori*, sea algae, plum wine, rice bran and *yuzu* (small citrus fruits) are fast becoming desired spa and skin care ingredients. In Tibet, people relied on locally grown barley, juniper, mustard oil and butter to nourish the skin, while plants and herbs like *gotu kola*, spikenard and *amla*, all classified as important ayurvedic ingredients, are gaining popularity in longevity supplements and skin care products.

Indonesia, which is home to the world's largest tropical rainforests, has a strong tradition of herbal medicine. Also influenced by ayurveda and TCM, Indonesia's centuries-old herbal medicine system is known as *jamu*. Experimentation with various plants along with knowledge introduced by Chinese, Arabic and early Indian traders, has resulted in literally hundreds of recipes, many of them handed down orally from generation to generation over centuries. There is also a record of over 1,700 healing remedies in an 1872 Javanese poetic text in several volumes called the *Serat Centhini*. Other medicinal formulae are recorded on *lontars* or palm leaf manuscripts as well as in medical journals and on statuary. Many Asian spas are researching these ancient traditions and use indigenous herbs, spices, fruits and flowers in their treatments.

Indonesians regard *jamu* as the ancient elixir of life. Created from local herbs, flowers, fruits, barks and roots, *jamu* is drunk as a medicinal tonic or applied through face and body masks, body wraps, massage oils and balms. *Jamu* is considered by many Indonesians to be the best way to increase blood circulation and metabolism, regulate digestion and increase longevity. Even today, millions of Indonesians take *jamu* daily as a preventative tonic and to promote endurance. In Bali, *jamu* elixirs were formulated and passed down by *balian* (Balinese medicine men). Used to treat fevers, headaches, muscle

the world is our spa

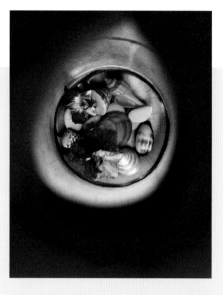

aches and chills, these herbal concoctions use natural plant extracts and herbs to benefit blood circulation and overall health. Many Balinese spas, and others elsewhere in Asia, offer *jamu*-inspired treatments with varying degrees of authenticity.

"At last, Western science is acknowledging that Asia holds the cures to some age-old ailments," says Feny Sri Sulistiawati, the woman behind the Indonesian spa range Jamu Jamu. "We're endeavoring to unlock some of those secrets and make them available for research." In addition, ancient remedies and cures recorded on palm leaf manuscripts are being deciphered and analyzed at centers across Indonesia. Many individuals are dedicated to preserving ancient medicinal formulae that are in danger of being lost forever. From the Himalayas to the islands of tropical southeast Asia, these people pay tribute to Asia's cultural diversity and rich botanical heritage in the revival of many ancient treatments.

Healing waters

As we have seen, Asian-based medicine systems and the cornucopia of Asia's natural bounty lie at the heart of the Asian spa. There is, however, one other important ingredient—water.

The human body is composed of around 70 percent water and the earth has about the same percentage. Everybody—and everything—is fluid filled: water transports nourishment in the blood to vital organs and is the medium that carries minerals and nutrients to plant life. Water enlivens, freshens and gives us energy. It is essential to present and future life on the planet—and an all-pervading element in the modern-day spa.

In Asia, water is at the core of bathing rituals, blessings and ceremonies. Thousands of people bathe in the holy Ganges River in India in a ritual symbolic of purification. In Tibet, water is regarded as one of the greatest sources of therapeutic medicine. An annual bathing festival is held on the banks of the Kishu River in Lhasa in August. In early September in Ladakh, Tibetan-speaking peoples of the western Himalayas wait until a special healing star called the *rishi* emerges in the sky before traveling to hot springs to replenish and renew. In Islamic countries, reverence for water traces back to the 7th century when the prophet Mohammed recommended water rituals for cleansing before prayer. An offshoot of this was the introduction of the *hamam* sweat bath: not dissimilar in aim and practice to the Japanese *onsen*, both men's and women's *hamam* are places for washing, scrubbing and socializing.

In pre-Buddhist Japan, communal hot springs or *onsen* were traditional meeting places where people came together to bathe. The ritual of bathing, like the ceremony of tea drinking, became an aesthetic expression of healing and beauty. Bathing in Japan's natural hot springs is a centuries-old way of returning the body to balance and is still regarded today as most beneficial. Many doctors often prescribe a trip to an *onsen* to heal various ailments, both physical and mental.

In accordance with the Islamic faith, bathing is an important element in Malay healing. The bath in Malaysia is more than a body cleanser. Blessings with water are made as silent *mantras* are intoned at important events and ceremonies. And in Indonesia, there is clear evidence of a profound bathing culture—both past and present. A relief at the Borobudur temple, built in 824 AD, shows the Buddha preparing to bathe in a pool full of flowers, aloe and sandalwood, while at Prambanan, a Javanese Hindu temple built in 781–872 AD, there is a sketch of a bathing ceremony used for sanctification. In addition, royal bathing pavilions are plentiful, and in the *Serat Centhini* text, mention is made of sacred springs, fountains and bathing places throughout the Majapahit kingdom. Later Islamic influences furthered the traditional culture of bathing in the region—and today bathing is practised both formally and informally.

At the Four Seasons Resort in Langkawi, guests are given a final blessing with rosewater to complete their Malaysian Mist spa ritual; and in Bali, the water element is seen as essential to spiritual life and an integral part of every ceremony. Ayu Martiashi from Maya Ubud spa explains that the Balinese pay homage to the god of water, Dewa Wisnu, with a shrine in the home and flower-filled foot baths are de rigeur at the beginning of treatments in a spa.

The global movement towards wellness has revitalized a fascination with water not only as a therapy but also as an element that may be used for togetherness. The revival of the European *thermae* (hot baths), Vichy showers, Turkish *hamams* and *rhassouls* together with Asia's own *onsen* and bathing traditions are all about taking to the waters as a way of having fun. Not all spas offer treatments; some simply have water therapies.

Asia is now developing its own therapeutic treatments using water. Technology and ecology merge with creations like the amethyst crystal steam rooms at Mandarin Oriental Spas; these combine the Eastern European *hamam* with Asian crystal therapy. Similar to this is the emergence of the color hydrotherapy bath, which is a blend of European bathing rituals with traditional ayurvedic color *chakra* influence.

With water being one of the most precious components for health, the best spa treatments use water consciously. As Dr Masaru Emoto, a Japanese scientist who has spent much of his working life researching the qualities of water, says: "The message of water is love and gratitude." No authentic Asian spa would be without this quintessential element.

massage

"TENSION IS WHO YOU THINK YOU SHOULD BE,
RELAXING IS WHO YOU ARE"

Chinese proverb

Travelling to far-off places helps us grow. Experiencing new sensations, aromas, people, cultures and food enlivens our senses, quickens the pulse and widens our view of life. Likewise, sampling different healing massages can open us up to new possibilities. Indigenous massages from the East vary from country to country and some will appeal to you more than others. Generally, these massages were not created for pleasure but for real therapeutic benefit. The unspoken purpose is to increase blood circulation, restore lymphatic, nervous and musculoskeletal systems, dissolve tension, tightness and stored emotions, and recharge the body.

When you arrive at a new destination, book a local massage to help you ease into the new surroundings. The exotic aromas of herbs and oils, the freshly made teas and the grace of the therapist's touch will allow your body and mind to surrender and soften. Gentle strokes and caresses, light pressure, holding, kneading, stretching, pulling and pounding are just some of the techniques. Others are more vigorous and involve the therapist walking on your back or using elbows to dig a little deeper. Feel free to tell the therapist if you prefer stronger or softer pressure.

So honored is the practice of massage in Asia that the therapist often performs a private ritual at the start of a treatment. This may take the form of a silent prayer or the chiming of two Tibetan bells. Some therapists ask for inner strength for both themselves and their guest. Mandara Spa therapists draw on the concept of oneness and take a few moments to relax and connect with the guest before the treatment begins. Giving through touch is the essence of the Asian massage.

What's exciting is that no two massages are ever the same, and in spas, the creativity is boundless. Many massages honor the village massage approach and merge local traditions with hot stones, flowers, energizing crystals, shells, sand and even jewels. Some spas offer a massage with heated crystals—white and green jade, jasper and adventurine—that deepens the healing experience. It is now recognized that we store most of our emotions in the abdominal area, so specific treatments like the *ch'i nei tsang*, a Taoist-inspired abdominal massage offered at Chiva-Som in Thailand, are an excellent choice for detoxifying, stimulating and strengthening the internal organs.

One cannot expect a therapist to drain away weeks or even years of personal tension instantly (although many do), so the best results come from the recipient working in synergy with the therapist. Communicate clearly what works for you and share any areas of your life you wish to transform—including physical and emotional. Breathe fully and be present.

Right Healing with crystals and stones has long been an integral part of Asian culture. At Six Senses Spas, massage with heated stones is a remarkably relaxing affair.

thai massage

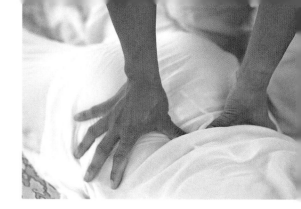

If you are drawn to a treatment that respects your space and need for privacy, increases your energy levels as well as encourages ease of mind, then Thai massage is for you.

With its origins in India, traditional Thai massage or *nuat bo'rarn* is often called "yoga massage" because during this massage the body is gently stretched into yoga-like positions. Similar to Japanese *shiatsu*, it is an oil-free massage where the recipient wears loose cotton pants and a shirt during the treatment. The therapist uses gentle and, if necessary, vigorous pressure, pulling and stretching the body. Utilizing all parts of the body, she or he may even walk on the back and use elbows and knees. The purpose is to unblock any stagnation in the 72,000 energy points or meridians to increase the flow of life force or *sen* as this is known in Thai. Some of the benefits of Thai massage include stress, muscle and pain relief, improved circulation in the blood and lymphatic system, body realignment and better flexibility and digestion.

As with many other Eastern disciplines, Thai massage techniques have been passed on from teacher to student since as far back as the 2nd or 3rd century, when a travelling Indian doctor, Shiva Kumar Baccha, introduced Buddhist practices and beliefs together with medicines and remedies to the people of Thailand. Prior to the advent of modern medicine, Buddhist temples were the main centers of learning, medicine and education in Thailand, with doctors being monks or former monks. Thai massage techniques were first practiced at the Temple of the Reclining Buddha or Wat Pho in Bangkok; here you can see sculptures in stone of various massage postures and even today take a 10-day course in massage techniques at the temple's massage school.

Opposite A traditional Thai massage given in one of the *salas* located in the tropical gardens of the Anantara Spa in Hua Hin. Surrounded by lotus ponds and tropical flowers, you are stretched and pulled to bliss.

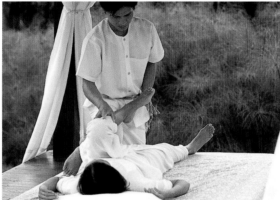

This page One of the chief benefits of traditional Thai massage is that you simply relax whilst the therapist does the work! Acupressure, and twisting, stretching, kneading and pummeling the body are some of the techniques used. The result is a rebalanced body with improved blood circulation and less energy blocks.

Many spas in Thailand offer Thai massage in a traditional *sala* or open pavilion. At the Anantara Spa (pages 70–73), these wall-free structures with soaring roofs are scattered around the garden. We heartily recommend their Traditional Journey, a two-hour treatment that includes a footbath, Thai massage and foot reflexology. Alternatively, at the Four Seasons Spa in Chiang Mai, take a Thai herbal steam before your massage (see page 239). This softens muscles and helps you to relax, so you are more open during the massage.

At the Mandarin Oriental Dhara Devi Spa in Chiang Mai (pages 82–87), some novel Thai-infused massage styles are offered: try the Lanna *tok sen*, a Northern village massage that translates as "tapping line." The treatment begins with the therapist tapping two thick blocks of wood from the tamarind fruit tree along the whole body. The continuous rhythm and sound of the tapping puts the mind at rest and it's surprisingly very relaxing. The tapping works on the various muscle groups, releasing and unlocking tension prior to a soothing herbal oil massage. As with other northern Thai massages, this is not a painful treatment. Another alternative is the traditional Mandalay massage—not unlike the classical Thai style, it is delivered with stronger and firmer pressure. What's special here is that every massage lasts at least one hour and 20 minutes and is followed by a 30-minute rest in a private spa suite.

Another Thai massage not to be missed is the one offered at the various Mandara Spas around the region. This is extremely authentic and reflects the essence of its

origins. A spokesperson explains: "From the Buddhist viewpoint, the giver of massage should be motivated only by the desire to bestow loving kindness with total concern and feeling. Massage given with these motives foremost is a healing experience for the giver as well as the receiver." Since Thai massage is strongly linked to the spiritual practices of Buddhism, it is believed that intrinsic life energy flows between the practitioner and the recipient as a result.

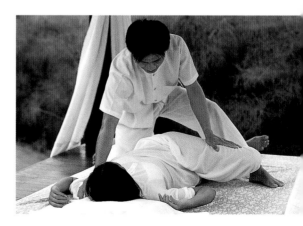

shiatsu massage

Shiatsu derives its name from the two Japanese words—*shi* ("fingers") and *atsu* ("pressure"). Traditionally performed on a simple mattress on a tatami mat floor, it is a graceful and simple Zen massage. Similar to the Thai style, *shiatsu* is oil-free and given to a recipient wearing soft cotton clothing. It is the perfect massage treatment for the relief of stress, headaches, back, shoulder and neck pain, and to combat fatigue.

Like most Asian massages, *shiatsu* is all about stimulating energy flow. Based on the same principles as acupuncture, it stimulates *ki* flow along the body's meridian lines to sustain wellness. *Ki* (*ch'i* in Chinese) is believed to be the basic essence of all living things—when it flows smoothly like a consistent stream, a person is fully energized.

According to Terry Liew, principal at the Shiatsu School in Singapore who trains many therapists at spas in Asia, the USA and the UK, Japanese views on health and beauty are derived from ancient China and have been continually refined over time. "The Japanese view is that once symptoms appear, the problem has already been present for a long time," he explains. "So the objective of the Japanese therapist is to discover any slight imbalances and treat them before they develop into disease." Massage is one such preventative therapy.

If you are travelling in Japan, stay at a traditional Japanese inn or *ryokan* and request an authentic *shiatsu* before bathing in the hot pools. During the massage, the therapist uses different parts of the body, including fingers, thumbs, palms, elbows, and even feet, to put both light and firm pressure on the acupressure points (*tsubos*) to stimulate energy flow. Afterwards a bath in a traditional *onsen* pool is highly recommended: its mineral-rich waters further soothe the muscles.

Shiatsu massage, as given here at a spa in Hokkaido, is a preventative therapy. It has also been used for centuries to diagnose and treat illness. Finger pressure techniques include the use of fingertips, thumbs and palms as well as elbows and even the forearm. Light to deep finger pressure applied to specific parts of the body restores balance. In turn, this promotes all over wellbeing. Not unlike the traditional Thai massage, *shiatsu* is based on the philosophy that the action of healing hands can return the body to equilibrium.

ayurvedic massage

Ayurvedic massages are among the most popular treatments found on spa menus today. To truly experience authentic ayurvedic therapies, a visit to a center in India or Sri Lanka is recommended. However, we are lucky that these treatments and massages are now available throughout spas in Asia. The Spa Village at Pangkor Laut and Mandarin Oriental Dhara Devi Spa in Chiang Mai are just two spas that have an ayurvedic physician on site—and offer authentic and excellent ayurvedic massages.

Developed over the past 5,000 years, Indian massages stimulate *ojas* or energy in the body resulting in outward radiance that shines from an inwardly balanced body. Ayurvedic massage may be given as a stand-alone treatment or as part of another treatment such as *shirodhara* (see page 215). It revitalizes the nervous system, promotes sound sleep, improves vitality and skin complexion, relieves fatigue and strengthens the immune system. By increasing bodily heat and the flow of life-supporting oxygen, it also stimulates circulation and helps the body flush out wastes more efficiently.

The best known style is *abhyanga*. Traditionally taken prior to bathing, this "exercise with oil" massage is an extremely oily rub-down given with *ghee* or sesame and coconut oils infused with herbs, depending on your *dosha* (body type). Dr Suchada Marwah at Mandarin Oriental Dhara Devi Spa says the blend of oils and herbs used varies according to *dosha* type, as does the rhythm and pressure of the massage. This style of massage tones the skin, strengthens the lungs and regulates the digestive system, having an overall re-juvenating effect on the body and mind. On an emotional level, it is known to improve concentration, intelligence, confidence and self-esteem, not to mention youthfulness.

Bombay-born Reenita Malhotra Hora, an Ayurvedic clinician and product designer, says that the therapist normally starts the massage by rubbing a little oil on the crown of the head to release any heat and negative energy. "*Abhyanga* is worked from the center of the body outward to the extremities," she explains. "This follows the body's natural energy flows, thus regulating tissue metabolism and providing for maximum distribution of *ojas*."

The *pizhichil* is another ayurvedic massage offered by many spas like the Prana Spa in Bali, and is recommended for rheumatic diseases, sexual impotence, high or low blood pressure, nervous disorders and for reversing the aging process. It involves two classical ayurvedic treatments,

snehana and *swedana*, with herbal oils massaged into the body by two or four trained masseurs working in a slow rhythmic movement together.

In India, at Ananda in the Himalayas and Sereno Spa in Goa, you can experience a wider range of ayurvedic massages. For daily cleansing there's the *nasya* where the face, shoulders and chest are massaged with specific herbal oils to induce perspiration. *Udwarthana* is a massage given with dry herbal powders to reduce cholesterol, combat obesity and skin problems, as well as to strengthen muscles and joints. For sports injuries, arthritis, rheumatism and neurological disorders, the Ananda offers *choorna swedan*, a massage that combines oil and herbal powders for detoxification. The *kathi basti* offered at the Mandarin Oriental Dhara Devi Spa, is a massage that focuses on releasing blockages in the spinal area (see page 216). Here, warm medicated oils are poured generously over the spine, and a gentle back massage relaxes and helps release tension.

Ayurvedic doctors advise against massage during menstruation and suggest staying clear of the stomach area if you are pregnant. If you want to try ayurvedic massage at home, there are varying styles of touch. Note the tips below—normally around 10 strokes for each point is plenty.

GENERAL MASSAGE TECHNIQUES

1. Soothing/rubbing movements: Use soothing rubbing movements on the surface of arms and legs. Legs: from sides of the feet to the groin. Arms: from the fingertips to the armpit.
2. Pinching techniques: Muscles are grasped between the forefinger and thumb, away from the bones. Apply pinching techniques only on the chest, arms, legs and back.
3. Kneading techniques: Grasp the larger muscles with the hands and coax them into vitality. Kneading can be applied to the entire body.
4. Pressing techniques: Press along the hard body surfaces with flat hands

moving in a circular manner. Caress and compress the softer areas of the body, applying wave-like pressure while constantly moving upward.

5. Thumb movements: Small, circular, clockwise and counter-clockwise massage movements are generally applied with the thumb to essential *marma* points (see overleaf) of the body.

VATA MASSAGE

When *vata* is out of balance, you may feel dry, cold and anxious, and would greatly benefit from a massage that uses lots of warm, smooth and nurturing oils. Stroking should be firm but should also be relaxing. Abrupt, rough movements can be irritating and disturbing to *vata* types. Lots and lots of warm oil is recommended as the excess oil can then soak into the skin to further soothe the body.

Recommended oils are sesame, avocado, walnut and hazelnut blended with essential oils of cinnamon and sandalwood.

PITTA MASSAGE

An imbalance of *pitta* often manifests itself as hot, intense and fluid emotions, so these types need a calming, relaxing massage. They do not need as much oil as *vata* types and the oils should be of a cooling nature. The massage is best kept deep and varied; too many fast movements may accentuate imbalances. Thus the massage is best performed slowly.

Recommended oils are coconut, olive and sunflower blended with essential oils of sandalwood and lime.

KAPHA MASSAGE

Kapha constitutions need a bit of a kick start and benefit greatly from a vigorous type of massage to stimulate an often sluggish metabolism and lack of fluid movement. Fast movements are most appropriate with as little oil as possible. During the massage it is important to draw *kaphas* into a conversation so they can explore and let go of their feelings, which they are usually reticent to divulge. A deep, stimulating, invigorating massage is best.

Recommended oils include a small amount of heated oils like almond, mustard and canola (you can also use powder), blended with essential oils of cardamom and lemon.

HOW TO GIVE AN AYURVEDIC MASSAGE

This massage is just the thing to give to a friend in need of a mood and energy change. Start by creating a gentle space enhanced with candles and an aromatherapy oil burner. If you have a bath, prepare this by filling with warm water and flower petals. If you do not have a massage table, improvise with a mattress on the floor covered with clean towels or *sarongs*. Fill a large bowl with warmed water and aromatherapy oils and put soothing music in your CD player.

Step 1: Offer your friend some tea and invite him/her to slip into a comfy robe. Place feet into a footbath for a pre-massage soak. Scrub the feet with salt. Find out what he or she would like to achieve from the massage, for example, relaxation or extra energy. Then, relax into silence.

Step 2: Invite your friend to lie down on a prepared massage table or bed. Close the blinds, turn on some music and light candles. Pour warmed oil into an attractive small bowl. You may be inspired to say a silent prayer to give your friend added vitality and wellness.

Step 3: Cover parts of the body that you are not massaging with a cloth, towel or *sarong* to keep your friend continually warm. Always have one hand on the body throughout the massage for nurturing.

Step 4: Begin with a soothing 10-minute scalp and head massage without oil. This helps banish worrying thoughts and encourages your friend to move into a space of deep relaxation. Massaging the head instantly calms nerves and energizes the cerebrospinal fluid; it is believed that regular head massage protects the brain from dehydration and the face from frown and worry lines. Oxygen in the blood is increased, which helps eliminate fatigue and tension.

Step 5: Dip your fingers into the bowl of warmed oil and rub into your hands. Start with light circular movements, moving down the back, hips and buttocks. Spend 10 minutes massaging feet to further relax your friend; this creates a sense of wellness throughout the entire body.

Step 6: Ask your friend what areas are particularly tight and spend a little time working into these. The shoulder and neck are often tight, particularly with those who work on the computer or are office bound.

Step 7: Work down the arms and massage hands for a while. Like our feet, the hands are enriched with reflex points connected with our organs and are sensitive to touch.

Step 8: Ask your friend to turn over slowly. Keep him/her covered all the while.

Step 9: Gently massage the arms, chest and the abdomen.

Step 10: Massage the back of the neck and the shoulders.

Step 11: Complete with a 10-minute facial massage, making sure to massage earlobes.

Step 12: Cover your friend with a towel so that he/she is warm; ask him or her to relax for a further 10–15 minutes whilst you prepare tea.

MARMA POINT MASSAGE

Ayurvedic texts reveal that there are 107 *marma* points in the body. These are similar to the Chinese acupuncture points, only they are found deeper within the body. Some are fine points whilst others may be several inches wide. The Vedic texts say that if *marma* points become damaged or clogged, disease can occur. According to ayurvedic physicians, keeping our *marma* points continually clear is one of the oldest secrets for retaining youth and beauty.

When booking a *marma* point massage, please check that your practitioner is highly experienced as this is considered a very therapeutic style that should not be undertaken lightly. It is best to experience *marma* point massage in a well-established ayurvedic center or spa, such as at Ananda in the Himalayas.

During *marma* point massage, the therapist's thumb is used extensively. First a drop of warm oil is applied to a specific point, then the therapist uses small, gentle clockwise movements on the point, moving outward and then back inward, with ever increasing pressure. Usually you will feel about five circles going out and five circles coming back, repeated three times.

Certain *marma* points are believed to be linked to specific ailments. For example:

Sthapani (the point between the eyebrows towards the center of the forehead): A gentle massage here is thought to relieve stress, worry or strain.

Hridaya (the point below the sternum at the end of the rib cage): A massage here is believed to help settle emotions.

Vasti (the point on the lower abdomen a few inches below the naval): Physicians recommend a massage here to regulate and soothe digestive problems and ease gas and constipation.

As a preventative measure, ayurvedic physicians have a few tips to keep *marma* points clear:

Left The ayurvedic *shirodhara* treatment given at Prana Spa in Bali begins with a mind soothing Indian head, neck, scalp and shoulder massage.

Above *Sthapani* is the point between the eyebrows towards the center of the forehead. Massage here is reported to relieve stress and worry.

Right and far right There are few things in life more soothing than having one's face, neck and shoulder area massaged into bliss. Pulling earlobes is particularly pleasant.

- Eat well and chew carefully. Undigested foods can end up clogging *marma* points.
- Try and keep your points actively toned through exercise. Yoga and swimming are recommended.
- Regular foot massages are excellent for maintaining rejuvenated *marma* points —use sesame oil.
- Cultivate and sustain good posture.
- Be mindful—meditation can bring us more often into presence and help keep us grounded.

INDIAN FOOT MASSAGE

Padabhyanga is similar to the Chinese art of reflexology. Feet and legs are massaged and pressed in certain areas to stimulate circulation and improve the health of internal organs. It also encourages deep relaxation. Massaging the feet relieves insomnia and nervousness and combats dryness or numbness of the feet. Further-more, massaging the legs helps energize the belly, pelvis and colon and improve general circulation. It's a most pleasurable way to maintain vitality.

Ingredients:
• Small cup of sesame or sweet almond oil.
Directions:
Step 1: Begin with right leg first. Use thumb to massage the point in the very center of the foot.
Step 2: Use thumb to massage the point located in the middle of the underside of the big toe.

Step 3: Massage the base joint of each toe, beginning with the big toe.
Step 4: Massage each toe and gently pull from base to tip.
Step 5: Press and massage both thumbs on the *marma* point located between the base of the big toe and the second toe. This is found on the top of the foot in the groove between the base of the big toe and the second toe. Press into the point with both thumbs one on top of the other and stroke one inch down towards the ankle using firm pressure. Repeat this three times.
Step 6: Using both hands, massage in an upward motion from toes to ankles. Use alternating upward strokes.

INDIAN HEAD MASSAGE

In the East, thick hair and a healthy scalp is a sign of strength and beauty. Traditional Chinese medicine (TCM) links the condition of hair with that of the lungs and large intestines, and, in the ayurvedic texts, the head is considered the most important part of the body. It carries eight of the body's ten sacred gates (the openings of the nostrils, eyes, ears and mouth, and the most auspicious point called *Brahma randhra* or the "gate of Brahma," situated eight finger widths upwards from the center of the eyebrows).

Ayurvedic physicians recommend a regular scalp massage or *shirobhyana* for people of all ages. Throughout history, Indians have carried out the spirited ritual of giving family members a regular head massage to keep the circulation moving and alleviate tension or stress. The tradition continues today. Regular massage of the *marma* points in the head and forehead area is believed to result in clarity of vision and improved focus and concentration.

At many Six Senses Spas, the Indian Head Massage is quite fantastic. It's a blend of shampoo, combing, ruffling, tugging and a delicious smoothing massage. It combines both gentle and stimulating techniques on the upper back, shoulders, neck and scalp and is designed to improve blood flow, nourish the scalp and induce a deep sense of calm.

Traditionally, Indian head massage is performed with the guest sitting upright, but at Six Senses Spas the guest is invited to lie on a massage bed for comfort. The therapist then works on scalp, upper back, shoulders and upper arms for additional relaxation.

At home, try this interpretation:

Ingredients:
• Small cup of sesame, coconut or jojoba oil.
Directions:
Step 1: Part the hair in the center and pour approx 1 tbsp oil on the *Brahma randhra* spot. Begin by massaging the oil into both sides of the head above the ears.
Step 2: Bend the head forward so that the chin touches the chest. Pour 1 tbsp of oil on to the crest of the head and spread the oil evenly over the back of the head, while firmly rubbing with both hands.
Step 3: Bend the head forward again, and apply 1 tbsp oil to the base of the skull and the back of the neck. Using both hands, rub the base of the skull and the back of the neck firmly. Press both thumbs on each side of the *medulla oblongata* (where the skull meets the neck) and hold for about a minute.
Step 4: Apply light pressure and massage in a clockwise motion on the middle of the scalp area (just above the forehead). Massage in the same manner above the crown *chakra* which is located at the top of the head.
Step 5: Complete further stimulation of circulation by moving both hands and finger tips quickly back all over the head and scalp. In addition, lift the roots of the hair, pull, and release them.
Step 6: Take some time out to rest quietly and drink a cup of herbal tea.

chinese massage

All traditional Chinese medicine (TCM) treatments, including the various Chinese massages, are designed to facilitate the regular flow of *ch'i* (life force). Outside China itself, spas are increasingly offering Chinese massage therapies, with many in Asia also employing the services of an expert TCM doctor. We recommend any of the following massages for both specific ailments and general rebalancing and revitalization.

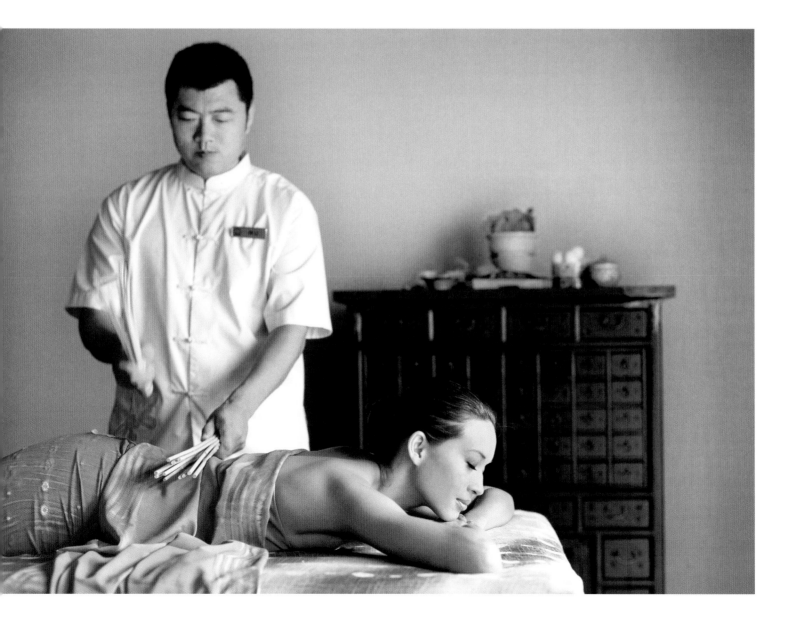

Opposite The bamboo stick tapping *qi gong* is part of the innovative Chinese Peranakan Treatment offered at the Spa Village in Kuala Lumpur.

This page The *tui na an mo* massage can be experienced at the Spa Village in both Pangkor Laut and Kuala Lumpur. The aim is to unlock tightness in the neck area, often caused by long hours sitting in front of a computer. The massage focuses on moving energy through the subtle channels of the body, with the therapist working on various acupressure points to further stimulate blood flow throughout the body.

ACUPRESSURE OR MERIDIAN MASSAGE

Employing the same principles as acupuncture, acupressure involves applying pressure to the meridian points in the body, but with hands instead of needles. It is based on the Chinese theory that there are 14 meridians within our body that carry energy connecting the brain to specific organs. Believed to have originated in Asia over 5,000 years ago, there are now several modes of acupressure. This form of massage is offered in many spas today either as a stand-alone treatment or combined with other therapies and massage styles.

Acupressure aims to stimulate the body's natural curative abilities by improving blood circulation and *ch'i* flow. Methods include pressing on trigger points, vigorous styles of pressure and rhythmic movements. Benefits include stress relief, increased blood circulation and energy levels, pain relief and detoxification, as well as overall rejuvenation and vitality. Normally, acupressure is administered in a one-hour session, and it is recommended a client experience a series of such sessions to fully benefit from it.

TUI NA

Tui na is probably the most popular Chinese massage style, and it is increasingly available at global spas and retreats. In Asia, the Spa Village in Kuala Lumpur and the Banyan Tree Spa Ringha in China both offer *tui na*.

Tui na is more than a relaxing massage. A combination of acupressure, massage and manipulation, it is now recognized as a healing massage with real therapeutic benefits. Practiced for thousands of years, *tui na* is a preventative massage that dramatically improves blood circulation and flow of *ch'i*. Taking its name from *tui* ("to push") and *na* ("to pull upward"), it is quite dynamic.

Tui na is performed on a clothed client and its overall purpose is to rebalance excess or deficiency in hot and cool conditions. It is not recommended if you are pregnant or have a heart condition. There are over 30 techniques in *tui na*, including *guen fa* (rolling), *yi zhi vi zhir chan fa* (one finger pushing), *na fa* (grasping), *an fa* (pressing), *rou fa* (kneading), *zhen fa* (vibration), *nie fa* (pinching), *bo fa* (plucking) and *ca fa* (chafing). The therapist may also use herbal preparations, oils, rollers and balms.

GUA SHA

With its roots in ancient China, this therapy takes its name from *gua* meaning "to rub" and *sha* which translates as "skin." It's a traditional Chinese healing treatment that uses a round-edged tool with strong pressure massage techniques; it is designed to stimulate acupressure points, remove stagnated blood and to expel heat or negative energy from the patient's body. *Gua sha* also encourages the unlocking of stagnated

ch'i and is a great remedy for those who suffer from chronic fatigue, pain and acute illness. It is used to treat asthma, bronchitis, cold and flu.

Using a special *gua sha* oil, the therapist concentrates on the neck, shoulder, back, buttocks and limbs. A specific *gua sha* tool, traditionally made of an Asian coin or water buffalo horn, is held at a 30-degree angle to

chinese massage

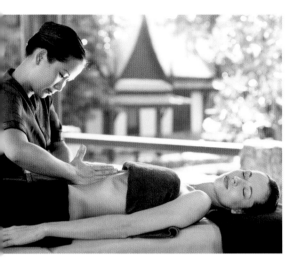

the skin with the smooth edge touching the skin; it is rubbed across the skin in downward strokes with moderate pressure. This immediately increases circulation of the blood and the client normally feels an instant change within the body. If the client has a chronic deficiency, *gua sha* may be complemented with acupuncture or acupressure on specific areas. *Gua sha* may be experienced up to three times weekly,

and is most therapeutic when used as a weekly treatment on chronic conditions.

At Rustic Nirvana Spas in Singapore, a gentler version of the *gua sha* is offered using chopsticks and a blend of *jamu* oil made from 21 Chinese herbs. The therapist taps the chopsticks along the meridians in order to stimulate energy and then uses the chopsticks to rub, press, scrape and knead the body. The invigorating qualities of the oil, combined with the unusual but effective massage techniques, makes this an extremely therapeutic experience for anyone.

CHINESE ABDOMINAL MASSAGE (CH'I NEI TSANG)

Like an inner medicine for the whole body, *ch'i nei tsang* abdominal massage, available at a few choice spas in Asia, frees up any blockages within to allow *ch'i* to flow more freely. For about an hour, your naval center or *hara* is pressed, kneaded and massaged gently to release stagnated energy and toxins, all the while reviving the body's natural healing ability.

Literally translating as "working the energy of the internal organs," *ch'i nei tsang* was originally practised by Taoist Chinese monks in the mountain regions of ancient China. It is said that the monks would purify their bodies in preparation for deep spiritual work with *ch'i nei tsang*; this gave them internal strength for their own path. Some of the techniques are based on the principles employed by *qi gong* and *kung fu*.

According to Mandala Spa in the Philippines, this treatment works on digestion and respiration, as well as the lymph, nervous, endocrine, reproductive, urinary, skeleto-muscular and acupuncture energy systems. At Chiva-Som, practitioners suggest a series of three treatments to restore vitality.

We now know that many problems, both stress-related and physical, affect the organs within the stomach area first; these, in turn, affect the body's natural ability to detoxify other organs like the liver and kidneys. Signs that you would benefit from *ch'i nei tsang* include poor digestion, bloating, irritable bowel syndrome, gas and constipation as well as general fatigue, stress and insomnia.

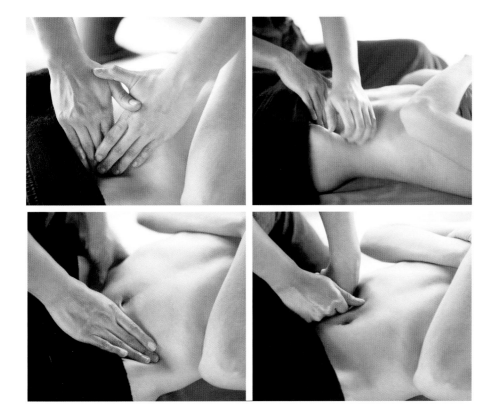

Left Movement is the key for moving *ch'i* at CHI spas in Shangri-La hotels and resorts. Chinese Abdominal Massage, also known as *ch'i nei tsang*, employs different techniques on the abdominal area to help detoxify and strengthen the body. Stress release is also one of the benefits to having all the tension in your abdominal area released. Authentic herbs and oils from the Himalayas are smoothed into the skin to heal and rejuvenate—then the massage takes place.

Bottom This massage sequence is part of the Himalayan Healing Stone Massage that can be experienced at CHI spas from Shanghai and Bangkok to the Maldives and the Philippines. Inspired by the traditions of the mystical Himalayan mountains, the massage includes rubbing, stretching and releasing techniques to help move *ch'i* throughout the body.

TIBETAN HEALING MASSAGE

Due to the harsh climate, massage did not develop in Tibet as a relaxing treatment as it did in tropical countries. As with most TCM massages, it was purely therapeutic. Its primary purpose was to encourage circulation of energy and to improve general health and wellbeing.

A synthesis of Indian and Chinese massage styles, it employs five techniques: stroking, rubbing, kneading, *shiatsu* or acupressure style, and cleansing. Mustard oil is massaged into the skin of babies and the elderly prior to massage, and a powder of chickpea and barley flour is applied afterwards to absorb excess oil.

Ian Baker, founding partner of Kamalaya, a Tibetan-Chinese inspired health resort, and author of *The Tibetan Art of Healing*, says: "Tibetan massage is used in a variety of contexts: combining the use of the 78 specific acupressure points with the medicinal effects of oils and plant extracts, Tibetan massage is used to overcome disease and enhance the life-force." He goes on to report that lengthwise strokes are used to release tensions and accumulated toxins, while circular strokes are said to charge the body with healing energy. Even today, massage is used to treat a variety of stress-related disorders as well as physical ailments, removing energy blockages in the body.

Tibetan-style massages are offered at the CHI spas at Shangri-La hotels and resorts and at the spa at The Banyan Tree Ringha, China. As interest in Tibetan-inspired therapies grows, many more spas are sure to follow.

reflexology

With its origins either in ancient Egypt or India, this treatment has long been practiced in Japan, India and China. Murals in tombs in Egypt dating back to 233 BC suggest a form of reflexology was practiced in Pharaonic times, but nowadays in Asia, you'll find reflexology in shopping centers and airports—and in ayurvedic and traditional Chinese medicine (TCM) influenced spas.

Reflexology works on the principle of treating the whole body as one, with our feet (and hands) acting as a mirror or a map to our inner body. Massaging the reflex nerves in the feet encourages internal organs to detoxify and release stored stress and tension within. Stagnation is unblocked and energy or *ch'i* is encouraged to flow freely.

Reflexology is recommended for people with acute problems, as it is thought to prevent illness, alleviate pain and reduce tension. Whilst one is sitting in a reclining chair, hopefully with an inspirational vista or in a dim-lit sanctuary, the therapist uses thumbs and fingers to stimulate, massage and apply pressure on various points in the feet (and hands) that correspond to specific glands and organs inside the body. A session normally lasts about an hour and can be soothing, painful, blissful or uncomfortable, particularly if there is an imbalance in a corresponding part in the body.

The reflexology pathway made with surface pebbles may be experienced at many ayurvedic centers and spas like Spa Botanica in Singapore, as well as in parks and public places in various parts of Asia. Chiva-Som in Thailand merges reflexology with hydrotherapy in their Bathing Pavilion. Walking barefoot on pebbles submerged in water is refreshing as the soles of the feet are stimulated, giving your body a gentle internal cleanse. This also helps to improve posture and spinal alignment and, whilst it may hurt a little, the feeling afterwards is quite rejuvenating.

FOOT REFLEXOLOGY AT HOME
Recreating a reflexology session at home is simple and easy to do.

To prepare, pour 2 tsp of base oil and 5 drops of essential oil (such as peppermint, sage, rosemary and lemon) into a glass dish or warm up the oil in a vaporizer. Smooth a little of this oil into feet and ankles.

Begin by massaging the ankle area. Using kneading and circular massage movements, massage the ankle and heel of the foot, stretching up the Achilles tendon which connects the calf muscle to the heel. Then move to the top of the foot and use your thumb to firmly stroke from the ankle between the tendons to between each of the toes. Continue by massaging each of your toes, using pinching and twisting movements. Pull and rotate each toe clockwise and anti-clockwise. Keep the area in-between the toes well oiled. Massaging the top of the toes is reported to energize and balance the sinuses.

Above The foot-stimulating reflexology path is found at spas, ayurveda centers, parks and other public areas all over southeast Asia.

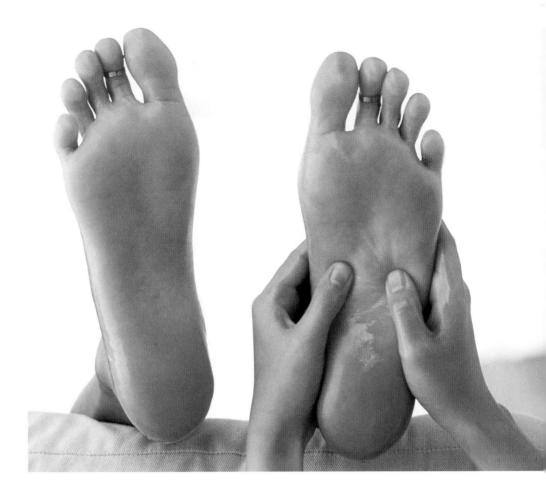

Now, massage the sole of the foot with your thumb, using pressing and circular movements to massage the heel of the foot, as this stimulates the intestines and colon. Move to the ball of the foot using similar movements, balancing and energizing the lungs, shoulders, heart, liver and spleen. The center of the foot portrays the stomach, pancreas, gallbladder and kidneys.

Complete by massaging the inner arch of the foot, again using your thumb in a snake-like movement starting at the inside heel and working all the way up to the big toe. The snake-like movement is like a push on the spot with your thumb, then releasing and slowly sliding up a little, pressing again, and repeating all the way up. This area represents the whole of the spine and the neck.

Try to spend about 5 to 7 minutes massaging your feet. Ideally do this when you are giving yourself a pedicure so one foot can rest in a bowl of water while you massage the other. Rinse in the water and apply a foot wrap (see page 209). Repeat on the other foot.

FOOT AND LEG TREATMENT

One of the rituals not to be missed at Kirana Spa in Bali is a refreshing foot and leg massage that uses reflexology massage and ordinary massage as well as rejuvenating oils and balms. Experienced in your own private spa villa overlooking views of paddy field, gorge and forest, the treatment promotes lipid metabolism, thereby enhancing resilience and firmness of skin. It also induces a deep feeling of relaxation.

The therapist begins the treatment with a foot bath, bathing your feet in essences while cleaning, brushing and massaging toes, feet and heels. Concentrating on lower legs and feet and working from the toes to the knees, the therapist stimulates blood and *ch'i* circulation through various massage techniques. This helps reduce fatigue and swelling and promotes smooth

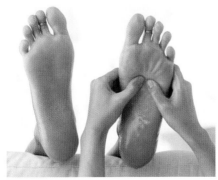

skin. At the same time, a shoulder massage takes place.

After this, feet are brushed to further stimulate circulation, while a blend of macadamia oil and birch and fennel extracts is applied to moisturize and energize. A strong, but not too hard, foot exfoliation follows with a scrub made from *Phellodendron ammuence* and birch extract; this helps to exfoliate old keratins and promotes healthy metabolism, thereby helping skin regain a smooth and sheer feel and look.

You can try something similar at home with 1 tbsp fine sea salt, 2 tbsp soy oil or apricot kernel oil (or a mix of both), 2 drops each of essential oil of white birch and tea tree and 1 tsp peel of grapefruit. Mix the ingredients together, adding the essential oils last. Scrub the feet with an upward motion towards the heart. Rinse and pat dry after.

As a finale, the therapist applies a hot massage gel infused with fennel, white lily extract and water lily extract and massages this well into the skin from the toes to the knees. This induces a relaxed, refreshed feeling. At home we suggest using a recipe of 1 tbsp aloe vera gel, 1 tbsp apricot kernel oil with 2 drops each of essential oils of peppermint, camphor and grapefruit.

Steaming towels remove the gel, and a final stretch, known as the Awakening, pulls legs, shoulders and arms into alignment.

indonesian massage

Massage plays a central role in Indonesia's spa culture. Traditionally used for healing and rejuvenation purposes, many people still have a daily massage to keep the body in balance. Indonesia is home to a variety of massage types: different massage styles are specifically paired with certain plants and oils for a variety of therapeutic effects.

Massage is used in Indonesia to nurture the body at different stages of life. In the early years, babies and small children are massaged with coconut oil blended with sweet fennel and cajuput essential oils. During puberty, a blend of rose or jasmine oil with nutmeg in a carrier oil is rubbed over the lower abdomen and lower back area to relieve menstruation cramps. And in adulthood, massage is part of the royal *mandi lulur* treatment (see page 189), amongst others. For the elderly, a carrier oil made from ginger or clove oil is blended and applied to help overcome back pain, muscle pain, ankle problems and fatigue.

BALINESE MASSAGE

Within family homes in Bali, massage is considered a silent way to communicate and bond and is practiced from an early age. There is no particular technique. The masseur is guided by the heart. The intention is to create harmony of body, mind and spirit and strengthen the connection between the giver and receiver.

The creators of Mandara Spa explain that Balinese massage incorporates stretching, long strokes, skin rolling and palm and thumb pressure—techniques commonly used in the village to relieve tension, improve circulation and to create a feeling of wellbeing. A spokesperson explains: "Long ago the Balinese realized that to achieve health they must focus equally on the development of mind and body. The most important ingredient of Balinese massage is the intrinsically Balinese way of giving from the heart."

JAVANESE BAREFOOT MASSAGE

This ancient massage developed in the royal courts of Java appeals to overactive people who are looking for a way to slow down. The techniques help unlock blockages and loosen knots in the muscles thereby releasing unwanted energy and

Right top "Massage is one of the most important aspects in our approach to beauty in Indonesia," says Dr Martha Tilaar.

Right middle At The Eastern Rejuvenation Center, the Indonesian Deep Tissue Massage is given with aromatherapy oils.

Right bottom Therapist stretching the body from head to toe.

rebalancing the nervous system. A blend of essential oils extracted from Indonesian spices and flowers is applied, while the therapist walks over the guest's back. At Bagus Jati Wellbeing Resort this massage is performed in a lavishly appointed stone enclave built into the hillside. Here guests recline with views across a celestial jungle valley, all the while being serenaded by the sounds of a mountain stream and waterfall below.

MANDARA MASSAGE

If you desire a fairly relaxing style of massage, the signature Mandara Massage performed in graceful synergy by two therapists is a good choice. It incorporates the flavor of a few exotic styles—Japanese *shiatsu*, Thai, Hawaiian *lomi lomi*, Swedish and Balinese—all in one session. Developed in Bali in 1996, it is based on the principle that we are all one, we all derive from the same source and are made up of the same elements. It may be experienced in dozens of spas around Asia and overseas.

The treatment begins with the two therapists simultaneously massaging the body with fluid and rhythmic strokes inspired by the Hawaiian *lomi lomi*; they combine this with the finger pressuring style of Balinese massage. This is followed by the long and gentle strokes of Swedish effleurage and *shiatsu* thumb pressure together with the stretching and squeezing techniques of Thai massage.

AT-HOME INDONESIAN MASSAGE

"Massage is one of the most important aspects in our approach to beauty in Indonesia," says Dr Martha Tilaar. She suggests routinely performing a traditional Indonesian massage on yourself as a route to health and wellbeing. The best time to do self-massage is before bathing in the morning or at bedtime. Always empty your bladder before massage and never massage directly after a meal, she advises.

Ingredients:
• ½ cup (100 ml) olive or soybean oil or a base oil blended with 20 drops of pure essential oils of lemon, orange and spearmint, or peppermint.

Directions:
Step 1: Feet
Start with your right foot. Using your thumb, massage the point located in the middle of the arch of the foot in a circular motion. Repeat the same movement in the middle of the underside of the big toe. Massage each toe, starting at the base. With both hands, massage the foot in upward strokes from toes to ankles. Repeat with the left foot.
Step 2: Legs
Again, starting with the right leg, use both hands to circle around the ankle bone in an upwards direction. Rub the lower leg using up and down stroking movements. Massage clockwise around the knee joint and back of the knee. Massage up and down from knee to groin on all sides. You can also knead the upper thighs to stimulate circulation. Repeat on left leg.
Step 3: Hands
Using your thumb, press the point in the middle of your right hand. Starting with the thumb, massage the base of each finger, moving towards the tip. Repeat on the left hand.
Step 4: Arms
Massage up and down from right wrist to

elbow with clockwise movements around the elbow and up and down movements from the elbow to the shoulder. Use whole palm massage clockwise around the shoulder joint. Knead the soft flesh between your shoulder joint and the base of the neck. Repeat on the left side.
Step 5: Back
With your palms, rub up and down your lower back and as far as you can comfortably reach to your middle back. Massage the buttocks in circular movements.
Step 6: Abdomen
With your fingers, gently massage around the navel in a clockwise circle. Then, using your palm, slowly make the circles bigger until you have massaged the entire abdomen. Reverse direction and slowly make the circles smaller and smaller until you are back at the navel.
Step 7: Upper torso
Massage the solar plexus point (located 4 inches or 10 cm above the navel) using the fingers in a clockwise direction. Massage the heart point, in between the nipples, at the center of your sternum. Place both palms underneath the breast or pectoral muscle and massage around the nipples in a circle moving from the outside towards the inside. Massage the throat using upwards stroking movements.
Step 8: Finish
With the outside portion of your hand, use chopping movements to both invigorate the shoulders and complete your massage.

massage oil blends

The aromatherapy massage remains the preferred massage on most spa menus around Asia, if not the world, and it's easy to understand why. Essential oils have the power to rebalance us on an emotional level and, when given with a massage, can be of real benefit. Indonesian, Balinese and some of the ayurvedic and Chinese massages prepared with oils from local flower, herb and plant life can be wonderfully relaxing.

Opposite When it comes to aromatherapy, follow your nose—and your instincts.

Below Secret healing recipes, blended from indigenous ingredients and passed down through generations, are at the heart of Jamu Jamu, a company that advocates botanical rejuvenation through natural Asian beauty treatments.

There are thousands of essential oils culled from common plants as well as more exotic essences like pink lotus and *ajowan* (both from India). The beauty of blending various oils is that it's really up to you to tune in and be creative in your mixing. Think of rose or lavender when you want to create an ambience of calm, whilst essences derived from citrus fruits are known to uplift and enliven. If your mind is overworked and you feel scattered, be drawn to an earthy blend containing sandalwood and vetiver. For those seeking clarity and motivation, herbaceous oils like rosemary or peppermint are good choices.

When exploring ingredients at home, follow your nose. It senses what you need. Inhale and learn to listen to the language of fragrance. Select oils that resonate with you. Use references as a guide, but your intuition as the leader. To create your own blend, use up to 2–3 drops of pure essential oil in 1 tsp of carrier or base oil. Base oils that are nutritious and penetrate the skin well are macadamia, sweet almond, wheat germ and soy oil. (Jojoba is also excellent, although it is technically a wax not an oil).

CHINESE EMPRESS MASSAGE OILS

These blends, created by Dr Marthar Tilaar using Chinese herbs, were formulated with the five elements of traditional Chinese medicine (TCM) in mind. In TCM, it is believed that emotions relate to different organs in the body and through herbs, oils, color and scent we are able to work to rebalance. Choose your blend intuitively, be it by feeling, taste, color or gut reaction, for a direct and firm pressure massage. This shifts any held energy or tension in the body and improves all over circulation.

Ingredients:

Wood: Yin liver and yang gall bladder. This is represented by the color green, a sour taste and a feeling of rage.

- 5 drops lemongrass essential oil; 10 drops ginseng essential oil; 1½ tbsp olive oil.

Fire: Yin heart and yang small intestines. This is represented by the color red, a bitter taste and a feeling of happiness.

- 5 drops rose essential oil; 10 drops cinnamon essential oil; 1½ tbsp olive oil.

Earth: Yin spleen and yang stomach. This is represented by the color yellow, a sweet taste and thoughtful feelings.

- 10 drops lemon essential oil; 5 drops fennel essential oil; 1½ tbsp olive oil.

Metal: Yin lung and yang large intestines. This is represented by the color white, a spicy taste and a feeling of sorrow.

- 5 drops peppermint essential oil; 10 drops eucalyptus essential oil; 1½ tbsp olive oil.

Water: Yin kidneys and yang bladder. This is represented by the color black, a salty taste and feelings of fear.

- 5 drops jasmine essential oil; 10 drops chamomile essential oil; 1½ tbsp olive oil.

SANDALWOOD AND LAWANG ROOT MASSAGE OIL

"Massage and the healing sense of touch to the human spirit are how we heal and connect with each other," says creator of this blend, David Haughton of Jamu Jamu spa products in Bali. *Lawang* root essential oil, originating from the mountains of Irian Jaya, is known to soothe and relieve tired muscles. Tenacious and warming with a spicy-sweet aroma, it is combined with stimulating oils of citronella, lemongrass and sandalwood. The blend is good for stimulating the circulation and is recommended for sports injuries. A touch of jasmine rounds it off with a subtle and floral aroma.

Ingredients:

3 tbsp cold pressed grape seed oil with 20 drop blend of pure essential oils of lemongrass, citronella, jasmine, sandalwood and *lawang* root (if unavailable, substitute with cinnamon).

BALINESE INSPIRED MASSAGE OILS

Recall scented moments of warm evenings spent in Bali with these soothing and restorative blends created by Four Seasons Spas. Each has been created to reflect a strong sense of place as well as to enhance mind, body and spirit. Although a massage at a Four Seasons Spa in Bali is what we all deserve, you can recreate the spirit of their spa philosophy in your own home through these fragrances.

Bali Santi

* 1 tbsp coconut oil blended with 2 drops each of caraway, basil, nutmeg, vetiver and patchouli pure essential oils.

Peace of Bali

* 1 tbsp grape seed oil blended with 2 drops each of sandalwood, ylang ylang, black pepper and ginger pure essential oils.

Bali Sunset

* 1 tbsp grape seed oil blended with 2 drops each of pure essential oils of lavender, lemongrass and nutmeg.

INDIAN MASSAGE OIL WITH ROSE AND SANDALWOOD

Revisit the mystical atmosphere of India via this nourishing massage oil blend from Prana Spa. Capturing the quintessence of Indian radiance, the Prana Spa experience is designed to nurture all the senses, enveloping you from the moment you enter the premises. This soft, woody, balsamic-like aroma combines beautifully with the intensely rich floral scent of Indian jasmine, creating an almost tea-like aroma. It is a most restful blend for mind and body.

Ingredients:

* 1 tbsp raw sesame oil with 1 tbsp coconut oil and 10 drops each of sandalwood and rose essential oils.

THE ANANDA HERBAL OIL DECOCTION

These decoctions have been created at Ananda in the Himalayas according to *dosha* type. They work to balance the *doshas*, bringing you into a more harmonious place. Embalm your being in these healing oils, and be transported via these exotic scents of the Himalayas.

Ingredients:

* 4 cups (1 l) water; 1 cup (250 ml) sesame oil; ¼ cup (50 g) herbs.

Directions: Bring water to the boil in a stainless steel pot, add oil and herbs, cover and simmer on low heat for 4–6 hours or until all the water has evaporated. Allow herbal oil to cool, then pour through a strainer into a glass jar. Cover and store in a cool place.

Add any or all of the following herbs to the oil decoction:
For Vata: Ashwagandha, *gotu kola*, liquorice, cloves, comfrey, ginger, ginseng.
For Pitta: Neem, *amalaki*, *gotu kola*, *shatavari*, peppermint, fennel, liquorice.
For Kapha: Gotu kola, neem, wild ginger, rosemary, sage, horseradish.

Before using the medicated massage oils, add these essential oils for each *dosha*:

Ananda Vata oil

* 1 tbsp base oil; 2 drops bergamot, 1 drop spikenard, 2 drops lime, 2 drops vetiver and 1 drop rosewood essential oils.

Ananda Pitta oil

* 1 tbsp base oil; 3 drops sweet orange, 1 drop *ajowan* or *ajwain* (*Carum copticum*, also known as bishop's weed; if difficult to find, substitute with thyme essential oil); 2 drops *tulsi* (Indian holy basil) essential oil; 2 drops myrrh essential oils.

Ananda Kapha oil

* 1 tbsp base oil; 3 drops black pepper, 2 drops spikenard, 1 drop lemon and 2 drops juniper essential oils.

Opposite top Fragrant jasmine flowers blended with aromatherapy oils make for a divine and unique massage at Martha Tilaar spas. Massages are usually the most popular treatments of choice in the Asian spa.

Opposite bottom Bottles of oils from The Ritz-Carlton Bali Thalasso & Spa.

Left A good quality carrier oil is the key to a long-lasting massage oil.

Below A serene therapist carries oils at Four Seasons Resort Bali at Jimbaran Bay.

Ananda Tridosha oil

- 1 tbsp base oil; 4 drops geranium, 2 drops coriander and 2 drops cypress essential oil.

SWEET ALMOND MASSAGE OIL WITH PATCHOULI AND YLANG YLANG

Evoke sensual summer days spent with a loved one via this Mandara Spa signature massage oil blend. The heady aroma released from the white ylang ylang flower picked in the early morning intermingles here with the warming and grounding scent of sandalwood and balancing patchouli. Together they create a scent that is perfect for couples' massages or simply to renew sweet memories of love.

Ingredients:

- 1 ½ tbsp sweet almond or coconut oil with 5 drops each of sandalwood, patchouli and ylang ylang essential oils.

JASMINE MASSAGE OIL

The scent of jasmine is intoxicating and lingering, and is especially calming when you are feeling disconnected and off center. The fragrance is grounding, and is known to instil confidence and bring one back to presence. This blend also comes from Mandara Spas. Widely known as an aphrodisiac, jasmine has been used for centuries by those who wish to shroud themselves with an alluring scent to increase sensual moments. It is also good for dry skin. Here we suggest you warm the jasmine oil and complete your journey with a jasmine-filled aromatic flower bath.

Ingredients:

- 1 tbsp sweet almond or macadamia oil with 5 drops pure jasmine essential oil.

Directions: After your jasmine oil massage, step into a warm bath filled with 1 cup (25 g) jasmine blooms.

heat therapy

Close your eyes. Dream. Drift. Relax. Warmth melts away aches, pains and tension in the body, and helps to still the mind. Therapeutic heat applications encourage detoxification, stimulate circulation of blood, restore equilibrium and dissolve stored and stuck emotions from the past. Whether we are talking about a hot stone therapy, a warm massage oil, a cosy body wrap or even the warmth of a therapist's smile, the feeling of being nurtured through heat is integral to the Asian healing process.

In ancient China, heated rocks and hot sand were wrapped in tree bark and applied to the body as hot compresses to relieve aches and pains. Later, these types of practices developed into therapies like moxibustion and cupping (see pages 244). Today, doctors place the herb mugwort (*Artemesia vulgaris*) on to the tip of an acupuncture needle and burn it as a way to relax the mind. Tibetans are known to heat small bags of herbs and place them on acupuncture points to move *ch'i* and hot stone therapy has long been practiced by American Indians. In Thailand, small tents were placed over pots of steaming herbs

and inhalation of the medicinal steam cleansed the respiratory and lymphatic systems. *Ashtanga* yoga is designed to heat the body internally so that the organs are cleansed and detoxification takes place.

Perhaps one of the most popular Asian treatments using heat to heal is the little poultice "pouch" that promises so much sweetness in a bundle! An increasing number of spas create alternatives to the Thai Herbal Hot Compress filling their hot pouches with Chinese or Japanese herbs and spices or even offering a 15-minute steam and pound post massage. At Per Aquum Spas in the Maldives, the Naplia

Herbal Poultice applied prior to a massage softens the muscles in preparation. Filled with lemongrass and Thai ginger as well as essential oils of rosewood and sweet orange, the poultice is first heated and then gently applied to the upper back, neck, shoulder and face area for the purpose of relieving stress and firming and toning the skin texture.

Today there are various interpretations of healing with heat on the Asian spa menu, many of which are easy to create at home. These treatments aim to detoxify and restore, so be prepared for some deep relaxing moments.

THAI HERBAL HOT COMPRESS

The Anantara Spa is one of many spas in Thailand that gives an insight into Thai healing through traditional treatments. This heat therapy was invented during the Ayutthaya period when soldiers treated their wounds and aching muscles with hot compresses. Practiced for over 200 years now, steamed herbal pouches are placed on to vulnerable areas of the body like upper back and shoulders to quickly melt away tension. They are particularly soothing for those with weak kidneys.

Drawing on local plants and herbs including *makrut* (lime leaves), *prai* (a type of Thai ginger), pounded lemongrass, tamarind leaves, turmeric powder, bark of the camphor tree and ground menthol, this treatment stimulates and encourages blood circulation. Other benefits include the stretching out of connective tissues, relief of aching joints, relaxation of muscles and a decrease in muscle contractions.

At the Anantara Spa, therapists combine the application of heat with some other treatments in their four-hour Traditional Thai Ritual. The journey begins with an exfoliating scrub of ground coriander seeds, nutmeg and other spices to cleanse and revitalize the skin, and is followed by a deep tissue massage in the back and shoulder

area. A herbal liquid made with menthol, *prai*, ginger, salt, camphor and oils is then massaged into the skin before the heated herbal pouches are applied. To recreate at home, try the recipe below:

Ingredients:
(makes two pouches)
- 10 tbsp lime zest; 6 ½ tbsp fresh ginger, grated; 3–4 stalks (40 g) lemongrass, cut and pounded; 20 eucalyptus leaves, crushed; 1 tbsp rock salt; 1 tbsp tamarind powder; 1 tbsp turmeric powder; 1 tbsp camphor granules; 2 x 45 cm terry cloth or calico; 2 m (6 ft) cotton string.

Directions: Mix all ingredients together and wrap in a terry cloth; tightly tie the edge of the compressed pouch with string. Use two pouches for each treatment. Bring water in a steamer to boil, lightly sprinkle the two pouches with water and steam for 10–15 minutes or until hot. The steam softens the herbal compresses, releasing the essential oils in the herbs and intensifying the aroma. Always keep one compress heated on the steamer while using the other one. Before putting the compress onto the skin, test the temperature by pressing the compress to your arm. Wait until it feels comfortable. Don't rest the compress on the skin for too long—just touch, press, lift and move in a constant and rapid motion. Each session should take 15–20 minutes, and, ideally, one morning and one evening treatment is best.

Here we have created Chinese and Japanese versions of the pouch recipes. The aromas of both are spicy and woody with the Japanese creation slightly more medicinal. These are for one-time use only, and should be prepared and used as for the Thai compress.

CHINESE HERBAL POUCH
Ingredients:
- 70 (20 g) cardamom pods (aromatic and calming); 4 tbsp cinnamon powder (good for arthritic pain); 6 tbsp ginger powder (anti-inflammatory); 2 tbsp galangal powder (analgesic properties); 1 tbsp turmeric powder; 9–10 tbsp barley flour; 2 x 45 cm terry cloth or calico; 2 m (6 ft) cotton string.

Directions: Grind the cardamom pods in a coffee grinder. Combine all ingredients together in a bowl and mix well. Follow the rest of the instructions as for the previous hot compress recipe.

JAPANESE HERBAL POUCH
Ingredients:
- 4 tbsp dried *kudzu* (Japanese arrowroot); 4 tbsp dried catnip; 2 tbsp comfrey root powder (good for muscle spasms and to heal bruises); 6 tbsp fresh ginger, chopped; 1 cup (120 g) cooked glutinous rice; 2 x 45 cm terry cloth or calico; 2 m (6 ft) cotton string.

Directions: As for the previous heated compress recipes.

heat therapy

Below Traditional *yam khang*, whereby heat is transferred from a therapist's feet to the muscles of the recipient, is practised at the Mandarin Oriental Dhara Devi Spa outside Chiang Mai.

Opposite Heat therapy does wonders to alleviate pain and stagnation in the body. The Indonesian herbal poultice at Bagus Jati Wellbeing Resort is part of the South Indian Malabar Rejuvenation package and is inspired by the old rituals of Indonesia, as well as ayurvedic teaching.

CAMPUR CAMPUR

The Malaysian-style *campur campur*, which translates as "a blend of varieties," is a signature treatment at Pangkor Laut Spa Village. Similar to the Thai poultice, it took two years to create and is one of the best loved treatments at the Spa Village. It is a lovely example of an authentic adaptation of a traditional healing greatment.

After a Thai massage to stretch muscles and a Malay massage using long kneading strokes that focus on the muscles, poultices filled with fragrant steamed lemongrass and pandan leaves are pressed gently on the body to stimulate and increase blood circulation. Through touch, tone and aromatherapy, the *campur campur* induces a wonderful relaxation in muscles and mind. It is sometimes also offered at the end of the *muka berseri-seri* or Malay Facial treatment (see pages 171–172).

YAM KHANG

Deriving its name from *yam* meaning "to walk" and *khang* ("to plough") in the Northern Thai dialect, this fantastic treatment originates from the Chiang Mai area. Practiced in ancient Lanna temples for hundreds of years, *yam khang* uses heat from a therapist's feet to rejuvenate and heal the body.

The therapist first heats up a type of hot plate made out of a plough tool used by farmers all over Thailand to grow rice using burning charcoal. Once the "plough plate" is scorching hot, the therapist dips his feet into bowls of herbal-infused water and oils, before placing them on the plate to warm them up. After this, he gently rests his feet on various parts of the guest's body to warm and nurture the system. Long-term practitioner, Yo Komrit, says that the therapist will need to have developed the art of spiritual inner calm before giving this treatment. Reminiscent of a fire walk, he says they must be in a meditative mood as this protects them from burning their own feet!

The treatment works in a similar way to other healing through heat therapies: muscle tension is eased, blood is stimulated and the warmth from the therapist's feet is nurturing, calming and relaxing.

LAOTIAN HERBAL POUCH

This recipe is inspired by a traditional Laotian treatment created by Thai spa brand, Ytsara, that can be experienced at the spa at the Residence Phou Vao, an Orient Express hotel in Luang Prabang in Laos. Ytsara are well regarded for their talent in uncovering old rituals and re-creating these in the spa.

Called the Mohom Indigo Healing Art Treatment, it is based on Laotian healing traditions and practices given by local shamans. Ytsara report that traditionally local herbs and plants were wrapped in indigo-colored fabric that was boiled in a clay pot filled with water and indigo plants. The purple-blue color is reported to represent the spiritual colors of Eastern medicine, as well as to enhance the detoxification process. In the Ytsara interpretation, local herbs of *yaanang*, as well as lemongrass, cinnamon, Borneo camphor, *prai* and ginger are used. The steaming compress is thoroughly pounded over the body before a deep tissue massage is given.

Ingredients:

- ¾ cup (150 g) cooked rice; ⅓ cup (80 g) fresh ginger or *prai*, crushed; ⅓ cup (70 g) fresh lemongrass, cut in pieces and crushed; ⅓ cup (30 g) fresh Thai purple basil or anise basil; ⅓ cup (30 g) fresh pepper leaf (*Piper sarmentosum*); 5 pieces cinnamon; 2 x 30 cm muslin cloth (optional to die it blue beforehand using natural vegetable dye); piece of string to tie muslin cloth into a pouch.

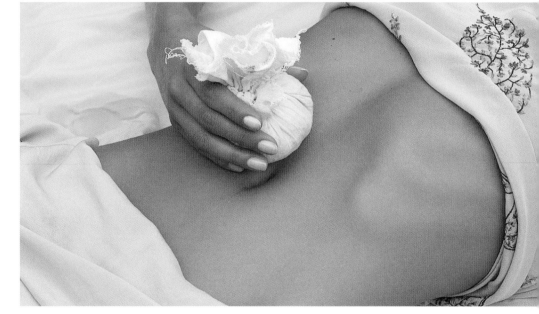

Directions: Bind all ingredients into a pouch and steam for 15-20 minutes. Apply to the skin using firm pressure, constantly moving from one area to the next.

INDONESIAN HERBAL POULTICE

This recipe takes around 30 minutes to prepare and is well worth the effort. Shared with us by Bagus Jati Wellbeing Resort, it is inspired by the old rituals of Indonesia. It relies on traditional techniques and medicinal powders, oils and herbs to restore physical and emotional balance to mind and body. Herbal poultices are rhythmically massaged over the body to help stimulate circulation and reduce general fatigue, insomnia and hypertension. The "bolus" of cooked rice softens skin, and also slightly exfoliates it; circulation is stimulated using up and down circular strokes.

Ingredients:
- ¾ cup (150 g) rice; 1 tsp dried ginger; 3 pandan leaves, chopped; 2 pieces *cempaka* flowers or substitute with 1 tbsp dried chamomile flowers; 1 tsp *akar wangi* herb (vetiver or *Andropogon zizanioides*) (optional); 1 tsp *lempunyang* (wild ginger or *Zingiber zerumbet*) or substitute with normal dried ginger; 2 tsp sandalwood powder; 1 tbsp lemon peel; ¼ tsp turmeric powder; 1 cup (250 ml) water; a cheesecloth square (16 x 16 inches; 40 cm x 40 cm).

Directions: Cook the rice until fluffy and put aside. Add all other ingredients to the cup of water, bring to the boil, and simmer for 10 minutes. Remove from heat, leave to cool, then strain. Mix the cooked white rice with the other ingredients, put in the cheese-cloth square and tie. Reheat the leftover water from the herbs and soak the poultice bag in the liquid until warm. Then apply over the body with circular movements, dipping the "bolus" back into the warmed liquid as needed.

HEALING BACK RECOVERY

A spa solution for hangovers! When we are feeling fatigued, it is often an indication that the *ch'i* flow within our kidneys is sluggish. As levels and movement of *ch'i* influence our vitality, it is important to keep them constantly flowing. With this recipe we rely on the warming and stimulating properties of ginger to move stagnated energy. For those in addiction recovery mode, this is a useful once-a-week routine. It helps to cleanse the body of toxins and increases energy and vitality in the long term.

Ingredients:
- 2–3 pieces whole ginger; 1 saucepan (about 3 l) water; 2 thin towels or a single sheet.

Directions: Chop or grate ginger rhizomes and bring to boil in a pot of water. Simmer for about 20 minutes. Add towels to the infused water and allow to soak. Create a space in your home where you can lay out a wet blanket or towels. Use tongs to lift the soaking towels. Wring out slightly and strain the water. Carefully drape the towels over your back and lie down to rest. When the towels cool, you may dip them back into the water to reheat. Repeat 2 to 3 times. Complete the ritual with an all-over self-massage with a body oil of your choice and rest for 20 minutes, ensuring you hydrate with water or ginger herbal tea afterwards. You'll find your energy levels begin to rise.

hot stone therapy

The sensation of having warmed stones smoothed across the body is deeply nurturing and relaxing, not to mention incredibly grounding for the mind. Whilst the origin of the hot stone massage is unclear, it is known that this therapy has long been practiced by native Americans, Tibetans, Koreans and Hawaiians, amongst others. In Hawaii, lava stones may be used during *lomi lomi* massage to soothe, and, in Tibet, the application of healing hot stones has long been a vital element in healing.

Hot stone therapy is very helpful during times of anxiety, sleeplessness and stress. The warmth from the stones dissolves tension, melts pain, strain and muscle aches away, and gently improves circulation. Stones are often placed on the soles of the feet and in the palms of the hands to stimulate the reflex points and on the back of thighs or upper shoulders to encourage deep rest. Those experiencing a warm or hot stone massage may notice an improvement in the following symptoms: muscular aches and pains, sprains and strains, poor circulation, rheumatic and arthritic conditions, back pain, stress, anxiety and tension, insomnia and depression.

According to therapists at Mandara Spas in Bali, ancient rocks are considered sacred and alive; they contain energy, even the life force of the universe. In Bali, therapists collect stones from the seashore and place them outside under each full moon to soak up lunar energy. If you visit the Anantara Spa, try the Hot Stone Therapy there: it starts with the therapist holding the guest up in a sitting position and placing six large stones on the bed. Then they cover the stones with a towel and invite the client to lie down on them, aligning the backbone

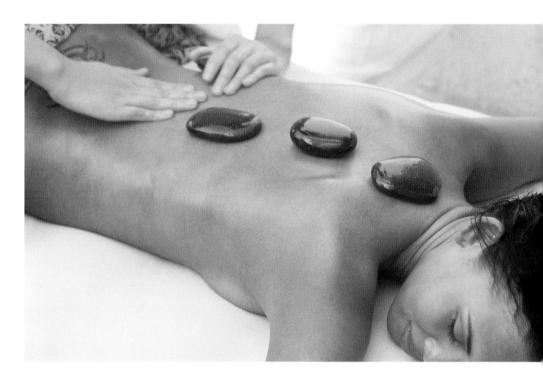

with the stones. More rocks are then placed on the body's different energy points, allowing the heat to penetrate deep within the muscles to melt away tension. Finally, the warm stones are massaged on various parts of the body, including the face, neck, chest, stomach, front and back of legs, and back, to encourage stimulation. This therapeutic

treatment is designed to relieve stiffness and soreness as well as to rejuvenate and relax the body.

Try the therapy at home: The warmth of the stones is nourishing for a friend in need of rebalancing. Based on the idea that we all have the power to heal ourselves, it is recommended that the warm stones be placed on the palms of hands and feet, as well as any sore areas, to energize the body's healing potential.

Ingredients:

- 7 flat stones (3 inches; 7.5 cm long); a warm oil blend of 5 tbsp carrier oil such as sweet almond mixed with 10 drops of geranium, mandarin and lime for vitality or sandalwood, orange and jasmine for nurturing.

Directions: Cover the stones in boiling water and heat for 10 minutes. Remove stones from water one by one with tongs, and dry. Ask your guest to lie face down, with arms relaxed and palms facing upwards. When the stones are just the

hot stone therapy

Below At CHI spas, the Himalayan Healing Stone Massage is inspired by the healing rituals of Lake Kokonar in Tibet. Creator of this treatment, anthropologist Carroll Dunham says: "Ways of healing need no borders or passports."

Opposite The Ritz-Carlton Hot Sand and Herbal Steam Massage is a most unique interpretation of the classical hot stone therapy.

Opposite below, clockwise from left Herbs in this treatment. The pouches are filled with sand from Kubu beach. The warm pouches generate a deep and lasting rest. A traditional cooker steams the herbal and sand pouches.

"right" temperature, place one each in the palms, two on each of their shoulder blades, one at the base of the neck, one at the center of the spine and the last stone in the center of the lower back. Leave for a few minutes to allow the warmth of the stones to energize and nurture whilst stimulating *ch'i* flow through the body. When the stones have cooled you can take them off one by one. Afterwards, choose one stone and oil it with the massage oil blend and gently massage the back with the stone. Take care not to massage the spine or apply too much pressure.

HIMALAYAN STONE MASSAGE

Tibetan treatments are a beautiful blend of Indian, ayurvedic, Chinese and Greek modalities, but it seems that neighboring Mongolia introduced this healing stone massage treatment into Tibet. "River stones have always been used by *horpas* (Tibetans of Mongol descent who live in the Hor desert region) who maintained this highly

effective treatment," reports Carroll Dunham, creator of all the Tibetan-inspired recipes in this book. She explains that to this day, the Mongol traditional medical system uses more minerals and stones in their pharmacopia than in neighboring Tibet.

"Stones and minerals are a common ingredient in Tibetan treatments," says Carroll. "Local ingredients like stones and barley were mixed with herbs for post oil massage, and minerals and precious muds from sacred places were also used. A small bolus or *pindu* was made using gems for cooling, and precious hot nutmeg dipped into hot mustard oil was applied to *marma* or acupuncture points on the body." Traditionally, Tibetan healers applied smoldering sticks of artemisia over critical acupuncture points to relieve wind trapped in the body. In addition, poultice bags filled with artemisia, nutmeg and ginger were dipped in hot medicated oils and applied to specific acupuncture points.

A place to experience a true Tibetan treatment outside Tibet is at one of the CHI Spas located at Shangri-La hotels. Their Himalayan Healing Stone Massage is based on Tibetan healing rituals and involves an ancient massage technique using a combination of hot stones heated in oils and herbs to ground the body and restore vitality, and cool stones to balance stress. Each stone is beautifully hand carved by monks with Sanskrit symbols to evoke the spirit and philosophy of CHI.

HOT SAND AND HERBAL STEAM MASSAGE

Drawing on the healing tradition of heated stones and crystals, the Spa at the Ritz Carlton Bali has come up with a creative invention that combines massage and inhalation with the penetrating heat of hot sand pouches. Small pouches filled with hot sand are placed on various points of the body to warm the muscles. This is followed by a massage—a blend of acupressure, *shiatsu* and deep tissue—and an inhalation

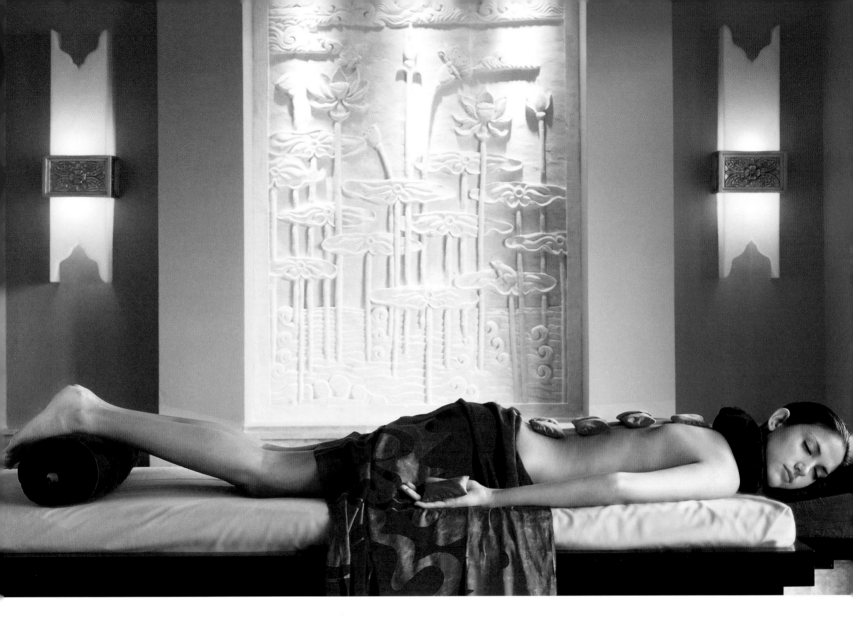

of herbs placed below the massage bed. The inhalation of lemongrass, wild ginger and cloves increases circulation and energy flow, removes toxins and relaxes tired muscles. Recreate the treatment at home.

Ingredients:
- 2 tbsp ginger, grated; 3 stalks lemongrass, cut and ground; 10 bay leaves.

Directions: Place ingredients in a bowl, pour hot water into the bowl and infuse. Fill some small cotton pouches with sand, and heat them by steaming over boiling water. Lie down on a massage bed, placing the bowl of ingredients under the face cradle. Before the massage commences, place the hot sand pouches on the *chakra* points on the back to warm and stimulate. During the massage, which should comprise the long strokes of traditional Balinese massage, inhale the steam from the bowl of ingredients. For the massage oil, we suggest you use a blend of 2 tbsp sweet almond oil or olive oil and 3 drops each of ginger, lemongrass and bay essential oil—and warm the oil before use.

reiki

Below Reiki is a hands-on healing system that has infinite wellness benefits. Here a therapist at Chiva-Som places her hands just above the patient's face.

Right The themes at Six Senses Spas are Holistic and Conscious. Masters are often invited to the various spas to give special sessions or courses with clients and, here, Tibetan reiki is being performed. Other offerings include guided meditations to help guests find a sense of purpose and self-empowerment.

Reiki translates as "universal life force energy," and its purpose is to channel universal energy to heal spiritual, mental or physical ailments. Tibetan reiki master and author, Derrick Gooch, explains that reiki (pronounced "ray-key") is "a hands-on healing system used to treat many different types of illnesses." According to Chiva-Som therapists, reiki originated in monasteries on the Tibetan plateau in Tibet and northern India and was introduced into Japan during the 19th century by a Japanese doctor called Dr Usui. Today it is taught throughout the world and it is believed that anyone can master it.

The experience of receiving reiki is profound, with insights, realizations, and visuals of colors and images of past lives commonplace. Like an artist, the therapist draws energy through them and, by placing their hands above the seven *chakra* points of the recipient's body, transfers it to the patient. It's not unusual for the patient to feel warmth from the flowing energy as the body falls into a deep, relaxing, sleep-like state.

Derrick explains that true healing comes from within and a practitioner's role is simply to open the door to awaken what is already there. Derrick advises that to truly benefit from Tibetan reiki, a course of two to four treatments is recommended. This way the patient understands what he or she is feeling by the second or third treatment. Calmness begins to expand and

instead of inducing sleep, more peace is felt from deep within. This helps the patient to make needed changes. It is advisable to take some quality time to rest after a reiki treatment.

Reiki is a holistic therapy and only a few notable Asian spas offer quality reiki sessions. These include Six Senses Spas at the Evason Hua Hin Resort and the Evason Hideaway at Ana Mandara in Vietnam, and Chiva-Som in Thailand.

"Reiki has infinite results," says Derrick. "It can be wonderful for pain management, headaches and chronic pain as well as for dealing with stress and worry." He adds: "Reiki is a great way to begin one's journey to knowing oneself better. This is because pure energy helps people to truly realize who they are and how they wish to be in the world."

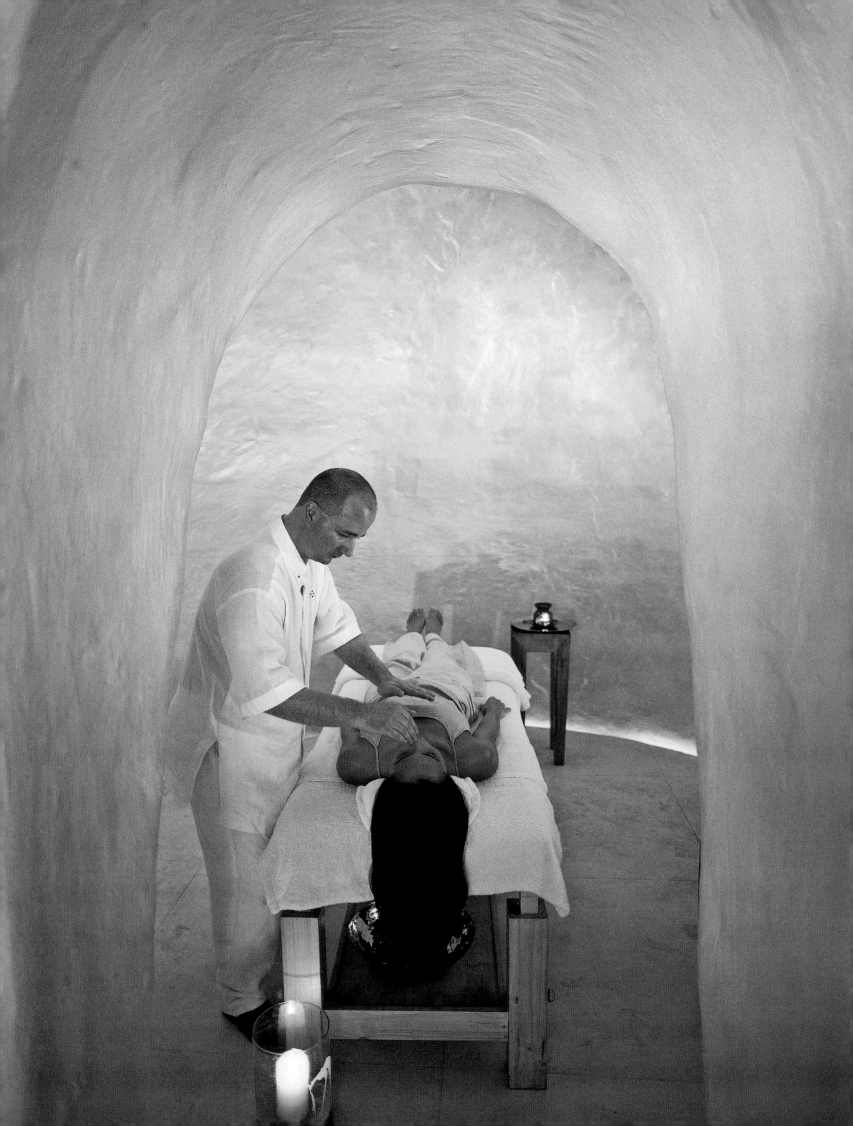

face

"LET THE BEAUTY OF WHAT YOU LOVE BE WHAT YOU DO"

Rumi (13th century mystic poet)

The ancient practice of physiognomy is experiencing a renaissance in facial treatments in Asian spas. Traditional Chinese and ayurvedic doctors have always diagnosed the health of the body through observation of the face, saying that each area of the face relates to a different organ in the body. They believe that inner beauty relates to outer beauty and certainly there is a connection between our emotional wellbeing and our external appearance. Outer joy can indicate inner happiness and a serene expression may reveal that there is composure within.

Spa therapists in Asia are now being trained to see the body as a whole and incorporate this knowledge in some innovative new facial treatments. Skin rejuvenating treatments that blend Eastern techniques with the very best from the West are the latest trend: facial acupuncture, acupressure and lymphatic drainage techniques to stimulate *ch'i* and blood flow are combined with hot and chilled stones and crystals, Chinese jade rollers, small poultices of steaming herbs and exotic plant ingredients for rejuvenating results.

Kirana Spa in Bali blends ancient Japanese acupressure techniques with modern scientific knowledge developed by Shiseido. Their serene facial treatments in a flower-filled tropical garden are extraordinary. Also in Bali, the Ritz-Carlton's Spa on the Rocks uses the well-regarded Crème de la Mer products and combines them with innovative East-meets-West treatments. In addition, many Asian spas offer wellness, lifestyle and diet consultations alongside facials, meditation and yoga sessions to encourage us to treat the body and mind as one.

One of the most beautiful aspects of Asian facials is the surroundings in which they are given. The same can be said about the gorgeous ingredients. Asian spa recipes are often derived from nature and draw upon the color, scent and texture of flowers, plants and sea-life to quench our thirst for beauty, touch, rhythm and love. To create spa recipes at home, start by gathering healing plants, flowers, crystals, clay, spices, herbs, essential oils and exotic accessories. Give your skin attention with regular cleansing, self-massage, scrubs and masks as well as a continual and hydrating shower of balanced and loving thoughts.

Awaken each morning with gratitude for what is. During treatments fuse your mind with positive thoughts. Embrace all of life's offerings—and encourage those around you to do so too. The results will be revealed in your radiant face.

Right Many Eastern practices advocate that inner beauty is a reflection of outer beauty—a fresh, radiant face indicates a well-balanced mind, body and spirit.

clean face

Awaken with a splash of cool water or pure rosewater on your skin and smile at your reflection. The secret of a bright exterior is to cleanse the skin daily with the purest of ingredients.

Opposite Water is the quintessential essence of many Asian beauty treatments.

This page The lotus root is renowned for its healing properties, and can be taken internally and externally for detoxification. The pure lotus cleanser below results in a smooth, shiny complexion.

Daily renewal of the skin can be approached in many ways. The regular practice of yoga, *qi gong* or *tai chi* can be a regular part of any beauty regimen, as can the choice of ingredients applied to the face. In ayurvedic India, cooling facial cleansers (facial *ubtans*) or pastes made from ground legumes and flours blended with milk or yoghurt and perhaps some ground or grated almonds, cucumber, figs and papaya with a pinch of turmeric, *tulsi* or neem act as great exfoliators. Other cultures use citrus fruits, full of alpha hydroxy acids, to speed up the skin's own shedding process. In the Himalayas, yak milk has long been regarded as an effective natural skin cleanser and the Mongolians continue to cleanse the face and body with mare's milk.

Cleansing and exfoliating the skin removes dead skin cells, toxins held on the skin's surface and sebum, and encourages cell renewal. Gently exfoliate your skin with ingredients that contain fine particles, or fruits that are high in natural exfoliating enzymes such as papaya. Use gentle circular movements to polish your skin, and always rinse with tepid water, gently patting skin dry afterwards. Bring fresh life to your skin by dedicating a few minutes to a daily cleanse and tone as well as a twice-weekly exfoliation. Always remember to moisturize afterwards.

JAPANESE CAMELLIA OIL WITH ALOE VERA

Believed to be the secret behind the silky flawless skin of Japanese women in traditional Japan, *tsubaki* is the cold pressed oil extracted from camellia seeds. High in oleic acid, it has been used for centuries to moisturize hair, skin and nails. This golden oil is valued for its color and viscosity; very similar to jojoba oil, it is fine to use undiluted on hair, skin and nails. After application, the skin feels super hydrated and has a shimmering appearance.

Ingredients:
- 7 tsp camellia oil (you can buy it in wellness stores and aromatherapy shops); 4 tsp aloe vera gel; 1 tsp vitamin E oil; 1 tsp vegetable glycerin; 2 tsp jojoba oil; blend of essential oils according to skin type (below).
- *Normal skin:* 7 drops each of basil, rosemary and lemon essential oils.
- *Dry skin:* 5 drops each of rose, sandalwood, jasmine and geranium essential oils.
- *Oily skin:* 7 drops each of bergamot, cypress and juniper essential oils.
- *Mature skin:* 7 drops each of lavender, frankincense and neroli essential oils.
- *Blemished skin:* 10 drops each of lavender and tea tree or 10 drops each of bergamot and lemon essential oils.
- The above are to be blended with sesame oil for dry and mature skin, camellia oil or sweet almond oil for normal and dehydrated skins, and jojoba oil for oily or blemished skin.

Directions: As this is a chemical-free cleanser it will separate, but only needs a quick shake before use to bring it back to the right consistency. Apply about 2 tsp to the face to remove the traces of the day. Massage in circular movements avoiding the eye area. Wet the fingertips and massage again in circular movements to create a very gentle lathering effect. Gently wipe off with damp cotton wool or a cloth. Rinse or splash face with lukewarm water. Lightly pat the face dry. Complete with a moisturizer.

PURE LOTUS ROOT CLEANSER

The exquisite lotus flower (*Nelumbo nucifera*) is the sacred flower of India and is linked to the goddess of prosperity, Lakshmi. A symbol of spirituality in many Asian countries, lotus essential oil is used in many perfumes. In Chinese and macrobiotic medicine, the lotus root is considered beneficial for the respiratory system. Available in Asian food stores and health food stores, it is consumed to detoxify and eliminate mucous build up and is full of vitamin B. This easy-to-prepare cooling cleanser results in a clean and glowing skin.

Left Organic facials given at Anantara Spa in Thailand are made with cucumber, green tea, bamboo, papaya and tamarind for a cooling and rejuvenating effect.

Below Moisturizing should always be the finale of any facial treatment. At Four Seasons Spa at Jimbaran Bay in Bali, a cooling moisturizer soothes, calms and refreshes the skin.

Opposite Four Seasons Spas are renowned for their facial exfoliations using indigenous botanicals, enzymes and sea elements.

with cool water, tone with rosewater lotion and apply moisturizer as the finale.

COOLING YOGHURT POLISH

From the highest mountains in Tibet to the royal palaces of Indonesia, yoghurt has long been valued as a cooling beauty ingredient. Its lactic acid content acts as a natural exfoliant that helps to smooth surface lines and improve overall skin texture. This recipe is particularly soothing and refreshing and is very easy to use. It's perfect for all skin types except the super sensitive. Expect to have freshened looking skin that feels soft and hydrated.

Ingredients:
- ¼ cup (60 ml) yoghurt; 1 tbsp rice bran or oat bran.

Directions: Mix the ingredients well in a bowl until the mixture has a creamy texture. Apply to face for 15 minutes. Wet fingertips and massage the face with small circular movements. Rinse off with cool water, and apply a moisturizer.

EGGSHELL EXFOLIATOR WITH ROSE PETALS

This little gem of a recipe, based on an ancient Indonesian remedy and presented to us by Dr Martha Tilaar, takes a little time to prepare but has fantastic results—pure skin brilliance and luminosity! Eggshells contain around 95 percent pure calcium carbonate (similar to seashells, coral and pearls), not to mention 5 percent calcium phosphate and magnesium—all of which help to enhance nutritional absorption in the body. We recommend this for all skin types as a twice-weekly gentle exfoliating procedure.

Ingredients:
- 1 tsp eggshell, ground to a powder; 1 tsp betel nut (*Areca catechu*) ground into a powder (or use 1 tsp almond meal); 1 tsp dried rose petals, ground; 2 tbsp jicama starch; 8 tbsp rice starch; 1–2 tbsp coconut cream.

Ingredients:
- 2 tbsp fresh lotus root, chopped (or 1 dried lotus root); 1 cup (250 ml) water.

Directions: Soak the chopped lotus root in cool water for up to 8 hours. Place in saucepan with a little water, bring to the boil and simmer until the water reduces to half. Strain and pour into a glass jar. Use within 2 days, storing in the refrigerator. Gently apply the tonic with a gauze or cotton wool to a freshly cleansed face. Rinse gently and follow with moisturizer.

PAPAYA CLEANSING CREAM WITH YOGHURT AND HONEY

Clean. Dewy. Radiant. This delicious fruity milk is perfect for cleansing normal to dry complexions and is gentle enough to be used both in the morning and at night across the face and throat. Yoghurt is known to be beneficial for cleansing and with regular use can slightly lighten the skin. Papaya is full of natural enzymes that effortlessly shed away dead skin cells and honey acts as a humectant to hydrate skin.

Ingredients:
- 50 g papaya, mashed; 2 tbsp yoghurt; 1 tbsp honey; 1 tbsp rosewater; 1 tbsp jojoba oil; ¼ tsp vitamin E oil; 5 drops pure rose essential oil.

Directions: Blend all the ingredients thoroughly together in a blender or use a hand-held mixer until the mixture is smooth and creamy. Apply with fingertips and massage into the skin. Rinse the face

Directions: Mix all ingredients, except the coconut cream, together and store in a glass jar. To use, mix 1 tbsp coconut milk with 1 tbsp of the dry mixture. Apply to the face using gentle scrubbing motions. Rinse afterwards and apply a moisturizer.

GREEN TEA AND PAPAYA CLEANSER

Two of the East's most precious ingredients combine here to create a recipe to exfoliate, cleanse, heal and re-feed thirsty skin of any type. Green and white teas are rich in antioxidant polyphenols: externally they help to vitalize as well as prevent damage from the sun and promote elasticity. We add bentonite clay as it's a highly absorbent clay that pulls oils and toxins from the skin and revitalizes dull areas.

Ingredients:

- ½ cup (125 ml) cooled infused green tea water; ½ cup (100 g) papaya, mashed; 2 tbsp bentonite clay or green clay.

Directions: Blend ingredients to make a light paste. Apply to face, neck and chest area (as well as hands) and gently exfoliate. Rinse in tepid water.

ORIENTAL OAT SCRUB WITH FLAXSEED AND ROSEBUDS

Created by Mary E. Wakefield and Sunanda Harrell-Stokes of Marisanda Skin Foods in New York, this recipe is a moisturizer, cleanser and exfoliator all in one. Full of minerals and vitamins, it is based on a combination of Western and Chinese herbs and may also be used as a body scrub. The flax seeds work to lubricate and soften skin whilst the rose buds and lavender leave a lovely fragrance. Apply by massaging with small gentle, circular movements.

Ingredients:

- 1 cup (100 g) oats or oat bran; 2 cups (200 g) French white clay; ¼ cup (30 g) almond meal; 1 ½ tbsp lavender flowers; 1 ½ tbsp rose buds; 1 ½ tbsp flaxseeds; 1 ½ tbsp kelp powder; 2 drops lavender, rose or geranium essential oil (or 5 drops vitamin E).

Directions: Finely grind the oats, lavender flowers, rose buds, flaxseeds and kelp powder in a mortar or food processor, then add this mixture to the French white clay. Coarsely grind the almonds, and combine all the ingredients. Store in a container, with a scoop in the refrigerator. Wet the face, and mix one tablespoon of the mixture with one tablespoon water to make a paste. Add the essential oils or vitamin E drops(or mix the paste with raw honey if you prefer), then gently massage into the neck and face. Wash off with warm water, gently pat dry and apply a moisturizer.

mask therapy

A mask is part of the finale in a facial sequence used to promote radiantly healthy skin. It cleanses the skin, absorbs excess oil, removes dead skin cells, softens blackheads, heals damaged or blem- ished areas, stimulates circulation and encourages healthy cell regeneration. Its function is to nourish and regenerate, helping the skin to fight free radicals from damaging pollutants. It stimulates the deep layers under the skin allowing healthy new skin to shine through.

When receiving a mask in a spa, you may be given a relaxing massage whilst your mask is drying. It certainly feels good to be wrapped up in a warm body wrap whilst your head and scalp are being massaged and your face is nourished with ingredients to deeply cleanse the skin. In spas today, there are many forms of cleansing facial masks for varying skin types and phases. Some are setting types created with clays, kaolin, fuller's earth, zinc, marine ingredients, sulphur and egg white: these cleanse, draw, tone and stimulate the skin. Others are non-setting masks that infuse active ingredients into the skin: they soothe, hydrate, calm, heal and refresh. These are often created with plants, fruits, vegetables, herbs, honey and gels.

In ayurvedic facial treatments, mask ingredients include rosewater, honey and neem oil in bases like natural clay and yoghurt spiced with turmeric root powder, black pepper, ginger juice and sandalwood powder. In Chinese treatments, ingredients may include crushed pearl powder, honey, egg, aloe vera, with flowers of chamomile, chrysanthemum and dandelion.

Clay is possibly the most common ingredient found in global spa treatments and skin care products worldwide, and the varieties are many. Like a magnet, clays draw out toxins and impurities from the skin. They are naturally enriched with the most nutritious of minerals including calcium, magnesium, potassium, zinc, iron and silica. Here is a simple round-up of their properties:

Red Kaolin Clay: Regulating and calming, red clay (reflecting its color) regulates blood circulation, calms sensitive or sunburnt skin and is beneficial for varicose veins, pregnancy and menopause. It is also used for drawing oils and toxins out from the skin.

White Kaolin Clay: Also known as China or white clay, this is basically kaolinite and is the mildest of all clays. Perfect for sensitive skin types, its texture is softening and delicate. It is highly recommended for mild exfoliating and cleansing.

French Green Clay: A most active clay for extracting oils and toxins from the skin, French green clay is naturally rich in minerals and phyto-nutrients. Hence, it is mostly applied as a therapeutic clay. Excellent for facials and body wraps, it stimulates the circulation and increases flow of blood, lymph and water.

Pink Kaolin Clay: Pink kaolin is a gentle clay, making it suitable for sensitive skin.

It helps stimulate circulation, all the while gently exfoliating and cleansing skin. Pink kaolin clay does not draw oils from the skin and can therefore be used on dry skin types. It is soothing, skin refining and balancing.

Yellow Kaolin Clay: Yellow kaolin is a mild clay making it suitable for sensitive skin. It helps stimulate circulation while gently exfoliating and cleansing skin. Yellow kaolin does not draw all oils from the skin and can therefore be used on most dry skin types.

Black Clay: Detoxifying and great for dehydrated skin, black clay also reduces water retention. In addition, it is moisturizing for sun-damaged skin.

Dead Sea Clay: Dead Sea clay is rich in the minerals found at the bottom of the Dead Sea. Used alone or mixed with other clays, it is recommended for facials, body wraps, hair wraps and soap.

Multani Mitti: Also known as Indian fuller's earth, this is similar to kaolin clay.

Derived from the decomposition of volcanic ash, fuller's is used to clean sheep's wool prior to spinning. It is highly absorbent and is good for drawing excess oils from the skin and stimulating circulation.

Rhassoul: Rhassoul is a super fine ancient clay that comes from the Atlas mountains in Morocco. Although it is difficult to obtain from the deep clay beds, it has been used for centuries by the ancient Romans and Egyptians. Rhassoul clay is rich in minerals such as silica, magnesium, iron, calcium, potassium and sodium. It helps detoxify the skin while it gently exfoliates.

As well as being one of nature's most detoxifying ingredients, the earthy quality of clay is also a restorative. At Spa Botanica in Singapore, the clays are presented like scoops of ice creams in an ice cream tray and you are invited to smother these on various parts of the body before entering a dome-shaped steam room. Many spa treatments in Indonesia use the clay from Lombok Island and, in Thailand, an indigenous white chalk-like mud called *dinsaw pong* is used to combat the tropical humidity by cooling and cleansing the skin. Traditionally it is sold in triangular white pellets that are dissolved in water and applied as a paste to the face and body. Spiritually, it is known to ground and bring one back to center and is used in ceremonial, healing and bathing rituals.

Try some of these masks for size: some use clay, others don't. And remember these golden rules:

- Steam clean your face before applying a mask. You can do this by holding your head over a bowl of steaming water for a minute or applying a soaked hand towel directly on to the face.
- Apply mask on to freshly cleansed and damp face, neck and if appropriate, the décolletage area, avoiding the eye and lip area.
- For best results, soak a gauze and then apply directly onto the skin.

- Take your time. Lie down and rest for the desired time or soak in the tub to allow nutrients to fully absorb into the skin.
- Remove gently with cool-warm water.
- Pat dry and apply moisturizer, serum or facial oil, delicately massaging for a few minutes.

ROYAL JELLY ENERGY MASK

We recommend this clay and royal jelly mask for dehydrated skin. Royal jelly is the vital food for the queen bee who lives 50 times longer than regular bees. As such, it is full of pure energy and considered effective for longevity and wellbeing. It is a most nutritious tonic that can be taken internally and applied externally. As a mask, the results are smoother skin with a velvety texture. Use twice a week to revitalize skin.

Ingredients:
- 1 ½ tbsp white clay; 5 ml vial royal jelly, pierced; 1 tbsp honey; 1 egg yolk; 1 tbsp oatmeal.

Directions: Mix ingredients into a paste and apply to the face, avoiding the eye area. Leave the mask on for 15 minutes, then rinse with warm water. Apply your regular moisturizer afterwards or give yourself a relaxing facial massage using warm oils for your skin type.

THAI WHITE CLAY AND ALOE MASK

Rejuvenating and regenerating for normal to dry and mature skins, honey protects and hydrates whilst clay cleanses and re-mineralizes. Here, we have added vitamin E for its natural antioxidant properties and evening primrose as a superb healing agent and moisturizer. This recipe helps renourish dry and flaking skin that is prone to eczema and irritations. Use once a week.

Ingredients:
- 3 tsp Thai white clay; 1 ¼ tsp honey; 1 tsp aloe vera juice; ¼ tsp vitamin E oil; ¼ tsp evening primrose oil.

Directions: Blend ingredients thoroughly and apply to a clean face; leave for 10–20 minutes. Rinse in tepid water, and moisturize.

GINSENG AND GREEN TEA MASK

This recipe relies on the nutrients of ginseng to heal and nourish the skin by stimulating cell growth and extending cellular life span. In *The Yellow Emperor's Classic of Internal Medicine*, a tome that introduces and analyses traditional Chinese medicine (TCM,) ginseng is referred to as "an energy tonic which replaces lost *ch'i* to the meridians and organs." Native to China, Japan and Korea, ginseng is believed to help alleviate stress-related conditions, combat fatigue and introduce vital energy or *ch'i* into the body. Here combined with green tea, it works to detoxify and restore health and radiance to the skin, as well as reduce any redness. Avocado is added for its nour-ishing and skin softening qualities. This recipe is best for normal to dry and mature skins, and is easy to prepare.

Ingredients:
- ½ avocado (90 g), mashed; ¼ tsp Chinese or Korean ginseng root liquid; ¼ tsp wheat germ oil; ½ tsp green tea powder.

Directions: Blend all ingredients together using a pestle and mortar or put in the blender until you have a creamy paste. Spread over face, neck and décolletage twice a week in the evening, ideally whilst in the bath when the skin is pre-warmed. Leave on for 8–10 minutes, then wash off and moisturize.

* As an additional bonus apply to the backs of the hands as a wonderful mini hand spa treatment. It leaves the hands super soft, refined and younger looking.

CHINESE EMPRESS PEARL MASK

We suggest using this recipe twice weekly for radiant skin. It's a very fine and gentle paste-like mix created with Chinese pearl powder (that can be substituted with eggshell powder). Ancient texts record that over 2,000 years ago pearls were used by the Ching Dynasty empress dowager with lustrous results. Fresh pearls were gathered, crushed and applied to the skin to clarify texture and reduce aging spots. Enriched in proteins, essential amino acids and calcium, pearls were also taken internally to detoxify and regulate the body system. This mask uses a more modern incarnation of crushed pearls and combines it with milk to brighten the complexion. The classical combination used human milk which was easily available in the Chinese palace from nursing nannies. For maximum benefits, this mask should be used at least twice a week before bedtime.

Ingredients:
- 1 tsp pearl powder or eggshell powder (from 1 egg); ½ tsp fresh lemon juice; ½ tsp fresh cow's milk.

Directions: Mix all ingredients together into a paste. After cleansing the face, dab and massage the mixture gently into the skin. Allow to dry and leave for at least 20 minutes to tighten and firm the skin. Wash off with cool water. Tone the skin with rosewater or your regular toning lotion. Apply moisturizer.

GREEN PAPAYA ENZYME BOOST

Poor digestion can result in illness, so any recipe that uses papaya with its natural enzymes works both internally and exter-nally. Green papaya enzymes speed up the digestive processes, in turn increasing overall wellbeing. Naturopaths, ayurvedic physicians and Chinese doctors all agree on this principle. Here, we apply papaya on the skin as a gentle exfoliant to help dissolve dead and damaged skin cells, gently cleansing and polishing the skin's surface to reveal fresh skin. Green papaya is reported to stimulate blood circulation and reduce the visual appearance of fine lines and large pores. This is quite an active mask, so we don't recommend it for people with

extremely sensitive skin types; however for people with dry and mature complexions, this is an ideal once-a-week, anti-aging treatment.

Ingredients:
- ¼ cup (60 g) mashed green papaya pulp (if you cannot find green papaya use a ripe papaya); 2 tbsp white clay.

Directions: Blend all of the ingredients together and apply the mixture to face. Lie

down and allow the ingredients to work into the skin for 10 minutes. Rinse gently and complete with facial moisturizer or oil.

JAVANESE FACIAL MASK WITH TAMARIND

This dazzling Javanese mask, formulated by the renowned Dr Marthar Tilaar, is easy to create at home. It works to soften facial skin as well as maintain its natural moisture levels. Ideally, it is recommended that this

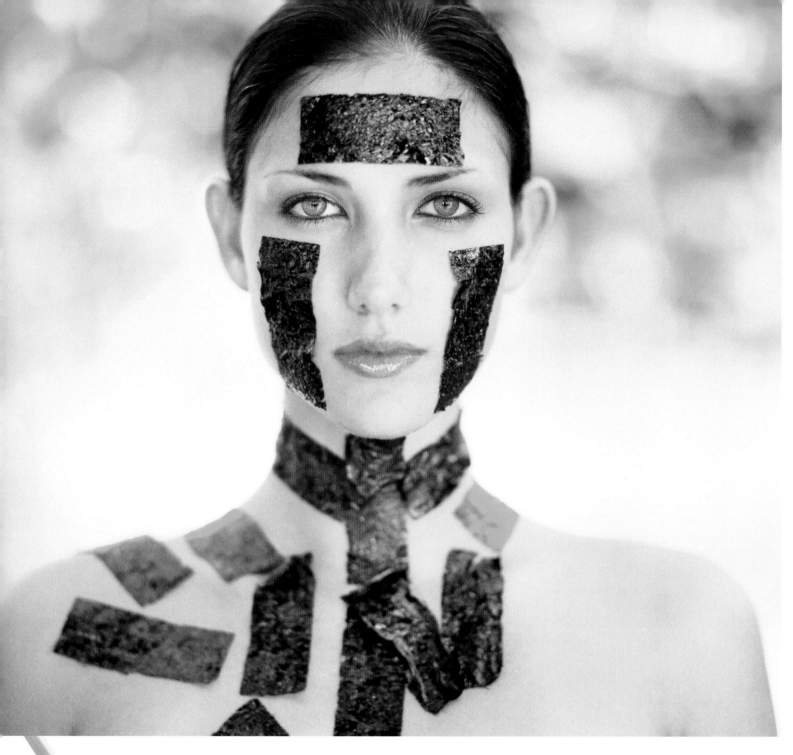

mask should be used once a week to leave the skin looking and feeling fresh and radiant.

Ingredients:

- 1 tsp fenugreek, ground; 1 tsp orange jessamine, ground (if unavailable, use 1 drop each of essential oil of jasmine and orange); 1 tsp dried tamarind; 1 tsp ylang ylang flowers, ground (or use 2 drops ylang ylang essential oil); 1 tsp turmeric, ground; 10 tbsp rice starch.

Directions: Mix all dry ingredients together and store in a glass jar. To use, take 1 tbsp of the mixture and add 1 tbsp water to form a paste. Add the essential oils last, if you cannot get hold of orange jessamine and ylang ylang. Apply directly on the face, leave for 15 minutes, then rinse with cool water. Tone and moisturize as usual.

SEAWEED ZEN MASK

Like taking a dip in the ocean, bathing your face in super vitalizing seaweed encourages and brings to the surface the skin's natural radiance. For centuries, the Japanese have used seaweed in both food and medicine, so its healing properties are well documented. Enriched with countless minerals, seaweed works to detoxify and re-mineralize skin cells and improve skin tone. This recipe is very smoothing and replenishing for facial skin.

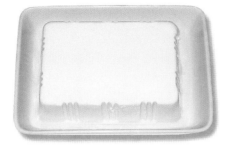

Ingredients:

- ½ packet dried *wakame*, or a handful of fresh seaweed.

Directions: If using *wakame*, rinse and soak the dried *wakame* in pure water for 15 minutes before use; if using fresh seaweed, simply rinse before use. Apply strips of seaweed to a cleansed face and leave for 20 minutes allowing the skin to absorb the nutrients. Remove and rinse with a cool splash of water.

WILD NEEM AND ROSE PETAL MASK

Neem is a good example of how plants from remote villages in Asia have "travelled" to become important ingredients in today's spa treatments. Indigenous to central India, neem has long been used in soaps, and neem oil, extracted from the neem tree, has been used in ayurvedic medicine for thousands of years. It is known to deeply purify the skin as well as heal skin irritations and inflammations. Today, it is a vital ingredient in bath, hair, nail and even tooth care products. In this recipe from Prana Spa, it is combined with *tulsi* powder, an Indian spice easily found in Indian grocery stores, to regulate sebum or oil secretion and reduce oiliness, blackheads and pimples. This mask is recommended as a once-a-week treatment for acne prone, oily or blemished skins.

Ingredients:

- 1 cup neem powder (or 2 tsp neem oil); 1 tbsp *tulsi* powder; 1 tbsp sandalwood powder or *multani mitti* clay; 1 tbsp rose petal powder; 1 tsp turmeric powder; 2 tbsp plain natural yogurt; 1 tbsp lemon juice.

Directions: Mix dry ingredients together and store in a glass container. Before application, mix 1 tbsp of the mixture with the yoghurt and lemon juice to form a thick paste. Apply to the face and allow the mask to dry. Rinse with warm water, and finish with a moisturizer.

SILKEN SKIN MASK

The most nourishing ingredients for the skin are often the most nutritious foods and drinks. Asian spa therapists are known for taking items from the kitchen and using them in fresh and zesty treatments, so it should be no surprise to find *tofu* (fermented bean curd) in a handful of spa recipes. Unlike regular *tofu*, the Japanese silken *tofu* called for in this recipe is made in a manner similar to yoghurt where the protein is not hardened into curds and no whey is drained off. This process gives the *tofu* its smooth, creamy velvety texture—a perfect base for any face mask!

Ground almonds, candlenuts and sweet almond oil are wonderful moisturizers for normal to dry skin; freshly grated orange peel and sweet orange essential oil give the blend a refreshing citrusy energy, while geranium essential oil balances and calms the skin. Fresh mint and celery are considered beneficial to tone and cleanse oily and acne prone skin. Spirulina and wheatgrass heal and nourish the skin with their oxygen and free radical fighting antioxidants.

Created by Adria Lake, these once-a-week treats are easy to make and perfect for the at-home spa.

Normal to dry skin

Created with Japanese silken *tofu* to soften and condition the skin, this recipe also uses a ground almond and candlenut emollient to moisturize. Results are silky soft and smooth skin texture.

Ingredients:

- 3 ½ oz (100 g) *kinugoshi* (Japanese silken *tofu*); 1 tbsp honey; 1 tbsp almonds, ground; 1 tbsp candlenuts, ground (optional); 1 tbsp orange peel, grated; 1 tsp sweet almond oil; 3 drops sweet orange oil; 2 drops essential oil of geranium.

Directions: Purée all ingredients except the essential oils in a blender until smooth. Pour into a dish or glass jar, then add the essential oil drops and stir well. This recipe makes enough material for 8 applications. You can leave this mixture in the fridge and use twice a week. Avoiding the eye area, apply mask over a freshly cleansed face and leave to dry for around 15 minutes. The orange peel acts as a gentle exfoliator, while the other ingredients soothe and nourishe the skin. Using circular movements, rinse the skin with tepid water, then pat dry and apply moisturizer.

Oily to acne prone skin

Created with astringent celery and the antioxidant and anti-aging properties of spirulina, this is a beautiful cooling mask with an uplifting aroma. Green clay helps to draw impurities from the skin, and results are a clean, fresh complexion.

Ingredients:

- 3 ½ oz (100 g) *kinugoshi* (Japanese silken *tofu*); 5 fresh mint leaves; ½ cup (50 g) fresh celery stalk; ¼ tsp spirulina powder; ¼ tsp wheatgrass powder; 1 tsp jojoba oil; 1 tbsp green clay; 2 drops grapefruit, 1 drop clary sage, 1 drop peppermint, 2 drops lavender and 1 drop rosemary essential oils.

Directions: Purée all ingredients except the clay and essential oils until smooth, then mix in clay and oils. Store in the fridge;the mixture will keep for four applications, used twice a week. Apply mask on face, avoiding eye area. Leave on for 10–15 minutes, wash with warm water and towel dry.

scented facial mists

Ceremonies and rituals combining water, blessings and prayer are part of daily life in cultures across Asia. Today's spas often adapt such ceremonies and introduce them into the treatment room. The Malaysian Mist ritual at the spa at Four Seasons Resort Langkawi ends with a blessing of floral water. Here, we create some natural scented mists—spray on to face or body for instant enlightenment.

Just as trees and plants need moisture to grow, so do our minds and bodies require fluids to keep us radiant. These enlivening mists and serums are created from water, teas, essential oils, plants and flowers to provide continual hydration for the face and body. They can be applied after a mask or before moisturizing and may even be used to scent the hair. They are also good as a natural room freshener or added to bath water as an added fragrance.

AROMATIC WATER MISTS

Scent is like poetry to our nose, an ancient language that subtly yet impressively influences mood. Smell travels immediately to the part of the brain that affects our emotions and the sense of smell is believed to be 10,000 times more powerful than the sense of taste. By combining essential oils with water, these spray mists replicate the traditional water blessings of the East. They encourage peace of mind and also hydrate the skin.

To make, fill a ¼ cup (50 ml) spray bottle with distilled or purified water; add 9 drops pure essential oils (see below) diluted in 1 tbsp carrier oil such as sweet almond or jojoba.

Ingredients:
Japanese Waterfall
Recall the aroma of temple visits, hot spring bathing and tea ceremonies with this exquisite, uplifting aroma. It is perfect for mature skin complexions.
- 3 drops neroli, 3 drops geranium and 3 drops lavender essential oils.

Indian River
Reminiscent of a fresh mountain spring, this more grounding aroma is somewhat mystical in nature. It is also recommended for mature skin.
- 3 drops sandalwood, 3 drops myrrh and 3 drops cardamom essential oils.

Thai Rain Shower
A tropical scented blend, this mist is recommended for oily and combination skin types.
- 3 drops lime, 3 drops lemongrass and 3 drops ginger essential oils.

China Monsoon
Exotic and energizing, this fresh, floral blend is recommended for normal to dry skin complexions.
- 3 drops jasmine, 3 drops geranium and 3 drops petitgrain essential oils.

Directions: The oil and water separates in the bottle, so shake well before use. Spray 11–12 inches (30 cm) from face and body.

CHINA WHITE TEA MIST WITH TANGERINE

A useful spa ingredient in Asian spa culture, tea from the *Camellia sinensis* plant is full of antioxidants. The rarer white tea, whose leaves are harvested before they open with the buds still covered in a fine white film, is considered the "champagne" of teas when it comes to nutritional benefit. Here we blend it with the strengthening properties of neroli (good for sensitive complexions) as well as the uplifting oil of tangerine. The overall nature of this recipe is translucent, sweet and light, yet medicinal.

Ingredients:
- 1 cup brewed white tea (1 teabag for 250 ml distilled water or use 2 tsp loose leaves); 4 tbsp neroli floral water; ¼ tsp grape seed extract; 5 drops each neroli, orange and tangerine essential oils.

Directions: Strain the white tea twice through a muslin cloth. Drink one half and mix the other half cup (125 ml) with the remaining ingredients. Pour into a 200 ml spray bottle. Use after cleansing by soaking 2 cotton pads with the white tea mist and sweeping over the skin. Alternatively spray on at any time of the day to fight free radicals and keep skin looking young and fresh.

CHINESE SKIN CEREMONY WITH GINKGO AND GINSENG

A beautiful recipe that honors ingredients from the Chinese dispensary, this serum has a liquorice-like aroma and natural anti-septic properties. Ginkgo is a large shade tree with its name derived from the Japanese *ginkyo* or "silver apricot" (referring to its fruit.) Traditionally grown in temple and monastery gardens by Buddhist monks, it is believed to carry the potent energy of vitality. Ginkgo, used in TCM and as part of the Japanese tea ceremony, is considered enlivening for male and female libidos. Anise star oil is warming and slightly spicy: extracted from the star-shaped fruit of the evergreen tree, it has been used in Chinese medicine for over 1,300 years. Combined with the antioxidant properties of green tea, this serum helps revive sallow skin and restores skin firmness. It is excellent for rebalancing oily complexions.

Ingredients:
- ½ cup (125 ml) strong green tea; 10 drops Siberian ginseng tincture; 2 drops ginger essential oil; 1 drop *Ginkgo biloba* tincture; 4 drops Chinese star anise essential oil.

Directions: Steep the strong green tea for about one hour, then sieve it through a muslin cloth and pour into a glass bottle with a spray top. Add the remaining ingredients and shake well. Store in the refrigerator. Spray on daily after cleansing, or pour on to cotton wool pads and cleanse the skin after mask application and before applying your moisturizer.

GREEN TEA AND GINSENG HYDRATION MIST

This energizing aromatic mist is uplifting, refreshing and cleansing, and also encourages clarity of mind. Created to appeal to both men and women, it may be used by all skin types on both face and body. Green tea is the perfect antioxidant to revitalize tired skin. Combined with the reviving qualities of ginseng, refreshing lime, chamomile flowers and aloe vera, skin is softened, hydrated and regenerated after application.

Ingredients:
- 1 tbsp dried *sencha* (Japanese green tea); 1 tbsp dried ginseng root (*Panax ginseng*), ground; 1 tsp lime peel; 1 tbsp whole dried chamomile flowers (or one teabag); 1 cup (250 ml) hot water; 1 tbsp aloe vera gel; 1 tbsp witch hazel (optional); 10 drops tangerine, 5 drops basil, 5 drops peppermint essential oils.

Directions: Place Japanese green tea, ginseng, chamomile flowers and lime peel in a glass jar. Pour the hot water over the ingredients and steep for 30 minutes. Strain the liquid and add the witch hazel (optional) and essential oils to the infusion. Store in a dark glass bottle and refrigerate. Spray on to facial skin as needed.

HIBISCUS AND ROSE HYDRATING MIST

This blend of blood-cleansing hibiscus and rose, shared with us by spa consultant Adria Lake, is recommended for *pitta* and *kapha* types. Rose works on an emotional level to nurture and increase confidence and feelings of security. It is well known for its regenerating qualities and for hydrating dry and mature skin types. Himalayan cedar wood is calming and stress-relieving, whilst sage is the perfect cleanser for both the mind and skin. Combine these ingredients with the cooling properties of aloe vera and you'll feel instantly nourished.

Ingredients:
- 1 tbsp dried hibiscus flowers or 2 fresh hibiscus flowers; 1 tbsp dried rose petals or ½ cup (125 g) fresh rose petals; 1 cup (250 ml) hot water; 1 tbsp aloe vera gel; 1 tbsp witch hazel (optional); 10 drops rose absolute, 5 drops cedar wood and 3 drops sage essential oils.

Directions: Place dried or fresh flowers in a large glass jar or bowl. Add the hot water, then the aloe vera gel and witch hazel (optional). Stir gently, then steep the concoction for one hour. Strain through a muslin cloth and pour half the liquid into a 200 ml dark glass bottle. Add the essential oils, shake the bottle well and add the remaining liquid. Store in the fridge. Use as a body and face spray when you are in need of a quick pick-me-up.

asian facial treatments

The revival of ancient beauty preparations in today's spas reminds us to take care of our skin. By supporting our appearance, we honor our existence. No longer should we feel a tinge of guilt if we spend too long on our appearance. The men and women of Asia have been doing so for centuries—and their rituals are increasingly being incorporated into global beauty routines.

Southeast Asia is home to a pharmacopoeia of rejuvenating plants and herbs as well as a treasure trove of massage techniques. Think of the shimmer of green jade rollers, the glow of energizing crystals or the warmth from heated stones and pouches of steaming herbs slowly relaxing facial muscles and inner tension. Fuse these with the life-giving ingredients of Asia's apothecary—pearl powder, rice bran, green tea, *gingko*, bamboo, plum wine, ginseng and aloe vera—and you have some of the most restorative facial rituals in the world.

Some of today's spa rituals blend Eastern and Western methodologies. Facial acupuncture and *shiatsu* finger pressure slow down skin aging, while *marma* point massage, color therapy and light therapy enhance blood flow and circulation. Combine these Oriental practices with Western technology, and the results are ground-breaking. The Aromatherapy Associates signature facial offered at Mandarin Oriental Spas, Spa Botanica and Chiva-Som combines such different techniques and applications. It begins with a 10-minute back massage to calm the nervous system which in turn relaxes the mind, and also includes a half-hour massage on both the face and the scalp as well as acupressure, pressure point and lymphatic drainage techniques.

VIETNAMESE COOLING FACIAL

Freshly picked aloe vera from the garden is the ultimate facial hydrator. Easy to grow at home, aloe vera is reported to hold over 75 nutrients and 200 active compounds, including 20 minerals, 18 amino acids and 12 vitamins. It's regarded as a natural miracle worker and is often used to smooth and rehydrate skin that has been exposed to intense sun. This recipe comes courtesy of Six Senses Spa at the Ana Mandara Resort in Vietnam, and makes extensive use of this spiky home-grown gem.

Ingredients:
- 1 blade aloe vera, unpeeled and blended; 1 tbsp vitamin E cream or 2 tbsp vitamin E oil if cream unavailable; 2 blades aloe vera, peeled and sliced lengthwise.

Directions: Clean the skin with the blended aloe vera on a cotton wool pad, and remove with a warm compress. Massage face with vitamin E cream or oil for about 10 minutes paying particular attention to the jaw line and eye area to soothe and relax. Apply a warm compress and remove any excess cream or oil. Afterwards, apply a mask of sliced aloe vera to the entire face, leaving on the skin for about 10 minutes. Remove, and leave the skin to breathe for half an hour, before applying your regular moisturizer.

CHINESE PERANAKAN TREATMENT

There is an encouraging trend in Asia, and around the world, for masterful healers and doctors to work in spas and retreats, or, at the very least, for therapists to be trained by doctors. At the Spa Village Kuala Lumpur, therapists are all trained by a TCM doctor and Malay practitioners. Treatments here derive from the healing heritage of the Nusantara region, an area that encompasses the mainland from Myanmar to Peninsula Malaysia, and the islands of Indonesia and the Philippines.

This Peranakan facial treatment offered at the spa pays tribute to the integration of Chinese and Malay traditional healing. *Peranakan* translates as "marry" and refers to a group of people that are descended from immigrant Chinese and local Malays. The Peranakans have a strong cultural identity that is reflected in many areas—architecture, arts and crafts, as well as in domestic rituals.

The three-hour ritual begins with a sensual bath. Warm milk mixed with sandalwood essential oil is poured over the body to calm the nervous system and lower blood pressure, as well as beautify the body. The facial treatment that follows includes an "egg undulation," Chinese jade roller and mulberry leaf eye compress. The former consists of two warmed boiled eggs rolled upon the face as a facial massage; this is followed by a classic Chinese whitening pearl and rice mask and cool jade roller massage. Dried mulberry leaves known for their eye clearing and vision improving qualities are brewed in liquorice and green tea and are then pressed on to the eyes.

In keeping with the traditional Chinese medical theory that a healthy digestive system is an important factor in staying balanced, the therapist then applies a herbal paste on the navel and warms it with a small *moxa* stick made of herbs. This is believed to help improve metabolic rate and the digestive system.

The finale of the treatment is a body massage, first a type of *qi gong* massage with two sticks of bamboo lightly tapped in a rhythmic movement along the meridian lines and second, a traditional *tui na* massage. This helps release excess wind or heat from within—and completes the innovative ritual.

CHINESE JADE RITUAL

If you cannot make it to Malaysia, we suggest trying this alluring jade roller facial recipe at home. During the treatment, the chilled surface of the jade gently caresses the skin to stimulate *ch'i* flow, while a cooling application opens pores and encourages lymphatic drainage. Considered the "froth of the liquid jade" by the ancient Chinese poets, this replenishing skin tonic is created from the dried leaves of the green tea plant. This treatment is perfect for normal, dry and mature skins with cooling and refreshing effects resulting in softened skin texture. Begin the ritual with the green tea tonic, and follow with a jade roller. You can also use chilled crystals as a good alternative to the roller.

Ingredients:
- 2 tsp Chinese green tea; ½ cup (125 ml) distilled water, boiled; 1 jade roller.

Directions: Steep the tea for one hour, sieve the mixture and pour the tea into a spray bottle or jar, and allow to cool. Apply it with cloth or cotton wool pad all over the face. Leave on to absorb. Store in the fridge and use every day for one week. Afterwards, roll a jade roller over the skin gently moving from the center of the face outwards. Do this at least three times starting at the forehead and moving down to the chin. On the neck, roll down the neck towards the collarbones.

FACIAL ACUPUNCTURE

For over 5,000 years, the Chinese have been fascinated with longevity and youth. Many TCM practices, using powerful plants and herbs, were aimed at keeping both the face and the body youthful. There are accounts from 221 BC of Chinese physicians who practiced what we now call dermatology alongside other more traditional therapies. These included procedures for enhancing longevity such as special diets, *tui na* massage, *qi gong* and acupuncture.

A modern-day pioneer of youth and longevity is Mary Elizabeth Wakefield, an American therapist who has trained hundreds of acupuncturists around the world. Her Consitutional Facial Acupuncture, a popular treatment in spas in the USA, is based on TCM. Mary says it is a safe, painless and effective method for renewing both the face and the body. "Fine needles

asian facial treatments

are placed on various acupuncture points on the face, neck and around the eyes to stimulate the body's natural energies," she reports. "During the treatment, increased *ch'i* and blood flow to the face improves complexion, so wrinkles start to lessen and skin tone improves."

Facial acupuncture is a non-invasive youth enhancing treatment designed to maintain vitality inside and out. Before commencing, the acupuncturist assesses the patient's *jing* (hereditary essence manifested in the bone structure of the face and body), then he studies energy levels and *shen* or spirit. After this preliminary assessment, the treatment begins.

KIRANA FACIAL RITUAL

Given in the breathtaking environment of Kirana Spa's gardens and developed by Japanese beauty company, Shiseido, this facial ritual is seductive and soothing. Blending essential oils of sedating valerian, soothing nutmeg and exquisite neroli with the Kirana's own signature *ki* releasing, flowing massage style, this facial is delivered with sensitive warm hands on the face, shoulder and scalp area. Be prepared to enter a new realm for an hour or so—and depart refreshed.

Replicating such a facial sequence at home is an easy route to achieving clear, blemish-free skin. Add it to your weekly skin care regimen—and note the improvement in skin quality. When purchasing products, we recommend those labelled petro-chemical free without artificial colors and fragrances. Alternatively, make some at home with recipes from this book.

Start your beauty routine by removing lip, eye and base makeup with gentle splashes of water or rosewater or alcohol-free and soap-free cleansers.

For deeper cleansing, use a good-quality cleansing foam on a brush and cleanse sebum, perspiration and dust from the face. Thorough cleansing washes away the remains of the past and prepares your skin for the application of products.

Gently massage the face using a subtle combination of touch and pressure techniques. Tap or pat the face to stimulate circulation if you feel inspired to do so. This promotes the metabolism of waste products and creates sheer, smooth skin. It also eases fatigue of neck and shoulders. Wipe the face clean afterwards with a steamed towel.

Applying a good quality mask restores equilibrium to stressed skin. Afterwards, wipe thoroughly with a sponge and finish with a cool towel.

The skin always needs plenty of moisture in order to maintain a supple and toned appearance, so applying a moisturizing solution gently and gracefully is the next step in this facial. Allow the skin to drink in the ingredients for a few minutes.

As a finale, spray an aromatic mist (see pages 168–169) into your hands and apply the essence to the skin by pressing your hands gently on to the face. This facilitates exfoliation of old keratins and leaves skin dewy and moisturized.

Massaging the head, neck and shoulders is a vital element in a facial treatment. It releases any held tension and improves blood circulation to brighten up the complexion. At the end of the Kirana Spa Facial, the therapist asks the guest to sit up on the bed and puts a steamed towel on the shoulder and neck area. The warmth has a tranquilizing effect and deepens feelings of relaxation. Do the same at the end of your at-home sequence—then rest quietly for 10 minutes or so.

MALAY FACIAL

Offered at the Spa Village at Pangkor Laut and Kuala Lumpur, this treatment pays tribute to the wonderful bounty of Malay herbal heritage. The ritual starts with a simple cleansing treatment followed by a herbal scrub made from turmeric, ginger and rice powder to exfoliate and remove dead skin cells. A traditional facial massage follows using yogurt, honey and a few drops of brewed oil to boost blood circulation and encourage growth of new skin. This nourishing concoction is left on the skin, and a mask containing egg yolk and white clay is then applied. Egg yolk is a natural collagen, while white clay draws impurities from the skin and heals blemishes on the surface. An aloe vera gel is applied at the end of the facial to soothe and reduce irritations.

We suggest you visit the Spa Village in Kuala Lumpur where you'll get a chance to experience the *bedak sejuk* or Malay face mask as well. This mask is a traditional

Left to right: The Kirana Facial Ritual is a two-hour extravaganza that combines the Kirana *ki* releasing, flowing massage style with Shiseido products. The therapist removes any lip and eye makeup from the eye area with a cleansing lotion and makeup remover. Preparing the massage oil. The foaming cleanser contains anti-bacterial and anti-inflammatory extract of *Philodendron amurence*. The head, neck and shoulder massage increases blood flow to the facial area.

answer to modern-day SPF (Sun Protection Factor) and is made in the age-old way: a mixture of rice and glutinous rice is steeped in a claypot with fresh water and flowers for three days, before being pounded into a fine powder and cone pressed with banana leaves on to a *mengkuang* mat and left to dry in the sun. Once all the moisture has evaporated, these fine rice pearls are kept in jars filled with dried pandanus leaves, rose and jasmine petals.

Before application, the powder is mixed with a little water to make a paste. The paste is patted on to the skin and left to dry. As it dries, the mask draws out toxins from the skin's surface, clears pigmentation and tightens the skin. This process occurs because fermentation of the rice produces a co-enzyme action on the skin. Afterwards, the entire complexion feels toned, scented and cool.

THAI WATERMELON AND HONEY FACIAL

We recommend trying this recipe at home with a friend as it's fun and uncomplicated to create. The ingredients have been used for centuries in Thai beautifying rituals: fresh cucumber is known for its cooling properties on the skin, yoghurt is a gentle exfoliator and honey a good nourishing and hydrating ingredient. Aroma-wise, it's like a citrusy brew that awakens the senses and delights the skin. This recipe is shared with us by Six Senses Spas. Their therapists say the secret is to use the freshest of ingredients.

Ingredients:

- 1 slice watermelon; 2 tbsp yoghurt; ½ tbsp honey; 1 medium cucumber; 3 tbsp fresh aloe vera flesh, equivalent to 2 or 3 big blades; 1 flat tbsp almonds, ground; 2 tsp almond oil; ½ cup (60 g) oatmeal; ¼ cup (60 ml) full fat milk; 1 vitamin E capsule, pierced; hot towels, sponges and spatula.

Preparation:

- *Step 1:* Crush the watermelon through a metal sieve and pour the juice into a bowl for the eye and lip cleanser. Cover with cling film.
- *Step 2:* Mix yoghurt and honey for the facial cleanser and place in a bowl. Cover with cling film to retain freshness.
- *Step 3:* Cut the cucumber, cutting off two round pieces large enough to cover the eyes, and juice the rest in a blender. Place in a bowl and cover with cling film. This is for the skin toner.
- *Step 4:* Remove the skin of the aloe blade and chop one quarter from the end. This will be used for the massage blend. Take the remaining aloe vera and slice into tiny pieces.
- *Step 5:* Mix the ground almond with the aloe vera to make a paste. Place in a bowl and cover with cling film. This is for the exfoliant.
- *Step 6:* With the leftover aloe vera, mash until juice is extracted. Pour into a bowl and mix with the almond oil until combined. This is for the face massage.
- *Step 7:* For the mask, mix the milk and oatmeal together and place in a bowl.

- *Step 8:* Slice open vitamin E capsule and place in a bowl and cover with cling film. This is for the moisturizer.
  *store any ingredients that will not be used immediately in fridge.

Directions: Once all this preparation is completed, you are ready to begin the facial. Wrap the head with a towel covering the ears—and begin. Using a cotton wool pad, cleanse eye area and lips with the watermelon mix, and the face and neck area with the honey and yoghurt cleanser. Tone, in a similar manner, using the fresh cucumber juice, then exfoliate with the ground almond and aloe vera mix. Massage the mixture with circular movements over the face and neck area, then remove this exfoliatiant with hot towels wrapped around the jaw and with ends folded over the forehead. Leave for 10 seconds and then use the end of the towel to wipe excess particles from the face. Massage the skin with almond oil and aloe vera combination, then apply the oatmeal and milk mask over face. Alternatively, you may first cover the face with a gauze and apply mask with spatula over the gauze. Cover the eyes with two slices of cucumber and leave the mask on for at least 10 minutes. After rinsing off the mask ingredients with tepid water, apply the vitamin E on to the face to moisturize. This ends your fruity Thai treatment!

* If ingredients have been in the fridge and are cold, it is important to first apply pressure to temples to allow the skin to get used to the temperature of the products.

stone and crystal facials

Below Ingredients for Sereno Spa's Crystal Healing Therapy include warmed rose quartz crystals that are massaged into the body to stimulate *marma* points and restore balance. The heat from the crystals feels deeply relaxing.

Right Face and body treatments using crystals and stones are an example of how today's spas are integrating ancient practices into modern-day treatments.

Innovative spa creators are constantly on the search for new holistic treatments and the current trend is to look to the past for wisdom. Inspired by the ancient practice of using gems and stones in healing, crystal therapy is experiencing a renaissance in Asian spas. A special place to experience crystal therapy at its optimum is in the crystal steam rooms at both the Four Seasons and Landmark Mandarin Oriental Spas in Hong Kong where the blend of crystal, steam and aromatherapy come together in a powerful and meditative way.

In ayurveda, it is believed that gems and precious metals hold energy from the earth, so they are regarded as grounding, detoxifying, healing and rejuvenating. The best way to absorb their powerful energies is to keep them next to the skin at all times. In Tibet, jewels and stones are integrated into healing and nourishing rituals; traditionally, astrologers selected a precious stone or metal to help rebalance and strengthen a person's energy levels. And in China, jade is considered to hold the essence of life force.

The Earthlight Ritual offered at Four Seasons Spa in Langkawi is a sensual experience where heated crystals such as white and green jade, adventurine, jasper and rhodonite are massaged on the body. Similar treatments are on spa menus at the Balé in Bali and Shinta Mani in Siem Reap in Cambodia. We offer you two alternatives, especially created for the face, to try at home.

HOLISTIC CRYSTAL FACIAL

Drawing on the reported vibrational healing powers of oxidized and purified precious stones and metals, this treatment stimulates the acupoints on the face. Having the capacity to both attract and dispel positive or negative energies, the stones' powers are received through having them close to the body. The stones below are reported to affect the emotions and are used for emotional healing in many parts of the world.

Ingredients:
Choose from the following list. Gems used in healing should be cleansed and purified in salt water for at least two days before use. Water from sacred places (sea, rivers, lakes or anywhere that resonates with you) may also be used.

Metals

Gold:	Warming and comforting, balancing for *vata* types.
Silver:	Increases vitality, cools hot flushes and heartburn; balancing for *pitta* and *kapha* types.
Copper:	Helps with spleen, liver and lymphatic problems.
Iron:	Rejuvenating and strengthening, increases bone strength and vitalizes spleen and liver.

Stones

Amethyst:	For composure, tranquility, mental strength.
Diamond:	For sensuality, healing, vitality.
Emerald:	For love, understanding and attraction.
Jade:	For longevity, protection, mental peace.
Lapis lazuli:	For relaxation, awareness, wisdom.
Opal:	For beauty, protection, power.
Pearl:	For rebalance, romance, purity.
Ruby:	For passion, love, protection.
Sapphire:	For healing, meditation, peace.

Directions: Apply a face mask (see pages 162–167) and put the stone in the middle of the forehead or on any of the facial *chakra* points. It may also be placed on the heart *chakra*, the navel or even in the bath water. Believed to resonate on an unseen energetic level, the stone helps cleanse and rebalance the *chakras* bringing one's entire being back to center. Leave the stone on the face as long as you wish.

AYURVEDIC GEM WATERS

It is known that water has the ability to change its molecular structure according to what it is combined with, so when it is blended with crystals the effect can be very powerful. Such water can increase people's energy levels, so they feel nurtured and rebalanced.

Rather than choosing stones according to books, select gems at home that you are intuitively drawn to for their color, shape, texture and emotional resonance. Place your selection in a glass of pure water and

let it sit in strong sunlight for at least thirty days. Transfer the water to a spritzer bottle and spray on the face once a day—or when you feel in need of a pick-me-up.

In ayurveda, the following stones are recommended for the three *dosha* types:

Vata types: emerald, jade and yellow sapphire to increase energy and vitality; topaz to help lessen fearfulness; ruby to increase concentration and strengthen willpower.

Pitta types: moonstone as it has a calming influence on the mind and helps

relieve emotional stress; clear quartz, emerald, jade and pearl all help calm both body and mind and are healing for the skin; blue sapphire because it is well known for its soothing and calming nature.

Kapha types: ruby, blue sapphire and amethyst are believed to balance the emotions and to promote a sense of dignity, compassion and love; garnet as it is an excellent semi-precious stone that is used to treat people suffering from depression.

facial self-massage

Many Japanese women are educated in the benefits of daily facial care from an early age. Their nutritious diet contributes to longevity, and regular facial massage enhances composure and grace. A well-delivered facial massage soothes away worrying thoughts, relaxes the whole body and improves the state of the internal organs. A serene appearance is the result.

It makes perfect sense to self-massage the facial and neck areas on a regular basis. Gentle movements help keep the skin plumped and vital, thereby naturally relaxing the facial muscles. Long term benefits also include improved circulation. As we age, our facial muscles become more rigid as repeated expressions, too many worrying thoughts and tense lips and mouths forge ridges into the face. Be aware (but not fanatical) about changes in your appearance. Think of your face as your mirror—and learn how to monitor your skin.

Kirana Spa is well known for its unique Kirana Facial where massage plays a major role. Concentrating on the face, scalp, neck and shoulders, therapists apply hot, cold, soft and pressure techniques to combat fatigue and promote metabolism of waste products and water in the facial cells. Adapting some of their movements, we've formulated a self-massage sequence as part of a daily self-help facial regimen. The movements release tension and stimulate blood flow in the face.

Ingredients:
- 1 tbsp sesame, almond or safflower carrier oil; 2 drops lavender and 2 drops geranium essential oil.

Directions: Begin your ritual with a deep skin cleanse. Pour carrier and essential oil blend into a bowl filled with hot water. Wrap your head in a towel or *sarong* and hold your face a little above the bowl. Allow the infused steam to gently clean your skin. This opens the pores and brings blood to the surface of the skin. The aroma helps to relax the mind and facial muscles so they respond better to the massage.

Using gentle strokes and circular movements, follow the instructions for the various areas at right. Do not in any way pull or push the skin off balance. Press down lightly on each point to ensure stimulation.

Face: Lightly tap fingertips all over your face, neck and chest area, five times in each area if possible. This stimulates the blood circulation and increases skin elasticity and rejuvenation.

Eyes: Pinch the skin between your eyebrows, starting at the bridge of your nose and moving outward. Strong horizontal lines on both sides of the inner eyebrow indicate a weakness in the spleen. Press your middle and ring fingers as if you were lightly pinching along the upper eye socket moving from inner to outer edges. Now repeat on the lower eye socket.

Forehead: Stretch and tighten the forehead muscles and hold and release three times. Use four fingertips of both hands and lightly stroke from the center of the forehead outwards ten times. Use four fingertips of both hands and lightly stroke upward from above eyebrows to hairline ten times.

Nose: Stroke fingers downward from the bridge of the nose to the tip ten times. Stroke upward from tip to bridge ten times.

Cheeks: Place forefinger and middle finger of both hands on the upper cheek, with the middle fingers resting next to the nostrils and forefinger resting by the nose, and stroke outward five times.

Mouth: Lightly stroke fingertips of both hands from below the nose outward to crease around the mouth. Do at least ten times. Repeat this technique below the lips and repeat ten times.

Neck: Stroke fingers downwards along the neck ten times on each side. On each side of the Adam's apple, use spiral strokes in a downward motion.

Chin: Spread four fingers evenly out over the face, so the little finger rests at the mouth level and the forefinger reaches the cheek-bone. Press ten times. Stroke forefingers of each hand upward from the center of the chin to lower cheeks ten times.

Clockwise from top left Our model demonstrates some of the techniques that promote skin elasticity and comprise the massage section of the Kirana Facial. Lightly tapping the forehead area. Pressing four fingers into the chin area. Lightly pinching the ear lobes from the top to the bottom. Lightly stroking fingertips from the area below the nose outward to the crease around the mouth area. Lightly pressing middle and ring fingers from the inner to outer edges of the upper eye area. Pressing four fingers evenly over the chin area.

ayurvedic facial rituals

Ayurvedic facial treatments take a holistic approach, considering not only the health of the face itself. They care for the skin, still the mind, correct imbalances elsewhere, and help develop the body's own healing ability. The routine *dinacharya* is more than just a facial cleanser: it involves scraping the tongue, exercise, bathing and self-massage as well as facial nourishment. By honoring our face, we celebrate the whole body.

Marma point facial massage, offered at authentic ayurvedic spas and resorts, is an important ayurvedic facial ritual. According to Dr Sanjay Khanzode at the Sereno Spa it is performed differently on different *doshas*. Thumb and finger pressure stimulates the *marma* points on the scalp, face and décolletage area. These, in turn, increase blood flow and energy to other areas of the body. Benefits include delay in signs of aging, increased suppleness in facial skin texture, relaxed facial muscles and a renewed outlook on life.

"*Marma* points are considered the energy centers of the body," Dr Khanzode explains. "They correspond to various organs and bio-chemical functions in the body, so stimulating a *marma* point has a "principal" effect on the organ or system that it corresponds with and also a "secondary" effect that influences the

local area. Both correct imbalances. The result is a stimulation of the entire organ system, thus bringing the internal body to a state of equilibrium."

Other ayurvedic facial treatments are offered at Taj spas all over Asia, at Ananda in the Himalayas and Prana Spa in Bali. Particular mention must be made of the ayurvedic-influenced Oberoi facial, offered at the stunning Oberoi spas in the palatial –vilas properties in Rajasthan. Delivered with locally grown plants and fruits and the humectant properties of honey, it is truly divine.

Another one to look out for is the facial *lepa*, a detoxification and nurturing facial treatment using a herbal mask with *shirodhara* at Four Seasons Spa at Sayan in Bali. The *mukha lepam*, offered at the Spa Village on Pangkor Laut is also interesting: it involves a facial massage with special oils and ingredients according to the individual's *dosha*, a herbal paste made from coriander powder and plant extracts from *Acorus calamus* to refine and heal skin texture, as well as a soothing scalp massage. Dr Xavier, the resort's ayurvedic physician, recommends that in addition to such external applications, we practice being kind to ourselves: with this type of inner beauty, outer beauty follows.

World renowned author of *Absolute Beauty* (1997) and ayurvedic skin care creator, Pratima Riachur, says no matter what type of skin we have, the three-step routine of cleanse, nourish and moisturize is vital. "It is essential to counteract the daily effects of environment, stress and the skin's natural process of cell degeneration," she says, "It is the minimum one can do to maintain a healthy, youthful complexion." She suggests that even if you do nothing else for an existing skin problem, follow this regimen every day to improve your skin condition. Ayurvedic texts reveal that facial care gives best results after exercise and before meditation.

Left Rich, ivory-colored natural cocoa butter is extracted from the cocoa bean and used in many ayurvedic treatments including the facial below.

Opposite The Indian *shirobhyanga* head massage is often given during an ayurvedic facial ritual at the Mandarin Oriental Dhara Devi Spa in Chiang Mai. Rhythmic pressure and deep relaxation techniques are used on *marma* points to improve circulation and help with conditions like insomnia.

Preparation: Cleanse the skin before you begin this ritual. It is best to massage the oil on to damp skin and use gentle strokes in an upward and outward motion; when massaging the eye area, use the ring finger to ensure the gentlest touch. In this area, the movement should go in a circular direction from the outside corner of eye to the inside.

FOR DRY SKIN (VATA)

Cleanse

Ingredients:

- 1 tsp almond meal; ½ tsp milk powder; ¼ tsp sugar; 1 tsp warm water.

Directions: Mix into a paste. Apply paste over the skin and massage gently. Rinse with warm water and leave to dry naturally. For extremely dry skin use 1 tbsp dairy cream and 2 drops of lemon juice instead.

Nourish

Ingredients:

- 1½ tbsp sesame oil; 10 drops geranium essential oil; 5 drops each neroli and lemon essential oils.

Directions: Mix all ingredients together and store in a dark glass container with a dropper. For a daily nourish mix 3 drops of the oil blend with 6 drops of pure water and gently massage for one minute into freshly cleansed and damp skin. Leave on for a minute to absorb before moisturizing.

Moisturize

Ingredients:

- 1½ oz (45 g) cocoa butter; ½ cup (125 ml) avocado oil; 1½ tbsp orange flower water; 4 drops each of geranium and rose essential oils.

Directions: Melt the cocoa butter in a double boiler, and add avocado oil. Turn off the heat, and, using a dropper, add the orange flower water one drop at a time whilst stirring the mixture. Allow to cool, then add the essential oils of geranium and rose. This is an extremely rich moisturizer

with a beautiful green color. Gently apply all over the face and neck area, but do not massage into the skin. Apply as needed throughout the day. It can also be used on other dry areas on the body, such as elbows and knees.

FOR SENSITIVE SKIN (PITTA)

Cleanse

Ingredients:

- 1 tsp almond meal; ½ tsp orange peel, ground; ½ tsp milk powder; 1 tsp rose-water.

Directions: Mix all the above into a paste, then apply over face and massage gently. Rinse in cool water and leave to dry naturally. For extra sensitive skin use only once a day. Alternatively, you may wish to wash your skin in the morning with plain dairy cream.

Nourish

Ingredients:

- 1½ tbsp almond oil; 10 drops each rose and sandalwood essential oils.

Directions: Mix the almond oil with the essential oils and store in a dark glass jar with stopper. In the palm of your hand, mix 2–3 drops of this nourishing oil and 4–6 drops of water and gently massage into damp skin for one minute. Leave to absorb before applying moisturizer.

Moisturize

Ingredients:

- 1 oz (30 g) cocoa butter; 4½ tbsp sunflower oil; 3 tbsp rosewater; 5–6 drops sandalwood essential oil.

Directions: Melt the cocoa butter in a double boiler. Add the sunflower oil, then

remove from heat. Using a dropper, add the rosewater one drop at a time whilst stirring the mixture. Allow to cool, then add the essential oil. This gives the moisturizer an extremely soft, sweet-woody aroma. Gently apply over face and neck, but do not massage. Apply as needed throughout the day.

FOR OILY SKIN (KAPHA)

Cleanse

Ingredients:

- 1 tsp barley meal; 1 tsp lemon peel; ½ tsp milk powder; 2 tsp warm water.

Directions: Make into a paste by mixing with the warm water, then apply over face and neck, massaging gently into the skin for one minute. Do not scrub. Rinse in warm water and leave to dry naturally.

Nourish

Ingredients:

- 1½ tbsp safflower oil; 10 drops lavender essential oil; 5 drops bergamot essential oil; 5 drops clary sage essential oil.

Directions: Mix ingredients and store in a glass jar with dropper. For a daily nourish, mix 2 drops of this nourishing oil with 4 drops of pure water and massage into freshly cleansed damp face and neck for one minute.

Moisturize

Ingredients:

- 1 oz (30 g) cocoa butter; 4½ tbsp almond, safflower or canola oil; 3 tbsp rosemary or basil tea; 1 drop camphor, 2 drops bergamot and 3 drops lavender essential oils.

Directions: Melt the cocoa butter in a double boiler, add the almond, safflower or canola oil and remove from heat. Using a dropper, add the rosemary or basil tea one drop at a time whilst stirring the mixture. Allow to cool, then add the essential oils. Gently apply over face and neck; do not massage. As this regulates and balances oil flow, you only need to use a tiny amount at night.

body

"WHEN YOU ARE MASTER OF YOUR BODY, WORD AND MIND,
YOU SHALL REJOICE IN PERFECT SERENITY."

Tibetan hermit, Shabkar (1781–1851)

Being scrubbed, wrapped and nourished in Asia's treasure chest of rejuvenating herbs, flowers and rituals is a memorable experience that brings us fully into the present moment. Whether it is a three-hour journey of steam, wrap, scrub, massage and bath with views across a Balinese rice field, or a grounding reiki and acupuncture session, the benefits for body and mind are many.

As Asian treatments are holistic, they focus on wellbeing in its entirety. Asian healers and therapists draw upon thousands of years of wisdom to harmonize the body and mind. We now know that our emotions affect the body and stressful thoughts can disturb our vital organs, so Asian spas offer many different internal and external healing treatments to balance the inner and outer. Whether you receive healing hands, indigenous plants, flowers and herbs, or crystals, jewels and stones (or a combination of the above), you'll be able to change the condition of your body effortlessly. You can detoxify, heal, rejuvenate or renourish with ease.

Take the steaming poultice, for example. An Asian speciality, it comprises a pouch filled with lingering, rejuvenating herbs that is placed on various parts of the body to melt away toxins within. The Malaysian *campur campur* version at Pangkor Laut Spa Village and the traditional Thai creation filled with lemongrass and menthol are wonderful. Offered at many spas in Thailand, it fills your being with a heady aroma.

Asian spas have a seemingly endless choice of body rituals. Alternatively, invite the energy of Asia into your own home. Healing plants, flowers and herbs from the East provide us with some enlivening spa ingredients. Used effectively, they can change the body—both internally and externally. Browse in Asian stores in the Chinatowns and Indian, Vietnamese and Arab districts of your local town to find Eastern offerings. Exotic looking medicinal herbs, teas, fruits and vegetables line the shelves. Take them home—and experiment.

Be inspired to dip your toes into the mind-expanding philosophies of the Himalayas via a Tibetan foot bath, wrap your energy in ingredients from Malaysia, experience Indonesian healing though a nourishing hair cream and bathe or salt your body with ingredients from the islands of the Maldives. Embrace your spa time with a full heart. Imbue your being with stillness by spending quiet time during your treatments. A truly nourishing experience will happen because of you!

Right The traditional golden *lulur*, here photographed at the Martha Tilaar Eastern Rejuvenating Center, is a staple on the Indonesian spa menu. It normally includes a massage, turmeric and yoghurt scrub and a flower and spice bath.

wrapture

Being embraced in an exotic wrap with the scents of aromatic oils and herbs infusing your skin is both reassuring and luxurious. In Asian spas, fresh-from-nature ingredients are smothered onto your body and held in place by natural materials like banana leaves, *sarongs*, blankets, and muslin or linen cloths. These serve to keep the body warm, as the ingredients detoxify, nourish and improve skin texture. As you lie, warm and cosy in your cocoon, you may be given a well-deserved scalp or facial massage. Once unwrapped, you are rinsed down with mineral-enriched spring water. What could be more nurturing?

How the wrap evolved remains a little bit of a mystery. We do know that some traditional wraps were given for the purpose of increasing heat in the body that in turn improved circulation. Other wraps were prepared specifically for women post-natally to slim and return the body back to shape. Even today, Malaysian new mothers are given a vigorous herbal oil rub and are then bound with meters of natural cloth.

Normally a wrap begins with the guest taking a quick shower to remove any bacteria; this is followed by a gentle exfoliation to gently shed dead skin cells and prepare the body for the wrap ingredients. After this, mud, seaweed, clay, butter or a combo cream is smeared over the entire body, and the body is wrapped up. The warmth of the wrap encourages rapid sweating, thus drawing out unwanted toxins and enhancing lymphatic flow. All the while, the ingredients are absorbed into the body system bringing vitality to the skin's surface.

A wrap can be partial (without arms and back) or whole. It's essential to only use natural, pure ingredients. A wrap is not recommended if you are pregnant or suffer from high or low blood pressure, heart disease, diabetes or certain other medical conditions. Once wrapped like a cocoon, you are encouraged to rest while the ingredients work to nourish and heal. Drink plenty of water before, during and after a wrap to encourage a further flush of toxins and to rehydrate. Take time out afterwards for rest and restoration.

THE WRAP AT HOME

What you need:

- A spray mist bottle filled with pure spring water or a hydrating mix such as rosewater or limewater.
- Wrap mix composed from either a salt scrub or volcanic clay or mud (see some suggestions on following pages).
- Massage oil mix such as 3 tbsp almond or olive oil with 6 drops relaxing essential oils like lavender and sandalwood.

wrapture

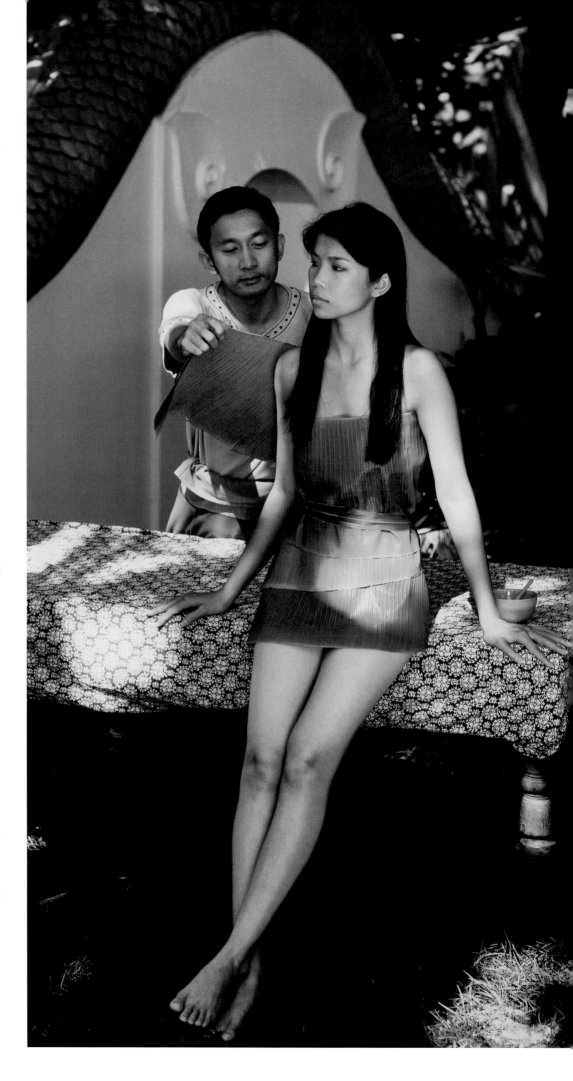

Directions:

1. Ask your "client" to remove their clothes and wrap a cotton *sarong* or sheet around their body and lie face down on the bed.

2. Start by giving them a 10-minute foot massage working gradually up to the lower leg region.

3. Spray entire body gently with mist spray (see pages 162–167), allowing the natural aroma to infuse the skin.

4. Sprinkle the body with your preferred wrap mix, be it a mix of salts and oils or volcanic clay or mud.

5. Massage wrap mix into the entire body both on the front and back, leaving face and neck free.

6. Spray the body with the massage oil mix to keep the mixture moist.

7. Sprinkle salt on to the skin and complete with another spray mist.

8. Cover the body with a wrap of your choice. Ask your client to relax for 20 minutes. Make sure pure water to hydrate is on hand, and do not leave the person alone for more than a few minutes.

9. Unwrap the body and massage the mix further into the skin, adding water if needed.

10. Gently lift your client up and escort her to the shower for a cool rinse. Whilst she is showering, clean the room and create a massage area with clean towels and sheets. Be creative: dim the lights or draw the shades, light an oil burner and put on soothing music.

11. Treat your client to a relaxing 20-minute massage using a massage oil that your friend likes. Use fairly light pressure, as the skin will already be very warm.

12. (Optional) To finish this complete enlivening experience, gently wipe off the oil from the skin and smother your friend with pure aloe vera gel. Complete by asking her to relax with a glass of water, juice or tea and fruit.

MALAY HERBAL WRAP

Many of Malaysia's beauty treatments, such as massages, steam compresses, herbal remedies and wraps, are inspired by ayurvedic and Chinese medicines and treatments. Malaysia has some of the richest rainforests in the world, so indigenous ingredients are plentiful. Chinese in origin, this wrap has a fresh, herbaceous aroma and is wonderful after or before a lukewarm bath. It uses a combination of rejuvenating and warming herbs to stimulate *ch'i* flow within the body. Camphor is believed to bring clarity to the mind, while lemongrass and ginger help to purify and ease tired or sore muscles.

Ingredients:
- 2 tbsp sesame oil; 4 drops camphor oil; 3 tbsp lemongrass powder; 3 tbsp ginger powder; 3 tbsp galangal powder; 1 cup (250 ml) warm water or milk.

Directions: Mix the camphor and sesame oils in a bowl, and warm slightly. In another bowl, mix the dried powders with the warm water or milk into a paste-like consistency. Massage the oil blend into the skin, then follow with the mask (there may be a slight tingling effect). Cocoon yourself in warm linen sheets and lie down for 15 minutes and rest. Unwrap, rinse and apply any left over sesame oil into the skin as a body oil.

BALINESE BOREH

Technically a mask, rather than a wrap, the *boreh* is therapeutic when you feel a cold or flu coming on or if your energy is low and you are in need of rejuvenation. Traditionally, farmers created this warming treatment to soothe tired muscles after a long day in the rice fields. After a preliminary massage, it was smeared over the body in gentle circular motions to exfoliate the skin. It was then left on for 15 minutes to allow the ingredients to absorb into the body. If you try the *boreh* at home, expect the heat from the spices to increase surface circulation in the skin, giving a heated, tingling sensation all over. This recipe, fresh from the rice fields of Bali, is shared by Bagus Jati Wellbeing Resort. Therapists there use pepper as well as rice powder for a powerful mix.

Ingredients:
- 1 tbsp pure dried ginger, ground; 2 tsp clove powder; 2 tsp cinnamon powder; 2 tsp nutmeg powder; 1 tbsp sandalwood powder; 2 tsp coriander powder; 1 tbsp black pepper, ground; 2 tbsp rice powder; 9 tbsp warm water.

Directions: Mix all spices together with warm water to create a paste. Apply liberally to the body. Massage well into the skin using circular motions. Concentrate on any areas where there is muscle soreness, as this is an excellent wrap mix for the computer bound with sore shoulders. Leave the *boreh* to absorb beneath a wrap, if wanted. Rinse in tepid water, and dry.

KURUMBAA KAASHI WRAP

Kurumbaa translates as "mature coconut" in dhivehi, the mother tongue of the Maldives, and the atolls here are covered in

wrapture

coconut palms. This recipe is shared with us by Six Senses Spas, a company with a strong environmental ethos that uses indigenous and organic ingredients wherever possible. Here they draw on local coconut to exfoliate and calm sensitive skin, humectant-rich honey to moisturize, and the enzymes in papaya to enrich it. Recommended for sensitive skins, the mixture has a cooling and calming effect leaving skin soft and smooth.

Ingredients:

- 1 dry coconut; a few strands of coconut husks; ½ a large papaya; 2 tbsp honey; 6 tbsp coconut oil.

Directions: Blend the coconut and husks in a food processor until a fine texture is achieved. Mix the papaya and honey, then set aside. Gently rub the skin with coconut oil using even pressure. Start on the legs and work around the entire body. Apply the coconut and husk mix using the same method. There is no need to rinse first. Apply papaya and honey mixture to the whole body and wrap the body with warm towels to allow the natural ingredients to absorb and nourish. Rest for 10 minutes and then rinse in a cool shower to rejuvenate the polished skin. You may apply leftover coconut oil as a body moisturizing rub if so desired.

VOLCANIC MUD STEAM WRAP

Another memorable recipe from Bagus Jati Wellbeing Resort, this treatment uses seaweed and nutrient-rich volcanic mud from the majestic Rinjani volcano on the island of Lombok. Here, you are smothered in seaweed and clays and take a steam in a private steam room overlooking a small lotus pond.

At home, try an adaptation of this deeply detoxifying ritual without the seaweed. Combine the healing properties of mud with a steaming wrap to re-energize the body.

Ingredients:

- 1 cup (200 g) volcanic clay (or mud); 1 tsp candlenuts, ground, or 1 tsp cocoa butter (melted); 10 drops (½ tsp) vitamin E oil liquid or cream; 15 drops lavender essential oil; 1 cup (250 ml) rosewater.

Directions: Mix all ingredients except the lavender essential oil together into a smooth, creamy paste. Prepare a large bowl (8 cups/2 liters) of warm water, a *sarong*, single sheet or light bath towel. Add the lavender oil and then soak the *sarong* or towel in the warm water. Smear the nutrient-rich volcanic mud over your body paying particular attention to legs, thighs, buttocks, chest and arms. Wrap your body in a *sarong* or towel and find a comfortable place to lie down for 10 minutes. Rinse in the shower with cool water and complete with body lotion or oil to re-hydrate the skin.

TRADITIONAL BANANA LEAF BODY WRAP

Indonesian spas are well known for their banana wraps. In the past, fresh banana leaves were wrapped around the body for warmth during the monsoon or at the first sign of colds, flu, rheumatism or fever. At Bagus Jati, king banana leaves are hand cut first thing in the morning ready to act as natural blankets after the application of herbs; the result is a complete detoxification, as impurities are drawn out from the skin.

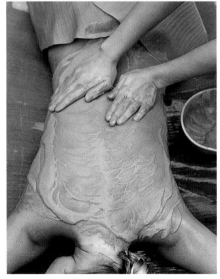

Ingredients:

- Use the pandan and cinnamon scrub from page 190 or create a creamy smooth paste from 10 to 15 pellets of white rice mixed with 100–120 ml water or rosewater.

Directions: Prepare a *sarong* wrap including banana leaves and coconut leaves (if available). Apply paste evenly to clean dry skin to create a light body mask. Cover the body with banana leaves and tie with coconut leaves and leave for 10 minutes. Massage the scalp with cananga oil during this time. Unwrap and rinse with warm water.

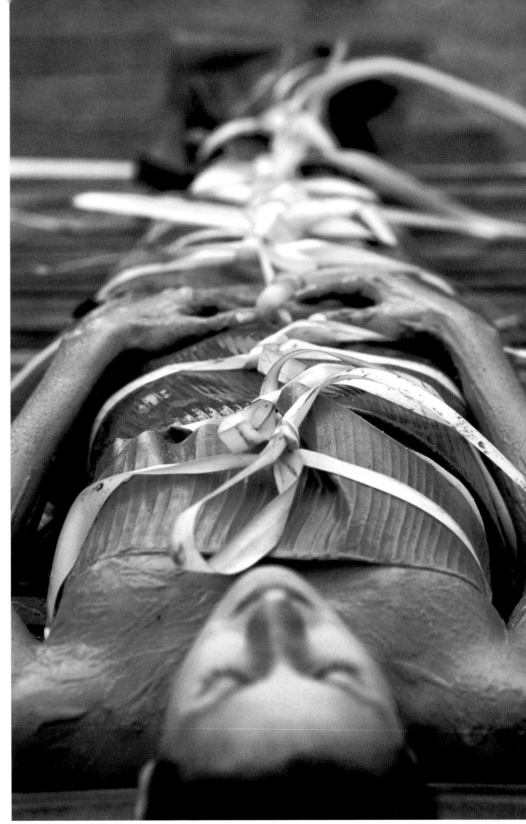

At Bagus Jati, the traditional banana leaf body wrap is a favorite treatment, both for its authentic recreation and its deeply nurturing feeling. At the beginning of the treatment, cananga oil is applied to the body, which is followed by an all-over massage. Then a gorgeous green paste made from a pandan leaf mixture is evenly applied to clean and dry skin. The paste creates a warming mask-like effect on the body that is exacerbated by a wrap of banana leaves, cleverly tied in place with strong banana fibers. While the client rests, a therapist gives a scalp and head massage.

body scrubs

Below Body scrubs at Four Seasons Spa in Chiang Mai are made with local ingredients including natural honey, sesame seeds, *prai* (local ginger), lemongrass, herbs and spices.

Right In Thailand, scrubs are often made from honey and sesame seeds. This one at the Anantara Spa in Hua Hin is a potent, enlivening mixture.

Far right Cinnamon sticks, when they are finely chopped or ground, may be used used in skin scrubs in the home spa.

A scrub is a simple ritual long practiced throughout the East. In spas, body scrubs are often given before a massage, and they are recommended prior to water therapies such as the *hamam*, Vichy shower or steam. After ayurvedic treatments, you may be scrubbed vigorously with a cleansing paste (*ubtan*) of ground lentils, flours and herbs to remove excess oil from the body. And in Japan, scrubbing the body before bathing is essential to cleanliness.

Asia's treasure chest of natural ingredients provides everything you need for a scrub. Indonesian recipes use coffee beans, coconut, clay, ground pumice stone and honey to scrub the skin. In Thailand, scrubs made of honey, seeds and rice are used to improve circulation and moisturize and tone the skin. Throughout India and Sri Lanka, the components for scrubs include ground nuts and flours, and in Japan, exotic ingredients include *adzuki* beans, buckwheat flour, rice bran, black sugar, pearl barley powder, soybean flour and various fruits, flowers, vegetables and green leaves.

Both the ingredients and the skill of the therapist are crucial to a good scrub. During a scrub, a potent mix of water, spices and herbs is massaged into the body, stimulating the metabolism and oxygenating the cells. Toxins are flushed out, thereby easing fluid retention and cellulite as well as removing dead cells from the skin's surface. Afterwards, skin becomes smooth and radiant. Heat, such as that from a steam, sauna or wrap, may also be used to enhance the scrub process.

SELF SCRUB TIPS
- Look for implements made from natural materials such as unbleached woods and natural bristles. Options include loofahs, loofah mitts, silk mitts, natural wood brushes and even a simple waffle or cotton hand towel.
- Dry brush your skin every morning with strokes towards the heart before showering or bathing.
- For a wet scrub, brush your skin towards the heart under cool to warm water until the skin turns slightly pink.
- Fill a muslin/cloth bag full of exfoliating ingredients such as seaweed, rice bran, oats and *adzuki* bean powder and scrub your skin under the shower with this. Using small circular motions, start at the feet and spiral upwards towards legs, hands, arms and torso.
- After rinsing off a scrub, we recommend massaging skin with an aromatherapy blend using upward strokes towards the heart.
- Use any of the following Aroma Active Blends daily for two months to help remove areas with cellulite and blood or *ch'i* congestion.
  Circulate Blend: 5 tbsp sweet almond or safflower oil with 20 drops juniper, 15 drops rosemary and 10 drops lemon essential oil.
  Tonify Blend: 5 tbsp jojoba or macadamia oil with 15 drops vetiver, 10 drops cypress, 10 drops lemongrass and 10 drops fennel essential oil.
  Stimulate Blend: 5 tbsp safflower or sweet almond oil with 10 drops peppermint, 15 drops rosemary and 20 drops pine essential oil.
  Rejuvenate Blend: 5 tbsp olive or macadamia oil with 15 drops frankincense, 20 drops lavender and 10 drops rose essential oil.

JAPANESE SELF MASSAGE DO-IN
In Japan, the ritual of the pre-bathing cleansing body scrub or *do-in* is considered as important as the bath itself. Daily scrubbing maintains healthy skin and circulation, while cool shower rinses are healthy and invigorating. Awaken your entire system with this early morning body rouser.
1. Make a soft fist with your hands and begin by pummelling your entire body. Start at your ankles and work up your legs, buttocks, arms and chest, completing by lightly patting your face and neck using the flat area of your fingertips.
2. Under warm water in the bath or shower, scrub your skin quite vigorously until it starts to turn a shade pinker. This coloring indicates that the blood has been stimulated and is circulating well to the surface.
3. Finish with a cool shower.

the marriage ceremony. Renowned for its skin softening qualities, *lulur* ingredients also lighten skin tone and sweeten skin aroma. Today, virtually every spa in Indonesia offers a version of this royal treatment. The scrub comes first, and is followed by a massage and flower bath. This particular preparation is adapted from a recipe of Dr Martha Tilaar's. She advocates that women indulge in a wide range of treatments to beautify body, hair and skin and to enhance sensuality. The ingredients stimulate circulation and help eliminate wastes and toxins from the lymph system.

We suggest you prepare a warm bath decorated with essential oils and fresh flowers of roses and jasmine for after. If you wish to self-massage, use a blend of 30 ml of base oil with 4 drops each of rose, jasmine and sandalwood essential oils.

Ingredients:

- 2 ½ tbsp rice starch; 2 tsp turmeric root powder; 1 tsp sandalwood powder; 1 tsp ginger powder; 1 tbsp dried jasmine flower powder (use jasmine flowers and grind them in a coffee grinder or mortar and pestle), if unavailable, substitute with 3 drops jasmine essential oil; 3 drops each pure essential oils of ylang ylang and sandalwood; ½ cup (100 g) plain yoghurt.

Directions: Blend all the ingredients except the yoghurt with a little tepid water until the texture is smooth and creamy. Apply all over the body except the face and rest for around 5 minutes until the treatment dries. Gently rub the skin to remove the paste and apply the yoghurt. Leave on for 10 or 15 minutes; you may wrap yourself up in a *sarong* to help the yoghurt absorb further. Yoghurt helps remove the slight yellow coloring left on the skin from the turmeric. In addition, its lactic acid content is skin smoothing. Rinse off in the shower and then prepare your self-massage oil or slip into a soothing bath.

LANNA HERBAL BODY POLISH

This is a smooth and fragrant exfoliating treatment that blends grounding sandalwood and herbal extracts of energizing *prai*, refreshing lemongrass and *bai nart* (a great muscle relaxant from the sage species). After the body polish offered at Four Seasons Spa in Chiang Mai, guests are treated to a drench of *prai* body milk to complete the treatment. A type of local ginger, *prai* hydrates and refines both skin and spirit. If you want to recreate the final body moisturizer, we suggest blending 1 tbsp vitamin E cream or sorbelene cream with 2 drops each of *prai* (or ginger), sandalwood and lemongrass essential oil. Smooth over the entire body.

Ingredients:

- 2 tbsp white clay; 1 tbsp dry *prai* or ginger powder; 1 tsp turmeric powder; 1 tsp cloves, ground; 2 tsp sandalwood; 1 tsp lemongrass powder (or 3 drops of lemongrass essential oil); 1 tbsp *bai nart* (or dried sage); 3 tbsp warm milk.

Directions: Mix all the dry ingredients in a bowl, adding the warm milk just before application. Apply on the body for an all-over exfoliant. Rinse off in the shower.

MANDI LULUR

This traditional beauty ritual was reserved for royal brides in Central Java and was given each day for 40 days leading up to

body scrubs

CLASSIC COFFEE SCRUB

This stimulating coffee scrub is easy to create and is found at most spas in southeast Asia. Of particular note is the aromatic coffee scrub at the Losari Coffee Plantation Resort and Spa in central Java: inhale the rousing aromas of coffee before stepping into their *hamam* steam chamber. Alternatively at Anantara Spa in Hua Hin, the treatment is given in a Moroccan-style treatment room. Here we have recreated their recipe using ground coffee beans (known for their stimulating effect on the psyche) and the bark of the *tanaka* tree. Cultivated in Burma as a natural face powder and sunscreen, it contains cooling camphor, while trace elements of vitamins B2, B3 and B6 help enhance beautiful skin.

Ingredients:
- 3 tbsp Thai coffee beans, ground; 1 tbsp rice flour, ground; 1 tbsp *tanaka* bark powder (you can purchase from a herbal supplier); 1 tbsp cinnamon powder; 6–7 tbsp water; 2 ½ cups (250 g) carrots, finely grated; 2 tsp set gelatin powder.

Directions: Mix the ground coffee beans, rice flour, *tanaka* bark, cinnamon powder and warm water. Mix the gelatin and carrots separately, and set aside. Begin the scrub, starting from the lower body and rub vigorously so that the mixture sloughs off. Rub the carrot and gelatin mixture all over the body to replenish moisture lost during the exfoliation process. Complete the treatment with a shower, and moisturize after.

ALMOND MASALA SKIN SCRUB

A gentle scrub that leaves your skin feeling soft and nourished, this recipe has a subtle warming and balancing effect and is suitable for all skin types. The *garam masala* or "strong mix" is used at Four Seasons Island Spa in the Maldives to create an exquisitely gentle and nutrient-rich body scrub.

Ingredients:
- 4 tbsp almond meal; 4 tbsp organic sugar; ½ tsp nutmeg powder; ½ tsp black pepper; 1 tsp ginger powder; 1 tsp cardamom; ½ tsp clove leaf powder; 3 drops each pure essential oils of nutmeg and cardamom; 3 tbsp plain yoghurt; 3 to 4 tbsp warm water.

Directions: Mix the spices together, then blend in the yoghurt and warm water to form a paste. Apply to body with circular motions. Rinse with warm water.

MALDIVIAN BLACK PEPPER SCRUB

This is a highly medicinal scrub sourced from Four Seasons Island Spa in the Maldives. It energizes the system, helping to alleviate fatigue. It is an excellent skin-enlivening and nourishing scrub that gently warms the body on coolish, winter days. Basil helps to clear the sinuses and black pepper is good for joint and muscle aches; both are natural stimulants and powerful toning agents.

Ingredients:
- 3 tbsp fine sea salt; 2 tsp black pepper; 1 tsp dried basil; 4 tbsp mix of sweet almond and grape seed oil; 4 drops black pepper essential oil.

Directions: Mix all the ingredients together. Apply to the body using gentle circular motions. Rinse with warm water.

CINNAMON AND PANDAN LEAF SCRUB

Created by Bagus Jati Wellbeing Resort in Bali, this mild exfoliating scrub is rich in natural vitamins and amino acids that help to oxygenate the skin. The fragrant pandan leaf makes the scrub mixture a little gooey, so wet the skin first under the shower, then take a little in the palm of the hands and scrub each area of the body. It is great for dry skin and is best used in the morning.

Ingredients:
- 3 tbsp pure dry pandan leaf powder; 2 tbsp cinnamon, ground; 2 tbsp sandalwood powder; 1 tbsp pandan leaf essence (if unavailable, substitute with 20 ml aloe vera gel); 7 tbsp warm water.

Directions: Mix herbs and oils with the warm water to make a smooth paste. Apply liberally to all parts of the body and exfoliate in circular motions. After the exfoliation process, clean up with a warm wash cloth and dry with a towel.

COCONUT AND GINGER SHRED

This is a very gentle scrub with a great coconut aroma that will remind you of tropical island holidays. Coconut is an important ingredient in both the Asian kitchen and spa. Here it is combined with the skin-soothing properties of soybean oil. Soybean is enriched with lecithin and vitamins A, E and K, and it, and ginger, boosts the production of collagen and elastin. The scrub leaves the skin looking more recharged and vitalized.

Ingredients:
- ½ cup (125 ml) base oils, such as almond, macadamia and soybean; ½ cup (40 g) desiccated coconut flakes; 1 tbsp fresh ginger, finely grated.

Directions: Grind the coconut flakes finely in a coffee grinder. Mix all ingredients together in a bowl. Before showering or bathing, rub over the body, massaging vigorously to stimulate circulation. Step into the shower or bath and allow the water to further hydrate the skin. Rinse off well and pat dry.

MOUNTAIN TSAMPA RUB

Tsampa is a barley powder that has been used as a body exfoliant by people in the Himalayas for centuries. Often rubbed on the body during Tibetan hot spring bathing, *tsampa* has a calming effect on the skin and is suitable for most skin types, in particular for oily skins. At CHI Spas at

Shangri-La hotels across Asia, you can experience a color "eternity light" or steam therapy followed by a massage using an oil to draw out toxins from the lymph systems; then the body is covered in an ancient barley recipe to absorb excess oil from the massage and gently remove dead skin cells. Use this at-home recipe as an exfoliant: it uses grape seed oil, rich in vitamins and proteins, and grapefruit essential oil to help congested and oily skin; mandarin essential oil promotes cell regeneration and juniper essential oil is well known for its detoxifying properties.

Ingredients:
For the massage oil
- 1 tbsp grape seed oil; 1 tsp olive oil; 2 drops grapefruit, 3 drops mandarin and 4 drops juniper essential oils.

For the tsampa rub
- 2 tbsp barley powder; 2 tsp Nepalese barberry root powder (can replace with goldenseal root powder if unavailable); 2 tsp neem powder; 2 tsp sandalwood powder; 2 tsp *Majitho* root powder (this is a Himalayan medicinal plant, if unavailable, simply delete); 2 drops juniper, 2 drops grapefruit and 3 drops mandarin essential oils.

Directions: Mix the oil blend in a bowl and set aside. For the rub, mix all the powders together first, then add the essential oils, and set aside. Begin by massaging the detoxifying massage oil into the body and follow with the *tsampa* rub to exfoliate dead cells. Rinse off in the shower.

HIBISCUS, SALT AND SUGAR SCRUB

Therapists at Four Seasons Spa at Jimbaran Bay share with us a scrub recipe that is super fun to do at home. The combination of salt and sugar gives two granule sizes to the scrub, so it is very effective, yet also smooth and lovely to use. In addition, it leaves the skin refreshed with a delicious fruity aroma.

Ingredients:
- 2 tbsp sugar; 2 tbsp fine sea salt; 4 tbsp sweet almond oil; 2 tsp dried hibiscus flowers (or use contents of 2 hibiscus teabags); 2 drops each of lemon, orange and grapefruit essential oil.

Directions: Mix all the ingredients together adding the essential oils last. Give skin a thorough scrub, then rinse off.

GLOBAL SCRUBS
INDOCHINE RICE AND ORANGE SCRUB

Ingredients:
- ¼ cup (45 g) rice, finely ground in a coffee grinder; 5 tsp orange flower water; 4 drops sandalwood, 4 drops orange and 2 drops jasmine essential oil; ¼ cup (60 ml) black sesame oil.

Directions: Make a smooth paste by blending all ingredients together. Scoop a handful of the blend and apply over your dry body rubbing well into the skin. Then scoop a little water in your hands and repeat the scrubbing motion all over the body for an uplifting, citrusy aroma.

BALINESE RICE AND FLOWER SCRUB

Ingredients:
- ¼ cup (45 g) red rice, finely ground in a coffee grinder; 2 drops jasmine, 3 drops ylang ylang, 3 drops clove essential oil; ¼ tsp turmeric powder; ¼ cup (60 ml) coconut oil.

Directions: Blend all of the ingredients together to make a smooth paste. Rub the scrub all over the body, taking care to avoid the face area. Turmeric is a powerful healing ingredient with wonderful antiseptic properties, but take care with the quantities as it can also stain the skin.

CHINESE SESAME AND GINSENG SCRUB

Ingredients:
- 2 tbsp lotus powder (or 1 dried lotus root, cut into pieces and finely ground in a coffee grinder); 1 tbsp ginseng powder (from *Panax ginseng* ground roughly in

a coffee grinder); 1 tbsp ginger powder; 2 tbsp sea salt; 4 tbsp black sesame or sesame oil; 1 tbsp rosehip oil; 5 drops each myrrh, Chinese star anise and mandarin essential oil.

Directions: Mix all of the ingredients together and then apply in circular movements before a shower.

INDIAN SPICE AND YOGHURT SCRUB

Ingredients:

- 1 ½ tbsp almond meal; 1½ tbsp oatmeal; 3 tbsp yoghurt; 1 tbsp water; 2 tsp sesame oil; 2 drops sandalwood, 2 drops ginger, 2 drops patchouli, 2 drops cinnamon essential oils.

Directions: Combine almond meal and oatmeal together in a bowl, mix in the yoghurt and water, add essential oils to sesame oil and add to the mixture. Blend well. Apply to the skin pre-shower and scrub the body all over.

THAI SALT AND HERB SCRUB

Ingredients:

- ¼ cup (60 g) fine sea salt; 3 drops lime, 3 drops ginger, 2 drops lemongrass essential oils; 1 heaped tsp fresh lemongrass, chopped finely; ¼ cup (50 ml) coconut oil.

Directions: Blend all to a smooth paste, then use circular movements to rub the entire body, before rinsing off. This scrub leaves skin feeling beautifully soft.

JAPANESE RICE AND SUGAR SCRUB

Ingredients:

- ¼ cup (30 g) rice flour or bran; ¼ cup (60 g) black sugar; 1 tbsp *agar agar*; 8 drops blend of lime, jasmine and orange essential oil; 1 tsp Japanese green tea powder; ¼ cup (60 ml) camellia nut oil.

Directions: Blend all the ingredients together and scrub over the entire body. Rinse off: the camellia nut oil will leave skin fully moisturized.

SEA SALT SCRUBS

Salt has been used for centuries to cure and heal and is regarded as a symbol of purity, wisdom, divinity and grace. The word salt derives from the sun (*sol*). The Romans named it after Salus, their goddess of healing. Our blood is made up of 0.9% Sodium chloride (salt). When we absorb mineral salts, we create electrolytes that are necessary for enzyme production; these, in turn, help us digest our food and absorb nutrients. Mineral salt benefits include improved muscle coordination, mental concentration and nerve and heart function as well as better fluid absorption.

In Asia, salt was traditionally used in Mongolia and Tibet as a body scrub, and other cultures have used it in various treatments. Today, a variety of salts are available and there are hundreds of salt-enriched skin scrubs on menus at spas and wellness centers. Be inspired to take your salt scrub prior to showering or as an all over body cleanser before a steam or sauna. Spiced and peppered with herbs, essential oils, flowers and extracts, salt scrubs are used to exfoliate the skin's surface and improve skin texture. Alternatively, these salts can be used in the bath as a water softener.

Hawaiian Red Sea Salt is a fine natural colored salt. Although not specifically an Asian ingredient, is well worth a mention as it is so pure and detoxifying. It is believed to draw out toxins from overworked muscle tissues. Also known as Alaea Sea Salt, it originates from both sea and earth, so is rich in sea minerals and high in iron oxide. Spiritually, it is used in healing rituals and to cleanse and bless homes.

Epsom Salts (Magnesium sulfate) are pure therapy for the body. The name derives from the eponymous spa town in England where mineral waters were evaporated to create salts. Epsom salts draw out toxins, reduce swelling and ease pain and muscle tension. We advise a once-a-week Epsom Salt bath or foot soak to give the nervous system a well-deserved rest. Epsom Salts are a good hangover cure and transform dull or anxious emotions into vitalized, confident ones.

Dead Sea Salts are believed to be as much as ten times more concentrated than other salts and are full of magnesium, bromide and potassium. They originate from the shores of the Dead Sea in Israel, the saltiest body of water on earth. They help regulate the body by eliminating toxins and promoting skin regeneration and hydration. Furthermore, they stimulate the blood and lymphatic systems and help to increase circulation to move any trapped fluid in the joints. Used to relax muscles, alleviate aches and pains and heal skin conditions, they are excellent for acne, eczema and psoriasis.

Himalayan Salts are beautiful soft pink beads and are considered the purest salts on earth. Salt crystals traced back to the Himalayan region around the borders of India and Pakistan—some 200 million years old and untouched by pollution—contain far more minerals than those from the sea. Enriched with over 84 minerals and elements, they are believed to holistically rebalance the bodily functions and keep the mind centered.

SEA KELP AND SALT SCRUB

Being by the sea is naturally rejuvenating. The abundance of unseen negative ions blended with the sea's mineral-rich salts and water are beneficial for our energy. This skin and mind enlivening recipe, shared with us by Island Spa at Four Seasons Resort in the Maldives, is a wonderfully refreshing once-a-week mineral-rich scrub.

Ingredients:

- 2 tbsp fine sea salt; 1 tbsp kelp powder; 1 ½ tbsp coconut oil; 1 ½ tbsp sweet almond oil; 1 tsp spirulina powder; 4 drops each of grapefruit, cypress, lemon and peppermint essential oils.

Directions: Mix all ingredients together well. Step into the shower and massage the ingredients into the whole body starting with the feet and working your way up. Turn on the shower and repeat the scrub all over the body by scooping water into your hands and massaging until the salt granules have disappeared. Skin feels soft and stimulated, and there is a faint citrusy aroma.

SALT GLOW

Offered by Anantara Spa on the Gulf of Siam in Thailand, this nutrient-rich treatment helps to gently remove dead skin cells and improve circulation, leaving skin soft and cleansed. With short circular massage strokes, dull skin cells are removed and circulation is improved. It is deeply moisture-giving, so there is no need to follow with a moisturizer.

Ingredients:

- 3 tbsp fine natural sea salts; 3 tbsp base oil like sweet almond or macadamia oil; a blend of 3 essential oils (see below) totalling 15 drops.

Dry skin: Sandalwood, lavender and geranium essential oils.
Oily skin: Cypress, lemon and ylang ylang essential oils.
Romance elixir: Ylang ylang, patchouli and orange essential oils.
Hangover elixir: Fennel, juniper and rosemary essential oils.

Directions: In a glass or ceramic bowl, stir essential oils into the macadamia nut oil, then add the salts and stir with a spatula until thoroughly mixed. Start the full body scrub using circular massage strokes, paying particular attention to the knees, elbows and heels. Complete with a shower.

YIN YANG SALT SCRUB

This recipe draws upon cooling and warming ingredients to return the skin to balance. The cooling *yin* energy of cucumber is very refreshing, whilst ginger is a more warming *yang* ingredient. Blended here with nourishing sweet almond oil and the mood-lifting quality of lime, this easy-to-prepare recipe is a good skin hydrator.

Ingredients:

- 2 tbsp sea salt; 1 tbsp fresh ginger, finely grated; 2 tbsp cucumber, finely grated; 2 tbsp almond oil; zest of 1 lime.

Directions: Blend all ingredients together in a bowl and apply before bathing or showering. Rinse in tepid water.

MALDIVIAN SAND SCRUB

Invigorate the senses and recreate the experience of a spa treatment in a most natural environment with this Maldivian sand scrub from Six Senses Spas in the Maldives. The treatment starts with the body being covered in cool, wet sand. The practitioner then works on all the acupressure points—along either side of the spine and down both arms and legs—almost pushing the goodness from the sea and sand into the skin. Once the acupressure points on the entire body have been treated, the client takes a dip in the sea. To complete the experience, pure coconut oil is massaged into the skin. Offer a loved one this wonderful experience on holiday.

Preparation: Place a large towel near the water's edge with something soft for the recipient to rest their head on. It's important that the sand near the water's edge is soft and smooth; remove all shells and pieces of coral. Ensure that a massage bed is set up nearby to complete the seaside ritual.

Directions: Ask your guest to lie face down on the towel with their feet in the cool water. Cover the back with a thick layer of wet sand. Using the heel of the palms, work your way up either side of the spine, applying pressure as you go along. Cover the entire left arm with sand. Apply pressure as you would in a *shiatsu* massage, ensuring that all pressure points are covered in the arm, extending down to the fingers. Do the same for the other arm. Now cover the entire left leg. Once again, work along the central meridian, applying even pressure down the leg. Ensure you pay attention to the foot: cover it with sand and apply pressure to the pressure points. Do the same for the other leg.

Your guest is now ready to turn over. Ensure their face is shaded from the sun. Begin working your way around the front of the body in a similar manner. After a refreshing dip, ask your guest to lie on the massage bed, and give an all-over moisturize with coconut oil. A tropical fruit drink completes the sand scrub.

skin nourishers

When we feed the body nutrients from both earth and sea, our skin—from the surface to the cellular level—becomes enlivened. Body coolers, creams and mists are a wonderful support system for the skin: the oils in them encourage rehydration and natural essences give a delicious all-over scent.

"Our skin absorbs nutrients more effectively when it is clean and shed of old layers," asserts cosmetic chemist, Arthur Lawrence. He says that the most nourishing ingredients in the spa world are those that are naturally derived from food grade sources. These include sesame, ginger, papaya, aloe vera and many other unprocessed food substances. "If it is great for the health of the body, then it's good for our skin," he adds.

In fact, most skin nutrients come from natural substances. They are absorbed externally by our skin cells and utilized to speed up skin metabolism, repair and encourage cell growth, and cleanse and detoxify as well. The positive effects can be seen both externally and internally.

"Our skin acts as a barrier to the outside world, protecting the body's organs and tissues from damage and infection," says Adria Lake, the managing director of A W Lake Spa Concepts, "It also prevents loss of water and other bodily fluids and keeps the body temperature in control." She says that maintaining skin hydration is also vital for sustaining healthy internal organs.

Travelling, stress, lack of exercise and poor diet affect the exterior of skin. If your skin lacks luster, is dry and has a flat appearance, you are probably depleted in nutrients and need a boost inside and out. Nurture your skin with easy-to-penetrate ingredients by preparing these recipes in the sanctuary of your home.

BODY COOLERS:

Just as a cool dip in the ocean awakens your energy and revitalizes the mind, cooling applications have a beneficial effect on the body. In the spa, mists and creams created with ingredients like rosewater, aloe vera and cucumber are sprayed or applied to cool down the face and body. Try some of these wonderful recipes and feel the results for yourself.

GREEN TEA FLIGHT THERAPY

This mist spray, created by Arthur Lawrence, is perfect for in-flight travel as it can be sprayed onto the skin as often as you want. Steeped, cooled green tea is linked to skin cell rejuvenation with its compound polyphenols high in antioxidants; sesame oil, a highly nourishing and protective oil, is high in minerals and blocks up to 45 percent of the sun's UV rays; jojoba oil is anti-inflammatory and has sunscreen properties; and soya oil is a known astringent that helps retain glowing skin. Essential oils of geranium are added to further hydrate and blue chamomile is to calm and soothe.

It is important to note that this spray has a water phase and an oil phase, so the water and oil will naturally separate. There's no harm in this; in fact, it makes a more nutritious formulation as most skin care products on the market add emulsifiers to blend the oil and water. Also note that glycerin is a humectant that helps the skin absorb and retain moisture; natural glycols, like natural glycerin or vegetable glycerin, are best (avoid the petrochemical filled products that are listed with glycol, glyceryl, ethelene glycol, PEG and propelene glycol as they cause more harm than good).

Ingredients (water phase):

- 1 cup (250 ml) strong filtered green tea; ⅓ cup (80 ml) pure aloe vera juice; 2 tbsp vegetable glycerin (only add if the environment is humid as glycerin in a dry environment will take moisture from the skin) or 2 tbsp sorbitol; 3 tsp liquid B complex (optional).

Ingredients (oil phase):

- 1 tsp soya oil; 1 tsp sesame oil; 1 tsp rosehip oil; 1 tsp jojoba oil; ½ tsp or 3 vitamin E capsules, pierced; ¼ tsp or 3 vitamin A capsules, pierced; ¼ tsp or 3 vitamin D capsules, pierced; 8 drops blue chamomile, 5 drops lavender and 5 drops geranium essential oils.

Directions: In a glass jar or bottle with a screw-top lid, mix oil phase ingredients together and shake vigorously. Add the water phase ingredients and shake the bottle well. Always shake before use and spray on face and body. Store in refrigerator.

SKIN SOOTHER WITH ALOE VERA

In ayurveda, aloe vera is sometimes called *kumari* or "princess with the gel" or *ghrit kumari* ("ghee of the princess"). In any case, Indian women are reported to have traditionally used aloe to nurture the complexion. It is understood to benefit all three *doshas*: it is soothing for *vata* types, cooling for *pitta* types and clearing for *kapha* types. If you've spent too long in the sun without adequate sun protection we recommend you slice an aloe leaf lengthwise and press the gel directly on to the affected area, then wrap in cloth to secure. This works well if you have cuts, burns or insect bites, too.

Alternatively, try this recipe created by the staff at Six Senses Spas. It is made with cooling lavender and aloe vera as well as nourishing milk. These work well together to soothe tender and reddish-colored skin. The formulation reduces skin temperature and helps to repair any damage caused by extensive sun exposure, and the lavender water and essential oils leave a lovely scent. In this recipe we used a 10 by 10 inch (25 x 25 cm) piece of gauze; depending on the area being treated you may need more, or less.

Ingredients:

- 3 medium blades of aloe vera, mashed; 2 tbsp aloe gel mixed together with 1 tbsp lavender water; 5 drops lavender essential oil; ½ cup (125 ml) milk; 2 pieces gauze; revitalizing body lotion.

Directions: Mix the fresh, mashed aloe vera with the aloe gel and lavender water. Set aside. Add lavender essential oil to milk and soak 2 pieces of gauze in this, then place in fridge to cool for about 15 minutes. Using gentle pressure, put one piece of gauze over the sunburned area. Gently pat on the aloe mixture, cover with the remaining gauze and leave for 15 minutes. After you remove, use a moisturizing body lotion or leave the skin bare. Repeat once a day until the redness disappears.

Opposite Local coffee is used a fair bit in Asian spas as it both stimulates circulation and nourishes skin.

This page Blending ingredients in a fresh coconut shell makes a most alluring home spa treatment. Salt may be added to most ingredients for an effective scrub.

COCONUT AND ALOE BODY OIL

Most of us know how cooling a sip of coconut milk can be. In Ayurvedic medicine, coconut is used to pacify *pitta* types and soothe burns and scars. In fact, coconut is one of the most common oils used in massage in Asian spas as it is so nourishing. Here we combine coconut with aloe vera, to create a remedial recipe for skin irritants and sunburn. Slather your skin with this oil and dream of tropical beach holidays where the wind swayed the coconut palms and cooled you into bliss.

Ingredients:
- 2 tbsp coconut oil; 1 tbsp aloe vera gel; 5 drops each of jasmine, sandalwood and neroli essential oils (these are all cooling to the body).

Directions: Mix all ingredients together and massage into the body after your shower or bath.

CUCUMBER AND MILK BODY MASK

This after-sun cooler, created with cucumber and milk powder, is for cooling, soothing and moisturizing skin. Native to India, and cultivated for over 3,000 years, the cucumber has been embraced worldwide for its cooling properties. It is a natural source of enzymes and vitamins and is a natural

hydrator, making it an excellent cleanser for problem skin. Milk powder is full of natural emollients and vitamin As and Bs help to restore lost moisture in the skin.

Ingredients:
- 2 cups (200 g) powdered milk; 6 large cucumbers, skin removed; 4 drops each of lavender, lemongrass, geranium and lime essential oils.

Directions: Purée the skinless cucumbers in a blender until smooth. Put in a bowl and stir in the powdered milk until thoroughly mixed. Add the essential oils and mix again. Apply the mixture directly to your body and lie down to rest for 20 minutes (you may want to envelop your body in a sheet). Place sliced cucumber wedges on your eyes for total relaxation. You can also use the mix by pouring into a lukewarm bath. Soak for 20 minutes. Finish with a cool/cold shower and rest the body. Drink plenty of water to keep your body hydrated.

BODY CREAMS:

The beauty of body creams is that they give your skin a subtle glow and scent that lingers for hours—perfect after a shower or bath. Here are four rich creams to massage into your body for deep moisturizing. They have been created with common Asian ingredients that are found worldwide together with pure essential oils to penetrate the skin and rebalance the emotions. Apply awakening blends like our Ginger Body Cream in the morning to get you moving for the day and try soothing recipes such as the Sesame Body Cream at night to help you sleep well.

CLASSICAL AROMATHERAPY CREAM

This is an exquisite and nutrient-rich recipe that leaves a lingering aroma on the skin. Created with almond oil and nourishing essential oils, this recipe stimulates the skin's metabolism and encourages skin vitality. It helps to rehydrate normal to dry

skin nourishers

Below left Rose essential oil and rose petals used in at-home recipes leave a wonderful lingering scent on the skin.

Bottom Fresh ginger rhizomes have detoxifying, warming and energizing properties—try the nurturing ginger body cream recipe below.

Right Cooling ingredients like fresh yoghurt are often applied to the skin after Asian spa treatments. Yoghurt's lactic acid content is refreshing and soothing on skin.

skin (*vata* imbalances) and is recommended for dehydrated parts of the body including hands, legs and elbows.

Ingredients:
- 1 tbsp beeswax; ½ cup (125 ml) almond oil; 6 tbsp rosewater; 10 drops rose, 8 drops patchouli, 8 drops sandalwood, 5 drops lavender, 4 drops bergamot essential oils.

Directions: Melt the beeswax in a double boiler. Add the almond oil gradually, constantly stirring until dissolved. Remove from heat and add rosewater gradually in a thin stream, vigorously beating the mixture all the while. When the mixture cools and turns creamy, add the essential oils. Use as necessary.

GHEE CRÈME

Ghee is a well-loved ingredient in ayurvedic cuisine and making *ghee* is a gorgeous visual experience. If you love cooking, the experience of observing the golden yellow color foaming when heated is one not to be missed. *Ghee* is pure clarified butter rich in vitamin E and beta-carotene; it is also an antioxidant that helps fight free radicals in the skin. In ayurvedic concoctions, *ghee* is often used to nourish *vata* and *pitta doshas* and is believed to enhance one's *ojas* or life energy. Ayurvedic physicians report that *ghee* also improves memory and other brain functions.

Ingredients:
- 16 oz (500 g) organic unsalted butter.

Directions: To make *ghee* at home, put the butter in a saucepan over medium heat until it comes to the boil. Reduce heat and simmer for an hour. When the water has reduced and the milk solids have settled, the *ghee* will appear as a transparent golden liquid on top. Strain into a clean glass jar. *Ghee* can be kept for several weeks at room temperature. Use daily as required as a body moisturizer, adding your favorite essential oil blend to the *ghee*. (Add no more than 20 drops of a blend of three or four essential oils to the *ghee*). It can also be used as a once-a-week eye cream to prevent lines; add a drop of rose or sandalwood essential oil first.

Vata Ghee

Symptoms of *vata* imbalances include worry, anxiety and nervousness. This recipe is grounding in nature, with oils selected for their reassuring and nurturing properties. If your stomach is feeling bloated, then massage well into this area.

Add to your home-made *ghee*: 5 drops ginger, 3 drops cardamom, 3 drops anise seed and 3 drops lemon essential oils.

Pitta Ghee

Pitta types are often hot and fiery and when off balance need cooling food and treatments to rebalance. This makes a relaxing moisturizer whenever you feel over-heated or bothered.

Add to your home-made *ghee*: 4 drops fennel, 4 drops coriander, 2 drops dill, 2 drops cardamom and 4 drops peppermint essential oils.

Kapha Ghee

Kapha imbalances include symptoms of extreme sluggishness and lethargy. This body moisturizer kick starts you for the day.

Add to your home-made *ghee*: 4 drops thyme, 4 drops juniper, 4 drops mint, 4 drops lemongrass and 2 drops ginger essential oils.

GINGER BODY CREAM

This is a superb, easy-to-create body cream that has a beautiful texture and a heady scent. Ginger is a vital ingredient in many Asian recipes as it has the ability to detoxify as well as warm and energize the body dispelling symptoms of cold and flu. In the past, the Egyptians massaged oil made from ginger into the lower back and leg

area to relieve sciatica. Today, ginger is recognized for both its calming quality on the nervous system and its high vitamin A, B and E content. In ayurveda and TCM, it is considered a medicinal ingredient and you'll often be served a nurturing ginger tea before or after a spa treatment.

Ingredients:

- 2 inch (5 cm) fresh young ginger; 1 tbsp sesame oil; 1 tbsp apricot kernel oil; 1 tbsp vitamin E oil; ¼ cup (40 g) cocoa butter; 5 drops ginger and 5 drops lavender essential oil.

Directions: Grate ginger root finely and squeeze out the juice to fill 1 teaspoon. Melt cocoa butter in a double boiler, add the

sesame, apricot kernel and vitamin E oils gradually, stirring constantly. Remove from heat. Add the ginger juice and the essential oils. Pour the mixture into a glass jar and store in the fridge. Use as needed.

SESAME BODY CREAM

Sesame is another nourishing ingredient used widely throughout the East. It has been cultivated for its mineral and medicinal properties throughout India and China for centuries. Long ago, the Chinese ground the seeds to a paste with water to soothe burns and insect bites. In ayurvedic medicine, sesame is well regarded as a protective and nourishing skin emollient. It is perfect for dry and *vata* type skin

complexions. Grounding in nature, it also helps reduce stress and tension held in the body. For *kapha* constitutions, substitute safflower oil.

Ingredients:

- 2 tbsp beeswax, grated; ¼ cup (60 ml) sesame oil; ¼ cup (60 ml) neroli or orange flower water; ¼ tsp vitamin E oil; 5 drops mandarin, 5 drops petitgrain and 3 drops jasmine essential oils.

Directions: Melt the beeswax in a double saucepan, add sesame oil, gradually whisking the oils together. Add the vitamin E oil and turn off the heat. Mix neroli water with oils; keep stirring. Pour into a glass jar with lid, allow to cool. Store in a cool place and coat the body as needed.

In Asia, for centuries women have hand blended fresh plants, fruits and herbs and applied them directly to the hair. In fact, the region has a long history of natural, nutrient-rich hair cleansers and conditioners. Today's spas celebrate these concoctions through an abundance of treatments for the hair and scalp.

Left and above Let it shine. Seaweed is an enlivening ingredient that stimulates hair growth and luster. At the Ritz-Carlton Bali Thalasso and Spa, it is used in a number of ocean-inspired treatments.

Some spa treatments have been adapted from home hair care tips and recipes handed down from mother to daughter—and many harness the bounty of the natural world. One good example is the centuries-old Indonesian Hair Smoke (see photographs overleaf). Formulated to scent and strengthen the hair, it was especially created for brides. Smoldering herbs were placed in a beautiful vessel and the smoke gently wafted over drying hair to leave a lingering aroma. Dr Marthar Tilaar has adapted what is most likely an ancient ayurvedic recipe with new technology to recreate the experience. You can either buy her product to try at home, or experience the smoke at one of her spas.

Another recommendation is the *Rawatan Ikal-Ikal* offered at the Village Spa at Pangkor Laut. This traditional Malay hair recipe is made with brewed oils, henna and betel leaves. Both henna and betel leaves contain properties that help draw out heat, so when the mixture is applied to the head area, it is an excellent remedy for migraine. Other Malay hair treatments use a variety of nourishing herbs and plants to prevent hair loss and soothe scalp irritations. Coconut oil is a popular ingredient, especially in Malaysia, Indonesia and India where coconuts grow

abundantly. In Goa, Sereno Spa's *Kalpa Moksha*, a therapeutic treatment that involves pouring warm medicated oil on the back and neck combined with a pressure point scalp massage, soothes the nervous system, helps prevent hair loss and improves muscle and nerve tone.

For something memorable, try the Hamam Classic treatment at the Spa at Four Seasons Hong Kong. Part of their water-inspired Aqua Collection menu, it is inspired by the rituals of the Middle East. The sequence includes a Morrocan soap massage with a luxurious Body and Hair Mask given on a marble slab in a private steam chamber.

Take time out, and try some of these washes, conditioners and rinses at home. After all, your hair speaks volumes about your health. An ayurvedic physician gets a sense of one's *dosha* by observing the condition of hair and, in TCM, it is believed that when *ch'i* is flowing well throughout the body, hair appears healthy and lustrous. During hair rituals, it is important to use ingredients that are cleansing and nourishing for the hair and scalp, and when rinsing the hair use tepid water. If the ends of your hair are split, there is no magic cure: you need a hair cut.

asian hair and scalp rituals

Below The traditional Indonesian Crème Bath is an amazing tension releasing treatment. Here a therapist from the Martha Tilaar Eastern Rejuvenating Center performs a scalp massage to lubricate and strengthen hair roots and stimulate circulation, then applies a conditioning crème to the hair. Indonesian crème baths are usually made from coconut blended with boiled hibiscus and jasmine flowers and leaves.

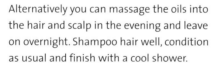

HOT OIL HAIR MASK

In some areas of India, women perform a weekly scalp massage with hot coconut oil to retain lustrous, thick and healthy hair. This blissful recipe is great for releasing tension in the head area, and also soaks warm nourishing oils into the scalp. For particular hair types, add the following essential oils.

Greasy/oily hair: 6 drops bergamot, 5 drops lavender, 2 drops cypress, 2 drops tea tree essential oils.

Damaged hair: 5 drops geranium, 5 drops sandalwood, 5 drops lavender essential oils.

Dry hair: 5 drops lavender, 5 drops sandalwood, 5 drops geranium essential oil. With regular use, condition of hair should improve.

Ingredients:

- 2 tsp avocado oil; 2 tsp macadamia oil; 2 tsp sesame oil; 2 tsp safflower oil; 2 tsp wheat germ oil; 1 tbsp calendula oil; essential oils, as above.

Directions: In a bowl, whisk all the ingredients together. Warm the oil slightly and work into the hair from roots to ends. Massage the scalp with your fingertips to encourage circulation, and release any tension. Wrap the hair in a hot towel and leave on for a minimum of 20 minutes.

Alternatively you can massage the oils into the hair and scalp in the evening and leave on overnight. Shampoo hair well, condition as usual and finish with a cool shower.

INDONESIAN CRÈME BATH

Like many Indonesian treatments, the crème bath developed in the palaces of East Java and was given to Javanese princesses as part of their beauty rituals. Today, there are very few Indonesian spas that do not offer this classic treatment. Usually offered as part of a sequence of hair rituals, the recipe is often created from crushed, ground and boiled hibiscus leaves and flowers, candlenuts, and ylang ylang and jasmine blooms blended with coconut oil. Dr Martha Tilaar reports that these ingredients, when combined with a scalp massage, nourish, lubricate and strengthen hair roots. Circulation in the scalp and hair follicles improves, leaving hair softer, darker, shinier and extremely manageable.

At Martha Tilaar Spas, the ingredients are massaged into the hair and scalp with a fingertip massage to stimulate pressure points, and then left, covered with a hot towel wrapped turban style, to nourish for 30 minutes. During this time, the massage continues from the head down to the neck, upper back and arms. Try either of these two recipes at home.

Classic Indonesian Crème Bath with Coconut

Recommended for shoulder length hair, eucalyptus stimulates and cleanses the scalp, rose tones and soothes, and rosemary stimulates circulation to the scalp, reduces oil build-up and prevents hair loss.

Ingredients:

- ½ cup (125 ml) coconut oil; 2 tbsp coconut cream; 5 drops eucalyptus, 5 drops rose, 5 drops rosemary essential oils.

Directions: Heat the coconut oil until warm, remove from heat and add the coconut cream. Stir well. Add the essential oils. Massage into the scalp and hair with firm fingertip pressure. Press the scalp and make small circular movements. Wrap a hot towel around your head and leave to absorb for 30 minutes. Shampoo well, rinse and condition as usual.

Botanical Crème Bath with Olive and Sesame

Created by Adria Lake, this crème bath recipe is good for longer length hair, and is compatible with the Wild Lime Hair Care treatment overleaf. You can use this recipe as a daily hair conditioner, or, for a deeper crème bath, apply the mixture into hair, wrap your head with a warm towel and leave in for 30 minutes. Rinse well.

Ingredients:
- 2 tbsp olive oil; 2 tbsp sesame oil; 2 eggs; 2 tbsp coconut cream; 2 tbsp honey; 1 tbsp coconut oil.

Directions: Blend all ingredients together well in a blender. Apply to the hair, leave in for a minute (or longer, as above), and rinse as usual.

SAMURAI SEAWEED RINSE

Seaweed, with its high mineral content, is a nutritious and enlivening ingredient for stimulating hair shine and growth. For centuries in Japan, it was used in a variety of beauty treatments. Today, this jewel of the sea is found in many innovative spa and beauty brands.

This simple yet effective rinse is best as a once-a-week treat to maintain silky, soft hair texture. An application of nutrient-rich water that has been soaked in seaweed has a cleansing effect, as it helps eliminate accumulated sebum. Also, by stimulating the peripheral circulation, you are oxygenating the skin, thereby creating a vibrant scalp and strong hair texture.

Ingredients:
- 2 cups (500 ml) pure spring water; 2 strips dried *kombu* or kelp (about 15 inches or 40 cm long).

Directions: Boil water and pour over seaweed; allow to cool for 30–45 minutes. Shampoo, then rinse hair. Remove the seaweed from the water and use the water for a second rinse. Pour it gently over the scalp and let the nutrient-rich water run through your hair. Massage well into the scalp for about one minute, then rinse again with clean water. Apply conditioner as usual.

TANGY LIME CONDITIONER

Therapists at Four Seasons Spa, Chiang Mai, recommend a reflexology pressure point massage on the feet while you let this conditioner do its work. Even though this recipe requires a bit of effort, your resulting glossy hair makes it worthwhile. It is also aromatic and uplifting.

Ingredients:
- 4 fresh limes; 2 tbsp conditioner.

Directions: Cut the limes in quarters and steam for 25 minutes. Put in a blender and blend until creamy. Strain through a metal strainer into a glass jar. Mix in 1 tbsp of your own conditioner for short to shoulder length hair, or 2 tbsp for longer hair, and stir well. Shampoo your hair as normal, then

Below The juice of freshly squeezed limes makes an excellent hair rinse. At Four Seasons Spa at Chiang Mai, the Wild Lime Hair Care treatment is uplifiting for both hair and emotions.

Right Infused flowers, like the ylang ylang flower with its exotic scent, make lovely additions to a hair rinse.

apply the conditioner from roots to ends. Cover with a shower cap or warm towel and leave to absorb for 30 minutes. Rinse and dry hair as normal.

WILD LIME HAIR RINSE

The Wild Lime Hair Care treatment made with locally grown ingredients and offered at Four Seasons Spa in Chiang Mai is pure bliss. Inhale the enlivening aromas of freshly crushed Thai wild lime or *makrut* as it is applied to your hair and scalp. This is

followed by the application of refreshing and fragrant wild lime shampoo, and completed with a moisturizing conditioner blended with pure lime essential oil. Then you are treated to a soothing head, scalp, neck and shoulder massage.

This lime rinse is an adaptation of their recipe for you to try at home whilst you dream of spa days in the mountains of northern Thailand. It encourages shine and lightens the hair.

Ingredients:
- Juice of 2 limes; 1 cup (250 ml) distilled water.

Directions: Squeeze the juice from 2 limes and add the distilled water. Mix well and use as a weekly rinse after shampooing. Apply conditioner after.

YLANG YLANG HAIR INFUSION

Infused flowers make fragrant hair rinses. Ylang ylang, in particular, is a most exotic aromatic white flower that grows abun-

dantly throughout Indonesia. In this recipe, it is combined with galangal, a pungent member of the ginger family. Used by both Indonesian village women and ladies of the court to strengthen and maintain silky, shiny hair, it is highly regarded for its balancing effect on both dry and oily scalps. This recipe, contributed by Jamu Jamu, also uses coconut oil and waxy candlenuts to moisturize hair and add shine. It makes enough for four applications.

Ingredients:
- 1 cup (250 ml) pure coconut oil; 10 pieces fresh ylang ylang flowers or 15 drops ylang ylang essential oil; 1 tbsp galangal root powder or ginger powder; 2 pieces (10 g) pandan leaf; 10 candlenuts or 1 tbsp castor oil.

Directions: Clean and slice all herbal and floral ingredients and place together in a medium-sized glass jar with an airtight screw-top lid. Warm coconut oil for 10 minutes on a low heat until around 30 degrees Celsius. Pour the coconut oil over the mixed ingredients in the jar and keep the infusion for 2 days. Just before use, strain ¼ cup (65 ml) of the herbal hair infusion and apply all over hair. Massage the scalp for 15 minutes, then wrap the head with a warm towel and leave to absorb for 10 minutes. Rinse with a gentle shampoo. Repeat weekly for one month for best results. The infusion should be stored in a cool dark place.

hand spa

Right Hand-made soaps from Four Seasons Spa in Chiang Mai keep hands cleansed and scented.

Below Water is an ever present element in the Asian spa. Always wash hands before treatments.

Bottom Thai white clay is the principle component in the Beautifying Hand Mask recipe.

When hands are soft, strong and well cared for, it is believed that *ch'i* is flowing smoothly through the body. Our hands reflect the way we treat ourselves and, according to scholars of Chinese medicine, the color, temperature and feel of our hands indicates the state of our overall health.

n Asia, looking after the hands is part of the daily wellness routine. Start cultivating graceful hands by dedicating a few minutes each day to cleansing, moisturizing and self-massaging. Reflex points exist in the hand area and they respond well to regular massage to keep them nourished and toned. Hand massage increases circulation and unlocks any stagnation, resulting in enhanced energy. Try, also, to incorporate a weekly hand bath.

Alternatively, there are some increasingly imaginative hand therapies offered at Asian spas. One such is the 25-minute Radiance Hand Treatment at Six Senses Spas. This well-deserved pamper starts with a warm compress, is followed by a luxurious jojoba bead exfoliation blended with lemon, lavender and geranium, and ends with a soothing massage to leave your hands feeling soft and smooth. Other ideas to try at home include the following:

ASIAN HAND RITUAL

This recipe was generously created for us by the Ytsara team. Ytsara is an organic Thai spa line founded by Florence Jaffre, who explains: "In Thailand, hands are a reflection of beauty and grace. This may be because Thais use them as a greeting and to pay respect to the Buddha, as well as in their beautiful dance." We suggest preparing all the treatments first to make this an easy and relaxing experience.

Cleanser:

Pour a few drops of lemongrass essential oil into lukewarm water and relax your hands for a few minutes. The lemongrass will help soothe and heal the hands as well as act as a natural antiseptic and deodorizer.

Hand scrub:

To gently get rid of dead cells while nourishing your skin, scrub hands with an exhilarating mixture of 2 tbsp freshly grated coconut or dried coconut and 2 tbsp coconut cream or coconut powder. Use circular movements.

Beautifying hand mask:

Apply this hand mask which is made from the most regenerating ingredients nature can offer. To obtain a thick paste, mix 4 tbsp *dinsow pong* (Thai white clay) with 1 tbsp rosehip seed oil (or substitute with olive oil), 2 drops rosewood essential oil, ½ tbsp pure honey, and ¼ tbsp water. Extracted from a rose that grows high in the Andes, a little of this rich rosehip seed oil goes a long way to nourish and revitalize dull, dry skin. Thai white clay is soothing, cleansing and healing; in olden times it was used like talc after a shower. It also has a natural SPF. Leave the hand mask on for about 20 minutes, then rinse off, and apply oil (see below).

Silky soft hand oil:

To keep your hands soft and elegant, mix 2 tbsp wheat germ oil with 3 tsp rosehip seed

Right Rose petals strewn in a foot bath are a beautiful accompaniment to the Rosewater Hand Wrap recipe below.

Below It is believed that hand reflexology works on the same principles as foot reflexology. Each touch, press and squeeze correlates to different parts of the body.

oil, 1 tsp lime juice, 5 drops of rosewood and 5 drops *palmarosa* essential oils, and rub into hands as a soothing finale.

ANTIOXIDANT GREEN TEA & AVOCADO HAND AND FOOT RITUAL

Antioxident-rich ingredients keep our body young and help prevent aging. With positive new evidence that both green and white teas contain high amounts of polyphenols that are beneficial when applied topically to the skin, it is not surprising that we are seeing more tea-based treatments in global spas. Known to prevent oxidation of skin cells and to protect the skin against aging, stress and sunburn, green and white teas also strengthen the immune system. Here we blend vitamin, mineral and amino acid-rich honey with nourishing avocado that is high in vitamin E, lecithin and phytoserols to help stimulate collagen metabolism. Avocado nourishes the skin with proteins and oils; oatmeal exfoliates dead skin cells; and lemon essential oil cleanses, refreshes, cools and stimulates. It also helps to lighten dull, stained hands and tone and condition nails and cuticles.

In between spa visits, create this once-a-week nurturing recipe to revive dry, wrinkled and rough hands and feet; it is great on elbows and knees as well. Results include softer skin with slower signs of aging.

Ingredients:

* 2 tbsp fine oatmeal; 1 tbsp avocado oil or 2 tbsp mashed fresh avocado; 1 tsp vegetable glycerin or honey; 2 tsp steeped green or white tea (use 1 tsp green or white tea with 200 ml hot water, steep for five minutes, take out 2 tsp for the recipe and drink the rest); 6–8 drops lemon or lime essential oil or 1 tsp lemon juice.

Directions: Mix together fine oatmeal, avocado oil or fresh mashed avocado,

vegetable glycerin or honey, green or white tea and essential oils in a bowl. Find a comfortable spot and gently massage this mixture on to your hands and feet, and leave in place for 20 minutes. Rinse off with cool water.

ROSEWATER HAND WRAP

This highly scented hand wrap is great for people with dry skin. Perfumed rosewater extracted from the distillation of rose petals creates a sweet, aromatic fragrance that is emotionally nourishing and balancing. The fine granules of oatmeal work to gently exfoliate and remove dead skin cells, softening the epidermis and improving elasticity and suppleness, whilst nourishing almond oil softens skin. This softening hand mask leaves hands smooth, hydrated and nourished. Please note that this mixture only keeps for one application. Use once a week.

Ingredients:

* 2 tbsp rosewater; 3 tbsp oatmeal; 2 tsp almond oil.

Directions: Mix all ingredients together and heat in a double saucepan until warm. Apply the warmed mask to hands (not the palm), wrap in cling wrap or warm towels, and leave for 10 minutes. Rinse.

SANDALWOOD HAND LOTION WITH ROSE OIL

Sandalwood is commonly cultivated in India and is renowned as a rejuvenating ayurvedic ingredient to balance *pitta*. Extracted from the heartwood of the sandalwood tree, it is a very earthy and emotionally balancing oil. This treatment has a lotion-like texture that is simple to create at home. For the cream, we suggest a natural vitamin E cream, as this is a humectant.

Ingredients:

* 6 ¼ tbsp natural sorbitol lotion; 5 drops of rose and 5 drops of sandalwood essential oils.

Directions: Blend the essential oils into the sorbitol lotion and combine well. Use other essential oils if you prefer, and apply all over hands to keep them fully moisturized.

foot care

Step into the world of the Orient and discover that clean feet are integral to long-term well-being. In most Eastern cultures, it is mandatory to remove shoes before entering either a temple or someone's home—so Asians generally take care of their feet. Many believe that the feet are like a map to the organs within the body. In TCM and ayurveda, it is thought that the condition of our feet mirrors internal imbalances. Ayurvedic physicians say that dry and rough feet relate to a *vata* imbalance, hot and sweaty feet indicate a *pitta* imbalance and heavy, swollen feet probably represent a *kapha* imbalance. A daily self-massage is usually recommended.

Spa sessions often begin with a cleansing footbath. Like an offering, they help purify and center the guest in preparation for the treatment to come. Foot washing is a symbolic part of certain ceremonies in Asia. For example, Balinese priests often end their day with a ritual foot wash in a floral-filled foot bath. The flowers represent the essence of nature, and serve to give thanks to the gods.

After a challenging day, soak your feet in one of these wonderful foot baths. Follow the soak with a scrub and self-massage to oxygenate blood and stimulate circulation. A wrap afterwards clears the mind of emotions and stored tension.

PRANA FOOT RITUAL

At Prana Spa, each guest is treated to a foot reflexology session before any body treatment, with attention given to the lower leg and calf areas. The procedure and ingredients relax sore calf muscles and act as a detox, at the same time invigorating and stimulating the feet and legs. At Prana, Karangasem salt found in the northern region of Bali and the local *delem* leaf are used. We've adapted their recipe for you with easy-to-find substitutes.

Ingredients:
- 5 tbsp rock salt; 3 drops peppermint essential oil; 3–4 pieces vetiver root or 3 drops vetiver essential oil; a few peppermint leaves; ¼ cup fresh rose petals; 1 pedicure brush.

Directions: Place all the ingredients into a bowl of warm water and allow the feet to soak for 2 to 3 minutes. Brush feet, nails and soles using a pedicure brush. Gently massage the legs, ankles and feet for 5 minutes to stimulate blood flow. Commence at the knee and work downwards with attention to ankles and calfs. Dry feet well after and apply moisturizer of your choice.

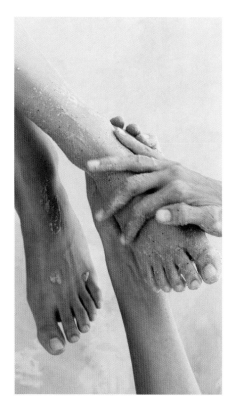

Opposite In ayurveda, a daily self-massage is recommended for overall wellness.

Left The Cinta Abadi treatment at the Ritz-Carlton Spa in Bali begins with a Flower Petal Foot Wash and Hot Towel Wrap followed by the Aromatic Petal Massage.

Below The Wild Mint and Clove Foot Salt recipe shared with us by Bagus Jati is cleansing and stimulating for feet.

FLOWER PETAL FOOT WASH

This recipe is inspired by the Flower Petal Foot Wash and Hot Towel Wrap at the Ritz-Carlton Spa in Bali. Their tropical garden spa is a riot of color with bougainvillea, banyan, water lilies and coconut trees, while the therapy villas boast soothing violet hues and rich mahogany furniture. Expansive ocean-to-forest views set the mood for this oceanic floral bathe.

Ingredients:
- 1 small bowl rose petals; 5 frangipani flowers; 1 tsp shower gel; 1 tsp bath salts; 1 tsp lavender body lotion; 1 pumice stone.

Directions: Lower feet one by one into a bowl filled with warm water, rose petals and frangipani and massage lightly. Scrub each foot gently with a mix of shower gel and bath salts followed with a stone scrub. Dip feet back into bowl to rinse the salt off. Dry feet. Work body lotion into feet, then wrap with a hot towel for a few minutes. Remove towel and then apply more lotion.

WILD MINT AND CLOVE FOOT SALT

Imagine bathing your feet in an earthenware bowl of enlivening ingredients whilst looking out over a jungle with the sounds of a mountain waterfall below. The experience of being at one with nature can be truly appreciated at Bagus Jati Wellbeing Resort delicately nestled in Bali's tropical rainforest. Here, they share their foot salt recipe.

Ingredients:
- 1 tbsp rock salts; ½ tbsp cloves; 3 drops spearmint essential oil; 3 drops peppermint essential oil; ½ tsp melted cocoa butter or 2 tsp apricot kernel oil with 2 drops each of clove and peppermint essential oil; 1 cup fresh flower petals such as rose.

Directions: Blend the melted cocoa butter or carrier oil with clove and peppermint essential oils, and set aside in a small bowl. Prepare a large bowl of warm water, add the salts, cloves and other essential oils and disperse well. Decorate with fresh flower petals. Soak feet for a few minutes, then scrub feet with pumice stone to remove any build up of dead and dry skin. Pat dry, and complete with a gentle massage using the cocoa butter mix.

CINNAMON AND CLOVE FOOT WRAP

The warming qualities of cinnamon and clove serve to calm and ground, while ginger root powder has a very distinctive spicy aroma; it is used to detoxify and warm the organs. This foot ritual is recommended for winter days or if you feel any symptoms of cold or flu coming on. It is also good as an antidote to a stressful day.

Ingredients:
- 1½ tbsp green clay; 1 tsp each of clove powder, cinnamon powder and ginger powder; 2 tbsp water or coconut cream; a foot bath filled with warm water; handful of fresh herbs or flowers.

Directions: Thoroughly mix the clay, spices, and water or coconut cream in a bowl to make a paste. Apply all over clean feet and ankles. Allow to dry for 15 minutes, then immerse feet in a bowl of warm water, adding the handful of flowers or fresh herbs for vitality. Wash off. Rest and complete with moisturizer.

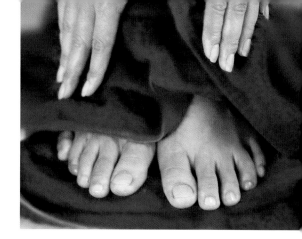

TIBETAN FOOT RITUAL

Carroll Dunham, an anthropologist working in Nepal, has adapted this local cleansing and grounding foot ritual for people to try at home. What better way to wind down than by pampering your feet in a sequence inspired by the spirited waters of Tibet? This is a four-part ritual, so ensure you have plenty of time to hand.

Dudtsi Safflower Cleanse

Saffron is considered an aphrodisiac in Tibet and is often added to love sachets, infusions and spells. When you visit a lama in Tibet, he pours *dudsti* (a blessing of safflower-infused water) into your cupped hands. This is ritually drunk, then your moist hands are placed on top of your head, clearing the entire body. Here we use safflower water in a foot bath to start this purifying ritual.

Ingredients:
* 3 tbsp safflower or saffron; 3 cups (750 ml) warm water.

Directions: Blend the ingredients and place in a teapot. Take a big breath and visualize the safflower water dissolving all agitation. Pour a small bit into a cupped palm and drink from your hand, then pour into a foot bowl. Place your feet in the water and let the mind become as spacious as the sky.

Chutsen or Herbal Foot Bath

Anyone with an appreciation of fragrance will love this part of the ritual. In Tibet, the leaf and flowering tops of artemisia (also known as wormwood) are often burned

with incense for symbolic protection. Tibetans also make a tonic from artemisia to cleanse the liver and improve circulation. Here, its properties cleanse in a foot bath.

Ingredients:
* 2 tsp safflower oil; 3 tbsp dried rosehip; 3 tbsp dried artemisia or dried sage: 3 tbsp dried nettles; 3 drops juniper or essential oil of your choice (sandalwood, cedarwood, spikenard, artemisia or rhododendron oils are recommended).

Directions: Place a collection of river stones in a visually pleasing bowl big enough to place both your feet in, and fill a teapot with boiling water. Add the safflower oil to the teapot and allow to steep for a few minutes. Rest your feet in the bowl, and gently pour in the steaming, but not scalding, safflower oil water. Curl and roll your feet over the stones. Soothing to the skin, the water symbolically cleanses and purifies not only the feet, but also the mind. Gently toss the herbs and essential oils into the bowl, add more water if necessary, and relax. Breathe deeply and allow your mind to empty completely.

Kangpartsayejukpa or Foot Salt Scrub

The next part of the ritual involves an easy-to-make scrub with a fresh, pine-like fragrance that has a slight woody undertone. Spikenard (*Nardostachys grandiflora*), called *dakpoe* in Tibetan, is a precious herb that grows only above 8,000 feet (2,430 meters). It is used in Tibet for treating fevers and wounds, altitude sickness and headaches, while the roots are used in incense to sedate; it is also an important ingredient in heart and head medicines in ayurveda. This recipe can also be used as a full body scrub.

Ingredients:
* ½ cup (140 g) Tibetan salt, sea salt or rock salt; 6 tbsp dried artemisia (or dried sage); 1 tbsp dried nettles (or dried

juniper); 2 tbsp safflower or sweet almond oil; ¼ cup (60 ml) apricot oil; 3 drops spikenard or rhododendron essential oil.

Directions: Mix ingredients together and place in a pleasing container that will not be stained by oil. Remove your right foot from the foot bath and rest on a towel. Scoop up the scrub and massage well into your feet, particularly in the heel and toe area. Start at the central point, pushing firmly and deeply with your thumbs toward the outer foot. Repeat with left foot. Rinse off afterwards.

Barley Flour Foot Powder

Inspired by the scent of the high mountain rhododendron (*Rhododendron anthopogen*) or *baluk karpo* used in Tibetan medicine for stomach disorders, indigestion and sore throats, this final section is very sweet scented. *Baluk karpo* is burned in incense for its fragrance to delight and invoke divine spirits. Here it is combined with various flours to create a foot powder rather like the *tsampa* or barley powder found in Tibet. Apply it after you have scrubbed and soaked your feet. It absorbs excess perspiration and keeps feet soft, cool, clean and dry for hours.

Ingredients:
* 3 tbsp barley and/or buckwheat; 3 tbsp chickpea or wheat flour; 1 tbsp dried artemisia or sage; 1 drop juniper, artemesia, cedarwood or rhododendron essential oil.

Directions: Mix all ingredients thoroughly in a bowl, dry your feet, then dust them with this soft floury mixture. It absorbs any excess oil. Results are fresh soft feet.

* Clear up your space well after your Tibetan Foot Ritual. Ensure you wash the stones with fresh water before putting them away. Make a cup of hot herbal tea, and have a restful sleep.

ayurvedic treatments

Below A consultation with diagnosis is given to a guest in the Ayurvedic Healing Hut at the Spa Village at Pangkor Laut Resort in Malaysia.

Right Medicated oil is poured over the back in a therapeutic spinal cord treatment at Mandarin Oriental Dhara Devi Spa in Chiang Mai, Thailand. It is one of the best ayurvedic treatments for soothing the nervous system.

Ayurveda is one of the leading disciplines in the modern spa industry. At its soul is the *tri-dosha* system of *pitta* (fire and air), *kapha* (earth and water) and *vata* (air and ether). It is believed that the universe is made up of these three elements and that, within each of us, is a unique proportion of all three *doshas*.

Enter the consulting room of an ayurvedic physician and you may well spend an hour or two there. First the doctor carefully studies your state of health by analyzing your *dosha* type (constitution) and any imbalances; then you are invited to participate in an overview of your diet, emotions and lifestyle and an examination of your body. Hands, eyes, ears, nose and skin texture are analyzed, and the doctor may also take your blood pressure and a stool sample. Many spas have on-site ayurvedic doctors nowadays —and many use computerized systems to back up their findings.

It is believed that everyone has a specific *dosha* at the moment of birth. Ayurveda ultimately aims to bring the patient back to his or her original *dosha* proportion from present imbalances. To this end, the patient is treated as an individual and very precise treatments are given according to different *dosha* types. All ayurvedic treatments first prepare the body for detoxification, then set about to rejuvenate and strengthen the constitution, slowly nudging the body back towards balance.

"Ayurveda is about balance," explains Dr Suchada from the Mandarin Oriental Dhara Devi Spa. "If our actions lead us towards living in balance, we stay away from disease." If, on the other hand, we indulge in too much of one thing and neglect another aspect of our life, she goes on to add, we are prone to falling ill.

The experience of having one's *doshas* balanced can be life transforming. It may involve treatments, medicines, specific yoga postures, meditation or massage, as well as diet and general lifestyle changes. The changes vary widely: Some patients report that their weight stabilizes and they have more energy. Others say that their voice changes tone and they are able to communicate better. The lucky few find their vocation in life and develop an inner fire to follow their hearts and dreams.

Many spas and retreats around the world offer ayurvedic treatments, although not all have in-house physicians to correctly analyze and diagnose. As a substitute, they take a more light-hearted approach by providing a simple questionnaire that aims to reveal the potential of one's *dosha*.

DISCOVER YOUR DOSHA

Six Senses Spas have formulated a chart that helps to determine one's *dosha* by looking at physical characteristics. Take a look and see if you correspond to any of these physical types.

Healthy *pitta* is revealed when one shows compassion, warmth and leadership.
Healthy *kapha* is revealed when there is endurance, calm and control.
Healthy *vata* is revealed when one is flexible, enthusiastic, creative and energetic.

	VATA	PITTA	KAPHA
Face	Small forehead, darkening, rough skin	Copper colored with plenty of pimples	Attractive, good looking, bright
Body weight	Light	Medium	Heavy
Body structure	Lean and tall	Medium sized	Heavy, short
Body strength	Weak	Moderately strong	Strong
Body temperature	Slightly less than normal	Slightly above normal	Normal
Body hair	Scanty	Few and brownish	Thick, dark and plenty
Body smell	None	Foul smell	Oily smell
Skin	Dry and rough	Soft and warm	Soft, glossy, cold, clear
Eyes	Protuberant, small, scanty eye lashes	Sharp, eye lashes are brown or copper/reddish in color	Large and attractive, thick eyebrows
Teeth	Cracked, irregular, dull white	Moderate sized, yellow	Large, white, strong
Nails	Rough, dry, less growth	Slightly glossy, copper colored	Long, white, strong and thick
Blood vessels	Prominent, reticulated	Less prominent with greenish-yellow color	Not at all visible, deep
Lips	Dry, thin, blackish	Red, soft, moist	Thick, glossy
Hands	Short	Medium	Long
Hair on the scalp	Brown, rough, dry	Scanty, tendency to early baldness	Plenty—dark, long and glossy
Joints	Prominent	Flabby	Strong, well formed and compact
Chest	Thin, narrow	Medium	Wide, strong, well covered with muscle and fat
Foot prints	Ill defined	Normal	Well defined
Tongue	Dark spots	Copper colored, thin	Clean and reddish
Abdomen	Thin	Normal	Large
Pulse	Irregular, quick	Fast pace, volume is less	Slow, full in volume

Whatever the approach, don't miss an opportunity to try one of the treatments.

Ananda in the Himalayas is one spa destination that has an extensive ayurvedic wing and numerous authentic treatments. A session here begins with the customary consultation by an ayurvedic physician to determine the natural body constitution and any *dosha* imbalances. This information is then used to select a treatment method and type of oil to balance body, mind and sprit. Generally, sesame oil is used with specific medicated oils to work on *dhatus* (tissues), *rasa* (plasma), *rakta* (blood) and *mamsa* (muscles), thus strengthening blood circulation, muscles and skin texture. The aim is also to improve the *agnis* or digestive system. Ayurvedic doctors undertake years of study and are normally well versed in yoga, nutrition, astrology, meditation and breath, as well as the "Science of Life."

Other Asian spas offering fantastic ayurvedic-inspired treatments include the Mandarin Oriental Dhara Devi Spa in Chiang Mai, Taj Spas all around the world, and the Spa Village at Pangkor Laut Resort in Malaysia. The *chakradhara*, offered at Four Seasons Spa at Sayan in Bali, includes

Left The *pizhichil* is part of the 7-, 14-, 31- or 28-day ayurvedic programs that can be taken at Pangkor Laut Spa Village in Malaysia. Here a prescribed warm oil is poured continuously over the body prior to a massage that is reported to assist in skeletal and muscular diseases, osteo-arthritis and neuropathy.

Below Ayurveda is so much more than a pot of oil. That said, *shirodhara* is an extremely oily experience, yet it feels like heaven in a cup for anyone in search of eternal calm.

the application of herbal oils over the *chakras* to promote energy flow and calm. And treatments that at first don't appear ayurvedic often have their roots in this ancient medicine. Many of the traditional treatments experienced in Thailand and Bali originate from India and are ayurvedic in nature. An example is the favored Thai poultice (see page 149): it was passed on by travelling Buddhists from India and has been adapted to include local Thai herbs. Furthermore, there are many medicinal treatments and courses available at guided ayurvedic retreats.

SHIRODHARA

Shirodhara is perhaps the best known ayurvedic treatment as it is offered in many spas around the world. It comes close to the experience of meditation and is one of the most beautiful ways to bring the body and mind back to equilibrium. Often given after a head and/or body massage, the guest lays down on a traditional neem wood massage table whilst a stream of warm medicated oil flows soothingly from a clay or copper pot on to the third eye area (the center of the forehead). The oil spreads generously across the forehead melting away any tension, smoothing out worry lines and encouraging a tranquil state of mind.

Shirodhara comes highly recommended for people with low energy levels and insomnia, and those who suffer from chronic headaches, fatigue and stress. Recent scientific studies show that it can improve neuro-muscular function, thereby increasing the strength of the immune system. Benefits include settling of the mind and central nervous system, as well as more superficial anti-aging benefits such as a line-free forehead.

According to Dr Srikantha Arunachalea at the Siddhalepa Ayurveda Health Resort in Sri Lanka, *shirodhara* is best taken for a minimum of three days to reap the full

Below The *kathi basti* treatment at the Mandarin Oriental Dhara Devi Spa in Thailand focuses on the lower spinal area. Flour and water are mixed to make a dough that is then placed on the lower back. This serves to trap medicated oil.

Right The *ubtan* scrub given at the same spa is made with turmeric, cinnamon, mint and rosewater and is part of a three-hour Ayurvedic Ceremony. A camphor-scented steam bath, Indian herbal wrap and *abhyanga* and *shirobhyana* massages are all part of this divine ritual.

benefits. He says it is important that the client be prepared for the treatment in advance. "We spend a few days detoxifying the client's body through massage, steam and herbs before administering *shirodhara*," he reports. "It's important that the client does not go out into the hot sun or harsh weather, swim, use the computer or listen to loud music during this time." The client is encouraged to stick to a strict vegetarian diet without spices and eat cooling foods such as coconut. Dr Arunachalea explains that the first treatment takes around ten minutes and from here is gently increased each day by about five minutes.

An increasing number of spas around the world offer authentic *shirodhara* experiences, with organic oils and well-trained therapists. These include Four Seasons Spas, Shambhala Spas in Como hotels and resorts, the Datai in Malaysia, Six Senses Spas in the Maldives and the Mandarin Oriental Dhara Devi Spa outside Chiang Mai in Thailand. At Prana Spa in Bali, their *shirodhara* begins with a 20-minute mind-soothing head and scalp massage. Techniques are based on *marma* point therapy (see pages 132–133). A warm medicated oil specially formulated for one's *dosha* type is then poured continually over the third eye.

HOW TO CREATE SHIRODHARA AT HOME:

This is a meditative ritual to try at home when you want to clear the mind and relax the body. Although not an exact reproduction of the authentic *shirodhara* (the treatment is extremely messy), it aims to instigate feelings of inner calm.

Ingredients:
- Select oil for your *dosha* type:
  Kapha: ½ cup (125 ml) sesame oil or equal parts sesame and coconut oil.
  Pitta: ½ cup (125 ml) coconut oil or equal parts coconut oil and *ghee* or cool milk.
  Vata: ½ cup (125 ml) sesame oil.

Directions: Fold a cloth, known in ayurveda as a *pichu* and soak in warmed oil of your choice for a few minutes. Lie down and press the *pichu* firmly on the *marma* point (also known as the third eye) in the center of your forehead. Rest for 15 minutes. Wipe away any excess oil with a hand towel.

KATHI BASTI

Rarely seen on spa menus, the *kathi basti* is normally only offered in ayurvedic retreats in India. The version offered at the Mandarin Oriental Dhara Devi Spa centers around rectifying lifestyle imbalances, but, on a micro level, concentrates on the spinal area. This is because many people now spend six to eight hours a day at a desk in front of a computer. "This is unnatural and stressful, especially if we don't counter-balance it with postures and movements," explains the director of their Holistic Center and Spa.

During the treatment, a blend of warm medicated oil, especially prepared for your *dosha* type, is poured along the spinal area and then massaged in well. The therapist then makes a doughnut-shaped ring out of a flour and water mixture and places it on the lower spinal area. Warm oil is poured gracefully into the ring whilst the dough holds the oil in place.

The *kathi basti* is believed to have a calming effect on the central nervous system and is thought to "open out" the spinal area. Be prepared for some pain during this treatment, but many patients swear by it as a prevention and/or cure for back complaints. They say that the *kathi basti* frees up the flow of both energy and blood circulation in the lower back—and the area is strengthened as a result.

For more ayurvedic treatments, turn to the Ayurvedic Massage section on pages 124–155 and the inspiring and exotic Ayurvedic Facial Treatments chapter on pages 170–173.

asian baths for cleansing the soul

Bath time provides a sanctuary-like space for "me-time." When combined with aromatherapy, sea minerals, candles and incense, it is also a way to let go of the old and embrace the new. A dip in a bath is wonderful when you require solitude to contemplate in restful surrounds.

A cross India, bathing is considered a route to ritual purification (see pages 230–233). Thousands of people dip themselves in the holy River Ganges every morning, while many others take an ayurvedic bath to rebalance the *doshas*. In Japan, a social gathering at an *onsen* or hot spring bath is similar to the cleansing *sento* or public bath of the past. In the Maldives the *lono vey* or traditional bathing place is a sea mineral paradise. Bathing is taken seriously in southeast Asia too: Indonesian and Malaysian bathing rituals are beautifully perfumed and, in Thailand, water is considered a significant elixir (see pages 234–235).

Today's spas offer some innovative bath creations including color baths, vitality pools and the classic *rasshoul* where you apply mineral-rich muds to the body before bathing in detoxifying mud pools. There are recreations of the classical *hamam* or Turkish steam bath, and spas like Spa Botanica in Singapore and the Spa Village at Pangkor Laut Resort have recreated the Japanese bath house experience (see the Malaysian Bathing Ritual on right). Per Aquum Spas in the Maldives have a *lono vey* floatation pool containing ten times more minerals and salts than the nearby Indian Ocean, while the thalassotherapy pool at the Ritz-Carlton Spa in Bali is the largest in Asia.

At home, we suggest keeping your bathroom sparkling clean with plenty of spa products, ingredients and accessories to play with. Bath salts and essential oils are staples, while more exotic additions may be picked up on your spa travels. Vary with candle-light and romantic music for evenings or opt for a morning bath filled with energizing ingredients to begin your day with vibrance. Winter baths taken in the early afternoon when the rain is pouring down with music, hot tea and lush warm towels make for a most nurturing journey. Try some of our Asian-inspired bathing suggestions.

MALAYSIAN BATHING RITUAL

A treatment at the Spa Village at Pangkor Laut Resort often begins with their unique Bath House Ritual, a voyage that includes some of Asia's most refreshing bathing traditions. It starts with a foot bath and an invigorating Chinese Foot Pounding, previously only enjoyed by concubines in feudal China. Feet are bathed in petal-adorned bowls, then kneaded, after which the soles are gently pounded with a small wooden hammer to revitalize circulation. From here, guests are escorted to the bath houses to enjoy a traditional Malay "circulating" bath (a representation of village bathing in streams and rivers) before adjourning for a cup of tea in the Japanese Bath House.

After the tea session, the bathing ritual continues with a Japanese-style cleansing using a *goshi-goshi* cloth to exfoliate, and is followed by a dip in the heated *rotenburu* pool (this translates as a "bath amid the dew under an open sky"). The finale is the signature Shanghai Scrub, where a therapist gently exfoliates and washes the body as you lie on a massage bed in a private scrub house. In Shanghai, this was traditionally offered exclusively to males. All these nurturing rituals take place in a glorious jungle setting with the sounds of water and nature as a backdrop, but some can be recreated in the privacy of your own home. Use a little imagination, and take your very own Malaysian bathing journey with a loved one.

OCEAN CITRUS BATH

This rich bath from Four Seasons Island Spa in the Maldives is filled with cleansing ingredients, perfect for when you need a pick-me-up. It contains spirulina, a single-cell type of algae that thrives in warm, alkaline fresh water, and is one of the best sources of beta-carotene, vitamin D and gamma linolenic acid or GMA. It also contains all nine essential amino acids. This colorful bath with slices of fresh fruit is uplifting and cleansing; it also re-mineralises the skin.

Ingredients:

- 1 cup (200 g) Epsom salts; 1 tbsp spirulina powder; 1 orange; 1 lime or lemon; 1 grapefruit; 1 tbsp coconut oil; 2 drops each of grapefruit, lime or lemon, peppermint and orange essential oils.

Directions: Cut the orange, lemon and grapefruit into slices. Fill the tub and add the Epsom salts, spirulina powder, coconut oil and essential oils. Add the fruit slices last. Step into your gorgeous, green-colored citrus bath and relax for 20 minutes. Finish with a cool rinse or just pat the skin dry.

GINSENG AND GREEN TEA BATH

It is advisable to take this bath when you are mentally fatigued and in need of a boost of positive energy. Ginseng is an Asian root used in tonics and teas as a pick-me-up. Here it enlivens by speeding up blood circulation, thereby increasing body heat. Blended with antioxidant-filled green tea, this is a powerful concoction with an herbaceous aroma.

Ingredients:

- 3 tbsp Chinese green tea; 6 (20 g) ginseng root pieces, dried; 100 g (4 x 3 inch; 7 x 10 cm) ginger, roughly chopped; 4 pints (2 l) water.

Directions: In a non-metal pan bring ginseng, ginger, green tea and water to the boil, then reduce heat and simmer for 15 minutes. Strain the herbal tea mixture through a sieve and add to your bath water. Soak for 20 minutes.

KOREAN RAINDROP BATH

An authentic communal Korean bath house offers a range of hot and cold water baths, steams and saunas, as well as therapists to vigorously scrub, pound and knead your body. Found in numerous cities around the world, many offer complimentary treatments like almond and cucumber masks, blueberry yoghurt body masks and scented oil massages. This interpretation of a Korean bath is a full-bodied blend of ginseng, a root known to revive the mind and enhance physical activity, cypress to stimulate blood circulation, ginger for grounding and warming, and lime for its pleasing fragrance.

Ingredients:

- 2 tsp (10 ml vial, pierced) Siberian ginseng; 2 drops each of essential oils of cypress, lime and ginger in 2 tbsp olive oil.

Directions: Pour ingredients into a filled bath and disperse before entering. Relax for 20 minutes. Pat dry.

INDONESIAN SPICE BATH

An easy-to-prepare recipe from Indonesian beauty guru Dr Martha Tilaar, this bath is calming in nature yet encourages alertness and presence. It uses turmeric root powder to detoxify and energize the immune system and nutmeg to realign emotions and increase inner strength. Fennel is added to clear an overworked mind. It has an enticing, spicy aroma.

Opposite A handful of zesty and spicy bath ingredients: lime and Kaffir lime leaves, with their citrusy scent, are great pick-me-ups, turmeric is detoxifying and lemongrass is soothing, invigorating and antiseptic.

Below A poolside foot massage in the gardens at Four Seasons Resort in Chiang Mai is a wonderful way to appreciate northern Thailand's natural beauty. To recreate some Thai bathing traditions, see pages 234–235.

Ingredients:

- 1 tsp fennel, dried; 2 tsp nutmeg powder or 4 drops essential oil of nutmeg; 2 tsp turmeric powder; ½ a handful dried *temugiring* (*Curcuma heyneana*) or 1 tbsp tamarind powder; 8 dried betel leaves (*Piper betle*) or 8 bay leaves or 8 lemon verbena leaves.

Directions: Mix all ingredients together, and put in the bath. Soak for 15 minutes, then rinse off. Alternatively, you can fill a muslin pouch with the ingredients and place in the bathwater.

SEAWEED AND ALOE PURIFYING BATH

Ingredients from the sea, such as seaweed and seawater minerals, are effective anti-aging skin boosters. They are increasingly found in skin care products, and are used here for a youthful effect. This bath concoction is full of nourishing vitamins and minerals that encourage skin to retain suppleness and firmness. Combined with detoxifying Epsom salts to cleanse and heal and aloe vera gel to hydrate, the result is skin glowing with vitality. This bath is best taken as a once-a-week purifying ritual.

Ingredients:

- 1 cup (100 g) kelp powder; 2 pieces dried *kombu* seaweed; 2 pints (1 l) boiling water; ½ cup (125 g) Epsom or sea salts; ¼ cup (45 g) aloe vera gel; 3 drops each of juniper, sage and orange essential oils.

Directions: Add seaweed to boiling water and steep for 30 minutes. Dilute the kelp powder, salts and aloe vera in the bath, then add the water combined with the *kombu* (strain the water if you don't want the actual seaweed in the bath). Add the essential oils last before stepping into your gorgeous sea mineral bath. Relax for 15–20 minutes. Pat dry and moisturize. Seaweed aloe baths can be draining, so don't over exert yourself immediately afterwards.

Traditional *ryokan* or inns are often sited adjacent to *onsen*. At such establishments it is habitual to remove your *yukata* (a cotton kimono-like robe traditionally worn after bathing) and *geta* (wooden clogs) and scrub away any toxins before immersing yourself in the natural steaming pools. Wooden buckets, tools and brushes are provided to help you with your pre-bathing scrub (see page 188). There may be a variety of pools to bathe in: indoor and outdoor pools with varying temperatures have different therapeutic effects. In addition, there is usually an indoor *hinoki* or cypress wood bath filled with steaming hot water. After trying the different baths and chatting with other bathers (most *onsen* are now divided into men's and women's areas and the atmosphere is social and friendly), you take a final scrub, wash your hair and prepare for tea.

This is usually taken in a *tatami* mat room where guests are seated on the floor. A sequence of over 20 dishes is served, beginning with local plum wine with fresh mountain leaf *tempura*, river fish, pickles, *sake*, and finishing with *miso* and rice. The ritual of bathing, scrubbing and cleansing, as well as eating and drinking, is all part of the traditional *onsen* experience.

Outside Japan, some spas are introducing Japanese bathing on to the menu. At Pangkor Laut Spa Village, enjoy tea in a Japanese tea house before scrubbing your body with a *goshi-goshi* cloth and bathing in an open-air bath (see previous page). Alternatively, try the purpose-built *onsen* at Four Seasons Hotel in Tokyo to experience a taste of traditional Japanese bathing.

If Tokyo isn't on your agenda, try an at-home Japanese bathing ritual. Decorate your bathroom with bamboo accessories, along with stones, rocks and plants. Start with a quick and vigorous exfoliation scrub before sinking into the bath. When reclining in the bath, take time to meditate and relax the mind. Afterwards, drink tea and rest.

SRI LANKAN FLOWER BATH

Sri Lanka's bathing history is as rich and diverse as the blossoming spa industry it hosts today. Beautiful bathing ponds and pavilions built for royalty in past times still remain, along with some of the old bathing traditions. For example, ritual baths are prepared at puberty and before marriage, and bathing in lotus ponds is considered auspicious. Such bathing was reserved for aristocrats in the past, as it was believed the water in which the lotus grew was cooling on the body. The Siddhalepa Ayurveda Resort offers a stunning flower bath: therapists take up to two hours to decorate this bathing masterpiece with indigo-colored flowers with a heavenly scent. Create something similar at home: gather fresh flowers and herbs from your garden or florist and create sculptures on the water according to shape and color.

Ingredients:

- 2 oz (60 g) brightly-colored fresh flower petals of rose and chamomile; 1 oz (30 g) refreshing mint leaves; 5 drops pure essential oil of rose or chamomile; 1 tbsp carrier oil such as sweet almond.

Directions: Sprinkle the petals over the water's surface, and add the oils under the tap for a strong aromatic soak.

JAPANESE BATH RITUALS

Open the door to Japan's bathing rituals and enter a hidden world of beauty. Within the home, the *furo* is the private bath, and the public bath still used today is known as the *sento*. However, it is the hot spring bath or *onsen* that is the most natural and by far the most beautiful Japanese bathing option. Dating back some 3,000 years to the Shinto period before the Chinese introduced Buddhism in 532 AD, *onsen* bathing in natural surrounds was a part of Shintoism's joyful respect for nature.

The more than 20,000 natural hot springs in Japan vary in mineral content depending on the nutrients that predominate in the ground around them. This influences their color too: From alkaline bright green to iron-enriched reddish waters, some are rich in therapeutic magnesium, calcium, iron and potassium whilst others are full of sodium chloride, known to aid digestion, heal arthritis and reverse infertility. There are earth baths, mud baths and sand baths, as well as hot spring waters flowing out of riverbanks, caves and underground volcanic streams. Enriched with minerals from underground geothermal activity, such waters are highly recommended for sports injuries, fatigued muscles and over-worked minds, as well as for anxiety and stress relief.

Left and below Lemongrass, ginger and ginseng are some of the enlivening ingredients used in Asian bathing rituals. Warming, energizing and antiseptic, they are also very exotic.

Bottom The hot spring culture of Japan is recreated via the *rotenburo* heated pool in a jungle setting in the Spa Village at Pangkor Laut Resort. Steaming, dreaming and relaxing the hours away is part of the spa experience there.

BLACK SEA SALT BATH

This skin softening, re-mineralising remedy reduces water retention—and is the next best thing to an *onsen*. Filled with citrusy Japanese grapefruit and essential oils, it is enlivening and refreshing. You need to make this fizz mix the day before your bath.

Ingredients:

- 1 tbsp citric acid; 2 tbsp sodium bicarbonate; 2 tbsp corn flour; 1 ½ tsp grape seed oil; 2 tsp *yuzu* zest (Japanese grapefruit—replace with zest of a lime or lemon if unavailable); 15 drops grapefruit essential oil; 3 fl oz (90 ml) spray bottle filled with neroli (orange flower) water (or distilled water); 1 cup (150 g) Black Sea salts (pink in color).

Directions: Mix sodium bicarbonate, citric acid, *yuzu* zest and corn flour. While stirring, drizzle grape seed oil into the mixture. Add essential oils one drop at a time. While stirring, spray the mixture with neroli flower water very slowly, taking care not to wet the mixture to the point of fizzing. Add neroli water until the mixture starts to clump together, then press the mixture into a tight ball. Let the ball dry on wax paper for 10 hours before use. Simply fill your tub with hot water, add the Black Sea salts and fizzy bath bomb and immerse in your home-made bubbling bath water.

WABI-SABI PLUM BATH

Wabi-sabi is a Japanese concept that dictates that real beauty exists everywhere in every moment, especially in imperfection. Here we have created an unusual bath recipe to celebrate this idea. *Umeboshi* plums are used in macrobiotic food to neutralize the acidity of blood; here, they give the bath water a slightly sweet aroma. Ginger is stimulating and warming for the body whilst antioxidant green tea gives the skin a boost. Pure lime essential oil is added to uplift and inspire positive thoughts and emotions.

Ingredients: 5 chopped *umeboshi* plums (available at health food and Japanese food stores); ½ cup (90 g) fresh ginger, grated; 1 pot strong Japanese *sencha* green tea (use 5 teabags with 2 pints (1 l) boiling water); 1 tbsp camellia or sweet almond oil blended with 5 drops lime essential oil.

Directions: Add the ginger and plums to the green tea infusion and let steep for 30 minutes. Strain the mixture through a sieve and add to a filled bath. Alternatively, you can fill a stocking or pack the ingredients into a muslin bag and add to a running bath. Mix in the oils just before stepping into your bath. Soak for 15–20 minutes, pat the skin dry and lie down to rest for 10 minutes or so.

SOYA MILK AND MANDARIN BATH

A bath of calm and quiet joy that is perfect if you feel a little stressed or off center, this recipe was recreated by Jamu Jamu and originates from the Sumatran royal court. It is a lovely warming and moisturizing affair that helps balance body temperature, and stimulates, softens and hydrates skin. Oatmeal is a good skin softener and nourisher and is regarded as hypo-allergenic. Native to China and Indochina, the essence of mandarin is expressed from the rind of the fruit and is well loved as an emotionally balancing and serene oil. We recommend taking this bath after a Balinese *boreh* or body exfoliation (see page 185).

Ingredients:

- 1 cup (125 g) hydrated soya milk; 1 tbsp oatmeal; 1 tbsp mandarin or orange citrus peel; ¼ cup (60 g) sea salt; 10 drops mandarin essential oil.

Directions: Blend oatmeal, citrus peel and sea salt together in a food processor until it attains the consistency of a fine powder. Then mix with the hydrated soya milk. Prepare a warm bath and dissolve the ingredients into the bath adding the essential oil drops last.

AROMATIC JAVANESE TEA BATH

With its origins in the royal courts of Surakarta, this is an easy-to-prepare tea bath that's very calming on the nerves. The Sultans believed this traditional bath purified the mind, body and soul. Its aroma is sweet and refreshing and has a grounding effect. Here it is recreated by Bagus Jati Wellbeing Resort; the folks there recommend you moisturize your skin after bathing and rest for 15 minutes.

Ingredients:
- ⅓ cup (20 g) *akar wangi* (if this aromatic root is unavailable, use 5 drops essential oil of patchouli or vetiver with 5 drops

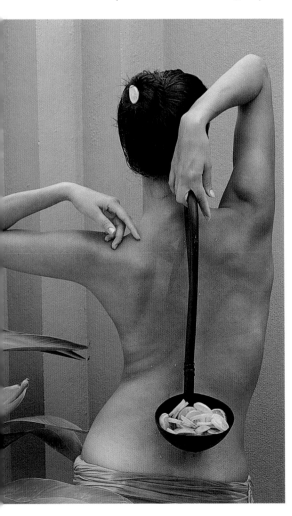

jasmine); ⅓ cup (20 g) citrus peel, dried; 3 pieces (10 g) pandan leaf; ¼ cup (5 g) jasmine flowers; 2 tbsp fresh ginger, grated; 2 tsp turmeric powder; 1 heaped tbsp sandalwood powder; 2 cups (500 ml) water.

Directions: Bring all ingredients to the boil in a saucepan, then simmer on a medium heat for around 30 minute., Remove and leave until cool. Strain off waste residue and add infusion to a warm bath. Soak in the bath for around 15 minutes. You may also pack mixture into a cheesecloth bag and place under the running tap of the bathtub and steep for 10 minutes, then step into the bath and squeeze the bag to release the aromas within.

RICE WATER TREAT

Created by Adria Lake, this recipe is inspired by the old Javanese tradition of using rice water to cool and moisturize the skin. Rich in essential nutrients, it is made with organic red rice water blended with coconut cream, white clay and sweet almond oil. It is a creamy, indulgent concoction that leaves skin soothed, supple and soft.

Ingredients:
- ¼ cup (60 g) organic red rice; 2 cups (500 ml) hot water; ½ cup (125 ml) coconut cream; 3 tbsp white clay; 1 tbsp sweet almond oil; 3 drops lemongrass, 3 drops ylang ylang and 5 drops mandarin essential oil, blended.

Directions: Soak red rice in hot water for at least 30 minutes and strain. Add coconut cream, white clay, sweet almond oil and the essential oils to the rice water and blend well. Pour into bath water—and relax.

BALINESE BATHING RITUALS

Watching Balinese women wrapped elegantly in batik *sarongs* bathing with their children on the river banks in rural Bali is a beautiful sight. The women gracefully pour water over themselves as the children

giggle and splash about. Using pumice stone and other tools, they make a ritual of cleaning and gleaming. Afterwards, they may rub coconut oil or a warming paste of crushed leaves, turmeric, cloves and nutmeg (see page 185) over their bodies for extra warmth and glow. Try these baths for size:

Late Afternoon Tropical Rain

Recreate the balmy atmosphere of a late afternoon tropical rain shower in Bali. Feel the peace, inhale its beauty and immerse yourself in the fragrant waters. Blend 1 tbsp coconut oil with 12 drops pure essential oils of ginger, ylang ylang and jasmine. Decorate your bath with pink frangipani flowers.

Balinese Morning Offering

Take part in the Balinese daily ritual of giving gratitude and blessings for self, family and the world. Celebrate life's simple offerings that often go unnoticed. Blend 1 tbsp (20 ml) coconut oil with 12 drops of ylang ylang, jasmine and clove essential oils. Sprinkle the water's surface with flowers, bark and petals.

Temple of Running Waters

Give thanks for life, friends and family as you bathe in this delicious aromatic bath syrup that reflects the sacred offerings of Bali. Blend 1 tbsp (20 ml) coconut oil with 12 drops warming essential oils of nutmeg, cinnamon and clove. Burn incense, meditate and be joyful.

Ceremony of the Sun

Celebrate the abundance of rituals and ceremonies in Bali with a tribute to Sanghyang Ratidya or the god of the sun. Symbolizing purity, this golden flower bath is made with as many varieties of Asian flowers, petals and leaves as you can find. Choose from lotus, jasmine, chamomile and ylang ylang.

water therapies

Water, with its myriad of energizing benefits, is the curative soul of the spa. In the same way that rainwater drenches tropical trees, plants and flowers with vitality, water revitalizes the human body. Water assists absorption of nutrients into the skin: continual hydration results in clean and vibrant eyes, hair and complexion and a strong immune system.

Left The Ritz-Carlton's thalasso pool provides a therapeutic union of water and massage. Jets massage the body submerged in warmed water to promote improved circulation and muscle and joint pain relief.

Right A gentle fall of rain can enhance all over wellbeing. The Rainshower Ritual at Four Seasons Spa at Jimbaran Bay's is an adaptation of the classic French Vichy shower.

Long before the term "spa" (taken from *salus per aquum* or "health through water") was invented, Asians were using the power of water (see pages 218–225). As their healing bathing rituals developed, so too did hydrotherapies in Europe. Today, Asian spas are building on these global bathing traditions, combining techniques and recipes from both East and West, to offer a fascinating variety of healing water options.

Hydrotherapy is a Western term that includes a wide range of water therapies including thalassotherapy, mineral baths, hot and cold plunges, hydro-massage and more. Its earliest incarnation was when the ancient Greeks (and then the Romans) took to thermal waters as a curative.

Today, in the Asian spa, you'll find hydrotherapy merged with steam treatments and saunas, along with ingredients like seaweed and sea minerals for complete cleansing. Water pressure facilitates the flow of lymph and stimulates blood circulation, helping to remove fatigue. Negative ions generated by showering activate an endorphin that energizes and vitalizes. Chinese-inspired hydrotherapy baths filled with ginger and ginseng are great for detoxifying and color baths to enliven the *chakras* are one of the spa industry's newer inventions.

In Bali at the Kirana Spa, you are encouraged to immerse yourself in their pools, so that your natural buoyancy loosens muscles and you become relaxed before a treatment. Kirana Spa water rituals include floating and hot and cold alternate bathing to balance nerves and refresh mind and body. At the Spa Village at Pangkor Laut Resort, the Malaysian tradition of the *mandi limau* where guests are purified with slices of lime and water has been resurrected. Try their Malay Bath Ritual made with aromatic oils, flowers and slices of lime placed in the bath water.

As water is an increasingly precious resource, new technologies for recycling, desalination and conservation are constantly being explored. Be sure to choose spas that use their water wisely.

VITALITY POOL

The vitality pool is a most invigorating way to begin your spa experience. Offered at Mandarin Oriental Spas at Landmark Hong Kong and Tokyo, guests lie on underwater loungers surrounded by water set at a temperature of about 35 degrees Celsius. All the while, jets massage the back, neck and shoulder area—preparing the body for the treatments to follow.

COLOR BATHS

An interesting addition to the Asian water experience is this colorful healing bath. Formulated from the premise that different colors have vibrations that influence mood, energy levels and even general health, they are a staple at CHI spas in Shangri-La hotels in Asia. As one sits meditatively in the bath, the color of the water alters from violet to indigo to blue, eventually covering each of the seven colors of the rainbow. In a similar vein, showers with multi-colored lights and massage jets are being developed for the ultimate shower experience.

VICHY SHOWER

It's definitely worth taking a Vichy shower at least once in your spa life, although the waste of water is a real concern and you should only experience it at a spa that recycles its water. Taking its name from the monastery town in France where people traveled to enjoy the natural spring waters, the Vichy shower is found in most luxury spas. In this treatment, the guest lies on a bed and fresh warm sea or mineral water cascades from jets positioned above on to the body below. The water stimulates the *chakra* points, revitalizing circulation and nurturing body and mind into bliss. You really feel a sense of renewal after a Vichy and many spas now offer scrubs and massages under the waterfall as well.

ICE FOUNTAIN

Easily one of the most rejuvenating water therapy delights on the Asian spa menu, the ice fountain is offered at a few select venues. Normally placed outside the steam and sauna areas, they have the same benefits as the icy cold plunge pool. Over-heated guests scoop ice from the fountain on to their skin to cool down the body, stimulate blood circulation and revitalize.

water therapies

WATSU

Increasingly common on spa menus across the globe, *watsu* is a type of water *shiatsu*. The body is swirled, waved, stretched and caressed through water by an experienced therapist. "Letting go" is the theme, with the womb-like nurturing qualities of water believed to encourage the recipient to return to his or her center.

According to practitioner, Frederik Vekeman, *watsu* usually starts and ends with the client against the wall of the pool. "This allows him to go into the three-dimensional world," he explains. "From there we bring the client into a horizontal body position and, once relaxed, the client is free to embark upon an inner journey." Vekeman says that some movements are for opening and lengthening the body and spine whilst others are for deepening and going inward. "*Watsu* is like a spiritual dance in water," he says. "After a few sessions when the client trusts themselves and the practitioner, they can go into a deepened trance-like state." Frederik also says that *watsu* practitioners often draw on Thai, Swedish and sports massage techniques as well as yoga and *tai chi* movements.

The type of *watsu* shown here is known as *wai ch'i* ("water energy") and was developed by Chang Wai Sing and Lee Wai Ching. The aim is for the client to return to the warmth, safety and genesis of consciousness in the womb, gently purifying the emotions and relaxing the body, ready for "rebirth" at the end of the session.

THALASSOTHERAPY

Thalassotherapy can be experienced at its optimum at the Ritz-Carlton Bali and at a handful of other resorts around the region. Deriving its name from the Greek (*thalasso*

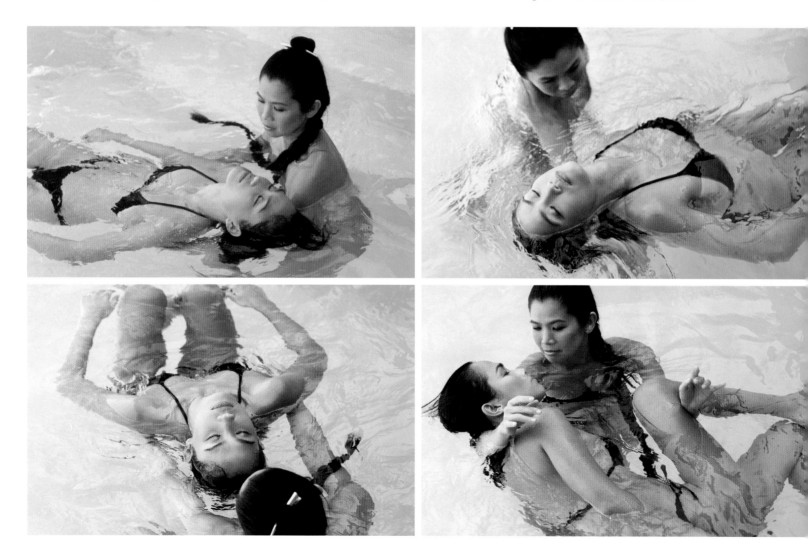

meaning "sea" and therapy meaning "care"), it is a holistic therapy that draws on sea water, sea grasses and the oceanic climate to heal and regenerate. For centuries, doctors prescribed trips to the seaside to recuperate after an illness, and even today, many believe that sea air and sea bathing can cure bone diseases, allergy problems, poor circulation, respiratory problems and various other ailments.

Authentic thalassotherapy spas are located no more than 800 meters (2,400 feet) from the seashore, so fresh seawater can be pumped into the complex. Seawater is the richest mineral water on earth. It is literally bursting with vitamins, minerals, plants and algae, containing as it does chlorine, sodium, magnesium, potassium, iodine, iron, fluorine, silver and brominates.

In a thalasso pool seawater is warmed to a certain temperature, so nutrients are quickly absorbed into the bloodstream. The salt-enriched waters are gentle on the body due to the body's buoyancy and there is little strain on muscles and joints. Many people use thalassotherapy to rehabilitate the body, as well as help with arthritis, hypertension, and respiratory and skin problems. It is also highly recommended for those suffering from insomnia or emotional imbalances.

In recent years we've seen a surge of sea-inspired water therapies in spas. There are sea-waterfalls, affusions and jet showers, open-air saltwater floatation pools, extra hot and cold plunge pools, and bubbling temperature pools for curative purposes. At home, you can rejuvenate and revitalize by recreating the *thalasso* experience with seaweed and marine-infused recipes for face and body. Combine them with some self-massage for maximum effect.

indian bathing

In India, ritual bathing is an act of purification—spiritually, mentally, emotionally and physically. Ayurvedic texts say that bathing improves sleep, appetite, sexual vigor, life span and enthusiasm. Ayurvedic clinician Reenita Malhotra Hora explains that warm water is believed to strengthen the body, while the face and head—the area that naturally releases heat—should be rinsed in cool water. The pre-bathing sequence of massage followed by prayers before a purifying bath is also an age-old custom.

PRANA CLEANSING BATH

Prana Spa in Bali offers a nourishing bathing ritual that involves the individual healing themselves through meditation whilst a Prana therapist gives a deep and nourishing Indian head massage with cooling coconut oil. Sometimes a facial cooler is also given during bathing time to keep the head area cool and refreshed.

We suggest recreating a similar bath at home using different ayurveda-inspired oil blends. Select base oils that are good for all *dosha* types, such as apricot kernel, hazelnut, jojoba, primrose or wheat germ oils. Use 1 to 2 tbsp of the base oil, and mix together with the ingredients below and right before combining with bath water and stirring vigorously. When relaxing in the bath, take cucumber slices from cold water kept in the freezer for 30 minutes, and place over eyes. Wring out excess water from a face cloth and place over the face after 5 minutes in the bath. Meditate, and focus on breathing. Relax.

Vata Bath

Too many late nights, unnecessary worry or fear can disrupt the balance of *vata*, resulting in feelings of anxiousness and dehydration. An essential oil blend that helps to wash away excess *vata* is 5 drops rosewood, 5 drops *jatamansi* (also called spikenard) and 5 drops yarrow essential oils. Or try 10–20 drops of citrus oils such as orange, lime, bergamot and lemon in sesame oil. Pour into the bath.

Pitta Bath

Feeling hot and bothered, angry, jealous or impatient can reveal an imbalance in *pitta*. Try a blend of 5 drops lavender, 5 drops sandalwood and 5 drops *champaka* essential oils to cool down. Or dilute up to 20 drops jasmine and chamomile essential oils in coconut or almond oil. Pour into the bath.

Kapha Bath

Lack of motivation, water retention, depression and sluggishness often indicates *kapha* is off center. A blend to help clear this and to return you to balance is 5 drops cypress, 5 drops juniper and 5 drops orange essential oils. Or try diluting 10 drops of eucalyptus, sage, peppermint or cedar wood essential oils with olive oil. Pour into the bath.

GODDESS OF MEDICINAL WATERS

Inspired by the Hindu Goddess of Medicinal Waters, this is the bath to take when you need to cleanse your mind and body of unresolved thoughts, emotions and memories and just be present. Epsom salts are known to detoxify and re-mineralize whilst white clay is selected for its cleansing and nourishing mineral properties. The combination of sandalwood and orange essences completes this splash, leaving you meditative in mind and composed in body. We also recommend this bath experience to help with dry skin and cellulite.

Ingredients:

- ½ cup (125 g) Epsom salts; ¼ cup (60 g) fine white clay; 1 tbsp sesame oil blended with 4 drops sandalwood and 4 drops orange essential oil.

Directions: Blend essential oils together with the sesame oil. Set aside. Pour the salts and clay into the bath to dissolve. Then add the oils. Relax in this re-mineralizing bath with the moisturizing benefits of the oils for 20 minutes.

AYURVEDIC CLEANSING RITUALS

In ayurvedic treatments, sesame, coconut and castor oils are the most popular oils. Castor oil is extremely moisturizing and lubricating as well as being rich in fatty acids to stimulate the lymphatic system; coconut oil is cooling for both emotions

indian bathing

and body; and sesame is an excellent anti-inflammatory and nourishing oil for rehydrating and protecting the skin's surface. Try either of these simple oily recipes to exfoliate, massage and cleanse prior to bathing.

Indian Summer

Devoted *yogi* practitioners in India often drink fresh coconut after their morning practice. Coconut is the ultimate ingredient for food and spa whenever you feel over-heated, hot or bothered.

Ingredients:

• ½ cup (125 ml) coconut oil.

Directions: Pour half of the oil into a warm bath. Take the other half and rub well into your entire body and leave on for 10 minutes to absorb before stepping into the bath. Relax for 15–20 minutes allowing the oil to warm and nourish your skin. Pat dry.

Indian Winter

A more warming oil, sesame has a deliciously nutty fragrance and is soothing in nature. It is used widely in *shirodhara* (see page 215).

Ingredients:

• ½ cup (125 ml) sesame oil.

Directions: As for previous recipe.

HINDU BATHING SEQUENCE

Recorded in ancient Hindu texts, this sequence is still practiced in India today. It outlines the order in which to bathe, and is believed to to purify and re-nourish the mind and body. Try it at home in the tub.

Majjana	Immerse your body in bathing water
Achamana	Rinse your mouth
Padya	Wash your feet
Abhisheka	Pour liquids such as yoghurt, honey and milk into the water
Kshala	Pour water over your body
Dhavala	Scrub and exfoliate your skin
Marjana	Dry the body

SPICY CHAI BATH

Cleopatra was not the only queen to bathe in milk, herbs and flowers for beauty and longevity. Royal queens and princesses from Indonesia to India also used milk baths in beauty rituals. In Mongolia, people bathed in mare's milk as it was regarded as a medicinal ingredient (in fact it contains loads of natural vitamins and antioxidants). Here, you can immerse in the signature tea of India: *chai* is full of heady spices that speed up circulation and warm the body on winter days and cool nights. The nutritious tea leaf adds antioxidant properties.

Ingredients:

• 2 cups (500 ml) fresh or 1 cup (100 g) dried milk; 1 tbsp honey; ¼ cup (25 g) oats; 1 tbsp cloves; 2 inch (5 cm) piece of ginger, chopped; 3 cinnamon quills, broken into small pieces; 1 tbsp cardamom pods; 1 tbsp black pepper; 1 drop each of ginger, nutmeg, clove, cardamom, cinnamon essential oils dispersed in 1 tbsp sesame or apricot kernel carrier oil; muslin cloth or stocking.

Directions: Fill the muslin cloth or stocking with oats and spices, and tie tightly. As you fill the bath with warm water, pour milk and honey under the running tap, adding the oil mix at the end. Immerse in your bath and give yourself a gentle exfoliation by rubbing the pouch over the skin. The oats will disintegrate and give off a milky liquid helping to soften skin. Soak for 20 minutes. Rinse under a coolish shower, make a cup of *chai* (tea) and rest.

REJUVENATING HIMALAYAN BATH RITUAL

According to Tibetan doctor, Dr Nida Chenagtsang, who trains practitioners in Tibetan bathing rituals, there are three styles of bath or *lum* therapy in Tibetan medicine. Water is known as *ciu lum*, vapor as *lhang lum* and the application of compresses as *jang lum*. This bath utilizes *ciu lum* practices, and is great for relaxation and personal reflection. Although best experienced at one of the Shangri-La CHI spas, try a simplified version of their

recipe in your home. We encourage you to take this after the Mountain Tsampa Scrub (see page 191) to complete the ritual. The pure essential oils, Indian herbs and salts cleanse and soften skin, promoting cell regeneration. The aromas from the water induce calmness of mind.

Ingredients:

- 2 tbsp Tibetan Plateau bath salts (substitute with Dead Sea salt if unavailable); 1 tbsp plain Indian salts; ½ cup (20 g) dried herbs such as nettle, ginger, neem, coriander and artemisia; 4 drops each of juniper, mandarin and grapefruit pure essential oils.

Directions: Fill the bath with hot water; add bath salts, herbs, and essential oils. Agitate the water to disperse the aroma and essential oils. Relax in the bath for 20 minutes. Pat dry the skin.

thai bathing rituals

The revitalizing waters surrounding Thailand and the Thais' relaxed approach to life make the country a restful retreat destination. Thailand is also home to some of southeast Asia's top spas, many of which utilize the country's plentiful water elements in enlivening bathing rituals. During the Thai New Year, a three-day festival, Thais pay homage to the cleansing and healing properties of water. It usually occurs in April, the hottest month in Thailand, and is a joyful occasion to celebrate the harvest.

SONGKRAN SCENTED BATH

This is an uplifting and inspirational bath to wash away the past and welcome the new. *Songkran* translates as "ever moving" and refers to the Thai new year celebrations when candles, incense, flowers, bottles of Thai scented water and three joss sticks are placed on the Buddha's altar. It is also the time when people take to the streets and drench each other in water! Our water fest uses citrus oils to move stagnated energy or emotions and lemongrass to cleanse.

Ingredients:
- 5 drops each of tangerine, grapefruit and lemongrass essential oils diluted in 1 tbsp sesame or coconut oil.

Directions: Decorate bathroom with candles. Pour blend into warmed bath water. Soak away the past year and plan for the new.

THAI DETOX WATER RITUAL

Inspired by Thai ingredients and practices, this one-and-a-half hour detox can be recreated in the quiet of your own home. Enriched with cleansing and nourishing ingredients, it includes a fatigue-relieving rub, a relaxing bath, a vitalizing scrub, shower and body moisturizer. Prepare your home first, so that an atmosphere of calm and quiet prevails.

Oil rub ingredients:
- 1–2 tbsp cold pressed oil such as grape seed, sesame or almond oil; 3 drops essential oils of *prai* or ginger, 2 drops bergamot and 1 drop lemongrass..

Bath ingredients:
- 1 cup (180 g) fresh ginger, grated; 1 cup (20 g) fresh jasmine flowers.

Scrub ingredients:
- 2 tbsp ginger powder; 2 tbsp Basmati rice, ground finely in a coffee grinder; 5 drops lemongrass essential oil; 1 tsp honey; 4 tbsp coconut milk.

Moisturizing ingredients:
- 1 tbsp cold pressed oil such as sesame, almond or olive; 1 tsp honey; 2 drops each bergamot, jasmine and *prai* or ginger essential oil.

Directions: Run a bath and add bath ingredients. Light an incense stick to cleanse the atmosphere, blend rub oils together, and massage all over your body with smooth strokes towards the heart together with kneading techniques to increase circulation. Soak in the bath for 20 minutes, celebrating the beautiful fragrance of jasmine. Mix the scrub ingredients together to make a creamy paste, then, starting with your upper body and using circular movements, rub in the paste. Work your way down to your feet. Rinse off in a cool shower to stimulate the circulatory system and to bring vitality to the skin. Towel dry. Mix all the moisturizing ingredients well to make a delicious body cream. Apply all over your body. Rest and drink a cup of ginger tea to complete your Thai ritual cleansing experience.

THAI SARONG BATH

Reflecting the Mandarin Oriental's belief that creating a sense of place is all part of the spa experience, this scented bathing ritual is inspired by the Songkran festival. Guests are clad in a traditional Thai sarong, then led to a secluded garden setting for what is aptly called the Thai Ceremony.

The first part includes a steam scented with cinnamon and the local *samoh* herb to improve blood circulation and relax the body. This is followed by a "flower shower" where the therapist pours scented floral water or *nam ob* all over you to cleanse and detoxify. It is an extremely refreshing and joyful experience.

If you opt to take the entire Royal Thai Ceremony, you also receive a royal Thai foot bath, a safflower scrub, a traditional *khraw kruea* wrap (*khraw kruea* is a local herb used for whitening and toning the skin) and a royal Thai massage. The whole ritual takes a little longer than two and a half hours, and you are guaranteed to emerge feeling revitalized and pampered. What could be a better start to the new year?

steam bath therapy

Regular sweat therapy is medicinally cleansing for mind and body. A good sweat opens the pores, releases stored toxins and clears the mind. The act of sweating flushes out impurities from the liver, kidney, stomach, muscles, brain and other organs and is one of the quickest ways to detoxify and bring our body back to equilibrium. Today, sweat therapies are fast making a comeback in our spa culture.

Opposite The bubbling jacuzzi at the Ritz-Carlton Bali Thalasso & Spa combines muscle toning, opening of the pores and steam therapy in one.

Below Flowers and herbs are often added to a steam room so that their fragrance soothes and restores. These white *cempaka* blooms from the magnolia family have an extremely strong scent —and are used in the steam room at Kirana Spa.

The writers of the ancient Vedic texts knew all about the benefits of sweat therapy. It was viewed as a medicine for the body. They noted that sweat rids the body of waste, regulates body temperature and keeps our largest organ (the skin) continually clean and refreshed. Even the ancient Romans used saunas and steams as part of their cleansing rituals. Other cultures that relied on sweat therapy were native Americans with their sacred sweat lodges, and the Nordics and Irish with their traditional sweat boxes. In Tibet, patients were enveloped in steam or vapor from a specially prepared bath to encourage a sweating reaction as a cure for various ailments. In Japan, steams and saunas were taken in natural steam caves.

Asian spa creators are looking back at these earlier practices, and recreating some of the ancient steam and water therapies in their modern-day spas. The Turkish *hamam*, dry sauna and *rasshoul* are currently experiencing a renaissance, but this time in an elegant and contemporary form. Another example is the Amethyst Crystal Steam Room at the Mandarin Oriental Spa in Landmark Hong Kong. Guests are encouraged to make use of this Zen-like chamber with its enormous amethyst crystal pre-treatment.

Today, the two major sweat therapies are sauna and steam, the former being partially dry, the latter moist and humid. Steam is condensed vapor formed by heating water, whereas a sauna works when water is poured on to hot stones raising the temperature level as much as 40 percent. They both work in the same way. When our body temperature rises, the pores open and toxins are drawn out through the sweat glands.

According to the creators of Six Senses Spas, the benefits of steam and sauna are numerous. They believe that integrating sauna and steam into your treatments brings about the following:

- increase and improvement of blood and lymphatic circulation
- warmed and relaxed muscles
- perspiration
- detoxification
- removal of dead skin cells
- improvement in the nutrient supply to the skin.

Combining sweat therapy with cool bathing is also considered beneficial to health and was embraced by many cultures. Today, some venues provide ice cold plunge pools to dip your body into after sweat bathing, whilst others recommend a tepid foot bath to slowly calm the body. Precautions vary according to doctors, but the general consensus is that people with heart conditions and high or low blood pressure should avoid sweat bathing —and should not participate in the hot-to-cold practices. It is also agreed that everyone should continually rehydrate with drinks and the application of cool towels.

THE SPIRIT OF SAUNA

A sauna is one of the best treatments at a spa and the good news is that it is normally complimentary! Whilst immersing yourself in such a hot temperature, your mind has the opportunity to rid itself of thoughts

and the body of toxins. In the past, many cultures developed their own version of the sauna, but it is believed that Finnish nomads in central Asia were the pioneers in bringing this form of healing to Europe. The Finnish *savusauna* was used frequently, not only to clean and refresh the body but as a rite of passage. Vapor in Finnish is *loyly* or "the spirit of life." The sauna attracted people because it was warm and clean, and it was often the place where surgery and childbirth took place.

The benefits of a sauna are many: a 15-minute sauna removes toxins from the body that normally takes the kidney 24 hours to excrete. It increases the body's metabolic rate and circulation, relaxes tired muscles, relieves fatigue and stress, provides temporary relief from arthritic pain, increases immune system function and improves skin complexion.

In Thailand, saunas are often filled with steamed fresh herbs such as lemongrass, lavender or chamomile. The natural fragrance that fills your lungs lasts even after you leave the sauna, gently easing mind and body. For the full relaxation effect, the temperature of a sauna should not be very hot (60–70 degrees Celsius is about right); this allows you to sit longer without strain.

To maximize the effect, follow these simple tips:

Before: To fully appreciate the thermal effect, enter the sauna with a dry body so that the skin can easily release toxins.

During: To warm your whole body evenly, balance the temperature of the air in the upper part and lower part of the sauna by swinging a towel around to circulate air. Fill a copper bowl with hot water and add freshly cut twigs of pine. Place bowl on top of rocks. Pine, known for its purifying properties, opens the sinus and breathing passages and removes lymphatic deposits from the body. It circulates a reviving aroma

steam bath therapy

throughout that uplifts mood. Five to 12 minutes is the most effective duration for a sauna.

After: Instead of taking an icy cold dip, doctors advise a lukewarm shower, just enough to cool down heated skin. Drink plenty of water to restore moisture in the body. For extra skin moisturizing, rub honey over your skin and sit in the sauna for a further 20 minutes.

STEAM DREAMS

Many spa treatments begin with a steam to cleanse both internally and externally. A steam room is usually a small room in which high temperature and high pressure generates steam. It is recommended that for a steam to properly cleanse, one stays in the steam room for between 10 to 15 minutes with the temperature of the body at around 38–39 degrees Celsius.

In Turkish *hamam* or bath houses, expect to find hot and cold plunge pools with day beds close by on which to recline and sip mint tea. Steam rooms here are often saturated with eucalyptus oil to help clear the lungs. For Turkish women, the *hamam* was (and still is) a haven for female socializing. Visits up to three times a day during wedding ceremonies are not uncommon.

Steams are a popular pastime in southeast Asia too. In the Buddhist country of Laos, where temples scatter the landscape in profusion and variety, traditional steam bathing is still practised. You can take a steam in a little wooden house on stilts adjacent the temple. Nuns collect local roots, barks, flowers and herbs like Kaffir lime, bergamot and orchid blooms and infuse them in a boiling cauldron in the hut. Sitting steaming in such a hut is a totally authentic experience! Locals use the steam bath as a social activity, as well as a remedy for such ailments as arthritis and respiratory conditions.

Spas today also infuse their steam rooms with herbs to give their guests a profound cleansing experience. At Prana Spa you are encouraged to take a 10– to 15–minute steam after the therapist smothers your body in natural volcanic mud from nearby Lombok island or marine mud from the ocean. In the steam rooms at Kirana Spa, *cempaka* and lemongrass are used and at Bagus Jati, therapists dilute *cajeput* essential oil in a bowl of water and place this in the steam room. *Cajeput* is known to be beneficial for respiration and is used with asthma patients. Another tradition here is to place dry cuttings of plants like *akar wangi*, pandan leaf, *cempaka*, jasmine, ylang ylang, ginger and sandalwood in a rattan basket over boiling water as a steam inhalation.

In ayurveda, heat is used to open the circulatory channels of the body both to release sweat and to allow medicated massage oils to be absorbed. Ayurvedic heat therapies include:

Bashpa sweda	steam bath containing herbs
Tapa sweda	exposure to dry heat near a fire, sunbathing in a sauna or sweat lodge
Upanaha sweda	poultices and hot compresses placed on specific areas
Nadi sweda	steam heat applied to specific parts of the body or joints through a heat resistant hose
Avagaha sweda	herbal bath
Drava sweda	bathing in hot herbal bath
Paga avagaha	hot herbal footbath
Hasta avagaha	hot herbal hand bath
Dhara sweda	sweat therapy by taking warm fluids
Anagni sweda	heat-producing compress made from mustard oil, tiger balm and ginger

In ayurvedic centers, the herbal steam bath derives from the word *bashpa* ("vapor") and *sweda* ("to sweat"). As part of the purgative *pancha karma* treatment, one sits or lies down in a type of handmade wooden box with only the head left exposed. Prior to this, cleansing herbs and oils such as ginger root, eucalyptus, bay leaf and other leaves are massaged with medicated oils into the skin. The idea is for you to sweat, so that the pores open and all the goodness from the medicated massage oils is absorbed into the skin and toxins are purged out of the body. It is believed that sweat clears the channels of the body where intellect flows and, by maintaining clarity in this area, the mind stays bright and healthy.

AROMATHERAPY HEALING STEAM

If you are feeling a little sluggish or off center, try any of these quick-fix aromatherapy-based facial steams. The essences here are selected specifically to have a therapeutic effect on the system. Steam cleansing the skin can be done daily and is great for city dwellers.

Ingredients:
- Bowl of boiling water; 3–6 drops of one of the essential oil blends below.
- For colds: 2 drops rosemary, 1 drop eucalyptus, 1 drop camphor essential oils.
- For flu: 1 drop thyme, 1 drop *cajeput* essential oils.
- For sinusitis: 1 drop each of angelica, eucalyptus, neroli, cypress and yarrow essential oils.
- For coughs: 1 drop each of hyssop, sage, anise and sandalwood essential oils.

Directions: Drop essential oils into the water and wrap towel around your head distancing yourself around 12 inches (30 cm) away from the bowl. Gently inhale and exhale, allowing the infusion to clear the sinus passages and gently open and cleanse the pores.

The steam room has come a long way thanks to the renaissance of the spa. This beautiful space at Bagus Jati Wellbeing Resort has a sweet picture window to the spa gardens outside.

We offer an at-home recipe using many of the same ingredients: lemongrass balances the nervous system; lime improves respiration and is recommended for throat and lung conditions; *bai nart* from the sage family soothes headaches; camphor is a natural cleanser and deodorizer that instantly clears the nose and sinus passageways; and eucalyptus is great for stimulating and clearing sinuses. The overall experience is excellent for relaxation, cleansing, detoxifying, better respiration and general wellbeing.

Ingredients:

- ¾ cup (70 g) fresh *prai* (or substitute with ginger); 5 stalks (10 g) lemongrass; rind of 3 wild limes (or limes or lemons), roughly grated; 1 tbsp *bai nart* (or substitute with dried sage); 1 block (2 g) camphor; 2 tbsp coconut oil; 10 drops eucalyptus essential oil.

Directions:

Step 1: Chop and smash fresh lemongrass stalks, put in a bowl and add the freshly grated lime rind, camphor block and sage leaves. Mix together, then pour into a filled bath.

Step 2: Add *prai* or ginger to coconut oil and apply the oil scrub on the skin, massaging while gently exfoliating. Spend a good 5 to 10 minutes massaging the skin while you inhale the fresh aroma from your bath.

Step 3: Before you step into your bath, add the eucalyptus essential oil. Soak in the bath for 15 minutes all the while continuing to massage your skin. Take full advantage of the fresh, reviving and cleansing aroma, by taking deep breaths, closing your eyes and letting the world drift away.

Step 4: After your bath, pat your body dry. This is a slightly stimulating and heating steam bath, so rest afterwards and drink plenty of room temperature water or herbal tea.

FRESH HERBAL STEAM VAPOR

As with many Eastern cultures, some of Vietnam's most precious treatments draw on centuries of knowledge passed down from generation to generation. Whilst spas are still in their infancy in Vietnam, the Six Senses Spa at the Ana Mandara Resort in beautiful Nha Trang is well worth a visit. It has harnessed many local Vietnamese traditions, including baths, footbaths and steam baths, into a variety of treatments.

The ingredients in the traditional steam here include lemongrass, grape, guava, eucalyptus and peppermint leaves, as well as mint, Indian borage and more. Together they all help to clear sinuses, stimulate the cardiovascular system, increase blood circulation and create supple muscles. It is reported that this treatment encourages a deep sense of relaxation in the body and mind and realigns as well as regulates breathing. If you can't travel to Vietnam, we've devised the following with the help of Six Senses' therapists, for your at-home spa. Take time to rest with a cup of mint tea afterwards.

Ingredients:

- 3 stems lemongrass, cut into 1 ½ inch (3 ½ cm) pieces; 20 eucalyptus leaves or 10 drops essential oil of eucalyptus; ⅓ cup (10 g) dried peppermint leaves; ⅓ cup (10 g) dried mint leaves; 12 cups; (3 l) boiling water; 2 drops each of myrrh, pine and cedar wood essential oils.

Directions: In a bowl, infuse the lemongrass and leaves in the boiling water, and just before inhalation, add essential oils. Sit down on a chair, lean your face over the bowl and put a blanket or towel on top of your head. Breathe in and out with deep breaths, all the while stirring the herbs with a chopstick or equivalent.

AROMATIC HERBAL STEAM BATH

This is a recommended treatment if you have been feeling stressed, haven't been breathing or sleeping properly and are generally a little fatigued. A traditional Thai recipe, it was originally available only in temples for visitors' use under the guidance of monks, but has now been preserved and adapted by Four Seasons Spa therapists.

balance

Over millennia, ayurvedic, traditional Chinese medicine (TCM), Tibetan and other Oriental doctors and healers have been gently encouraging their patients to return to balance. Most, if not all, Eastern spiritual and medicinal practices aim to restore imbalances in mind and body. Developed and practiced in temples and monasteries in the past, nowadays they are offered in studios, spas, wellness centers and retreat destinations. They can also easily be practiced at home.

Ancient texts from India, Indonesia, Thailand and elsewhere emphasize that true wellness in the body stems from a balanced mind. Learning to master balance is an empowering tool in today's world—and is something many of us strive for. Balance is when our mind and body align and we feel a sense of equilibrium flowing throughout. It is a place of personal retreat where we can gather inner strength and willpower to move forward.

Disciplines like Chinese and Japanese acupuncture, *tai chi*, *qi gong*, silat, yoga, dance and meditation are all balancing in their intention. Using breath, stretching, mind clearing techniques and more, they aim to enrich spiritually and emotionally, as well as physically. Many are offered in spas around the region. Particularly noteworthy are Sereno Spa at the Park Hyatt and Ananda in the Himalayas in India, and the Mandarin Oriental Dhara Deva Spa in northern Thailand. All have ayurvedic doctors on site, as do Chiva-Som and the Spa Village at Pangkor Laut Resort where ayurveda is integrated with Chinese disciplines. Six Senses Spas around the region are enthusiastic about *tai chi* and *qi gong*. Otherwise, be inspired to travel to one or more of the ayurvedic or yoga centers in India and Sri Lanka.

Increasingly, Western doctors and healers are spending time in the East training under Eastern masters to deepen their understanding of Asian modalities. The message is clear: don't leave your state of health last on the list. Put yourself first and live a life full of well-being—and encourage your friends to do the same. Your life force will increase, you'll learn to breathe correctly and become more aware.

Be inspired to dedicate time and energy to self and cultivate a regular practice at home. A 20-minute yoga stretch will do wonders for your energy levels and the same amount of time spent in meditation after work will bring you back to earth. Accept that quiet time is empowering as well—and use it to live in harmony with self and others.

Right Water *tai chi*, yoga, *pranyama* breathing and *tai chi* are just some of the wellness activities that are offered at Six Senses Spas.

the harmony of yin & yang

The underlying principle of traditional Chinese medicine (TCM) is to bring one's health into a state of pure and rewarding balance. TCM is now a recognized healthcare system in both the East and West, so TCM treatments, under the auspices of expert Chinese doctors, are increasingly being offered at spas. Indeed, China is becoming one of the world's most exciting new spa destinations, offering a variety of enlivening experiences. We give a brief outline of the philosophy of TCM —and tell you what you can expect in some of Asia's best spas.

According to the head physician of a TCM clinic called Sanctuary Your Health in Singapore, the underlying principles of TCM are derived from the ancient theory of *yin* and *yang*. This involves living in harmony with the universe as well as with one's fellow man.

Dr Liu Xing explains the theory of *yin* and *yang* as a kind of world outlook: "These two opposites are not stationary, but in constant motion," she says. "If we imagine the circadian rhythm, night is *yin* and day is *yang*; as night (*yin*) fades, it becomes day (*yang*) and as *yang* fades, it becomes *yin*. *Yin* and *yang* are therefore changing into each other as well as balancing each other.

"The theory holds that all things have two opposite aspects, *yin* and *yang*, which are both opposite and at the same time interdependent. This is the universal law of the material world. The ancient Chinese used water and fire to symbolize *yin* and *yang*; anything upward, moving, hot, bright and hyperactive is *yang*, and anything downward, quiescent, cold, dim and hypoactive is *yin*," Dr Liu Xing explains.

TCM is partly based on five elements that are said to reflect certain internal organs: wood (liver and gall bladder), fire (heart and small intestine), metal (lung and large intestine), earth (spleen and stomach) and water (kidney and urinary bladder). They are interconnected—for example, water can nourish and help a tree grow just as the kidney has a direct effect on the liver. Each organ has an element of *yin* and *yang* within it. The histological structures and nutrients are *yin*, and the functions are *yang*. Some organs, such as the *wei* (stomach) and *gan* (liver), are predominantly *yang* in their functions; while others, such as the *shen* or the kidney, are predominantly *yin*.

In TCM, diagnosis revolves around discovering what is out of balance or how the *yin* and *yang*, or heat and cool, are out of sync. Chronic *yin* or *yang* insufficiency or excess can take up to six months to set right. Causes of imbalance include genes, travel, lifestyle, diet and general habits. "However, being out of balance does not mean you are not healthy," cautions Dr Liu Xing. "In fact, *yin* and *yang* are continually moving in and out of balance. On its simplest level, a cooling tea will help if your body is too *yang* or you may need to take some medicines to bring down your *yin* if it is too high."

BALANCING YOUR CH'I

All TCM treatments encourage the flow of *ch'i* throughout the body to improve organ function and circulation of blood. Also known as *ki* (in Japanese) or "life force", our *ch'i* is what gives us strength, energy and balance of mind. Dr Li Hongke, the TCM doctor at the Spa Village at Pangkor Laut Resort, explains that healthy blood circulation means healthy *ch'i*. "If people are highly active they have lots of *ch'i* and if they exercise less then their *ch'i* is low," he says. Good quality blood produces good quality *ch'i* and vice versa.

Overall, when our *ch'i* is healthy, we are filled with quiet inspiration. It helps us in our work, business and relationships. Herbs like ginseng are taken to promote *ch'i* in the meridians and organs and Chinese licorice is believed to promote *ch'i* in the blood. On another level, exercises like *tai chi* and *qi gong* are thought to keep *ch'i* flowing well when they are practiced regularly. Increasingly we are seeing these disciplines alongside yoga and meditation sessions at many holistic and destination spas.

In addition to these straightforward treatments, there is a fast growing trend at high-tech spas to develop new treatments that incorporate elements of TCM. Chiva-Som in Thailand has an extensive range that includes EQ4 Meridian Testing to measure one's energy, detect food and other allergies —and offer remedies. At Simply Spa in Singapore the Wuxing Diagnostic Facial is

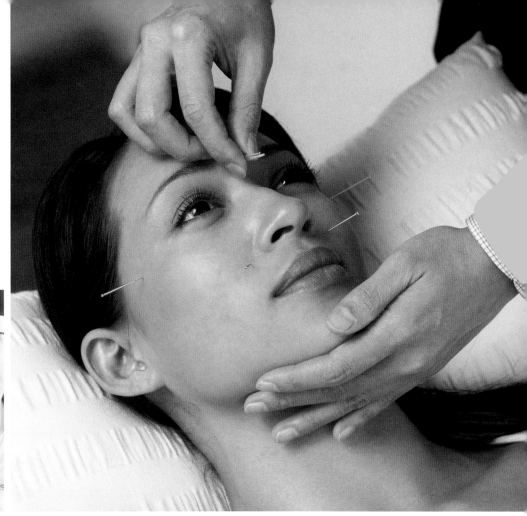

Right Facial Acupuncture is one of the most effective holistic facial rejuvenation therapies.

Below Acupuncture can be used to treat many health conditions but works best as a preventative medicine.

Bottom Moxibustion is still fairly new to spas outside of China but with traditional Chinese medicine becoming more widespread, this is set to change. At the Spa Village in Pangkor Laut, the doctor applies a lighted herbal stick upon specific acupoints as a way of increasing *ch'i* flow.

based on the Oriental art of physiognomy. A clay-based facial treatment, it accurately reveals imbalances in specific organs from signs on the exterior visage.

ACUPUNCTURE

If you're a newcomer to TCM, don't miss an opportunity to take this treatment. Believed to have developed over 2,000 years ago in China, its original roots were in India. It is believed to be a derivation of ayurvedic *marma* point massage, with the needles being inserted at the points where the pressure massage used to be given. The needles act like antennae either to bring more universal energy into the body to warm or uplift, or to release excess energy to cool or calm. Over time acupuncture has evolved to become a most respected therapeutic treatment for rebalancing.

The technique involves inserting fine needles into certain acupuncture points along the meridian lines. It is practiced to stimulate energy flow on a mental, physical and spiritual level. Once the acupuncture vessels open, *ch'i* within the body moves more freely and thereby unblocks any stagnation stored in the mind or body.

Acupuncture has been likened to a regulator that reflects the workings of *yin* and *yang* perfectly. It increases whatever is deficient in the body and reduces what

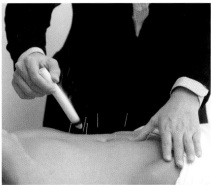

is excessive. It helps warm what is cool and cool what is hot.

There are reportedly over 356 acupuncture points, although new acupoints are being discovered all the time. Most practitioners generally work with around 100. Each session is highly individual as different combinations of acupoints affect the body differently.

Although used in China mainly for acute pain relief, in the West it has been embraced for a number of ailments. It is believed to help ease stress, and treat addiction, depression and insomnia, to name but a few. Regular recipients have no doubt that it calms and stimulates the nervous system, and has an overall effect on emotional stability.

To train to be an acupuncturist in China takes a minimum of six years. Other schools also conduct training programs elsewhere.

TAI CHI

The introduction of *tai ch'i chuan* (known as *tai chi* for short) into destination spas and retreats is yet another stunning demonstration of how the world is turning inward to find balance. *Tai chi* looks and feels like a graceful blend of moving yoga, meditation and martial arts. With its origins in ancient China, the Chinese characters translate as "Supreme Ultimate Force." The movements in this discipline help practitioners to learn balance, yield and force—or *yin* and *yang*.

Practitioner Derrick Gooch says: "*Tai chi* is thought to have been developed by a Taoist monk in the 12th century. It is an exercise that, when practiced correctly, strengthens our deep inner muscles and joints and benefits us all over." By repeating certain set movements at a slow pace, he says *tai chi* improves health in mind and body.

A *tai chi* teacher instructs students about control through push and pull exercises, rhythm, alignment, balance and poise. Health-wise, the focus is on vitalizing *ch'i* throughout the body which in turn energizes the nervous and vascular system resulting in overall mind/body balance. Some of the benefits include better balance which results in fewer falls, body awareness resulting in correct posture,

prevention of osteoporosis, increase in lung capacity and improved blood circulation, reduction of stress and improvement of heart rate, not to mention calming of the mind and increase in clarity and focus.

If you are interested in combining a visit to a destination spa with a course in *tai chi*, you would do well to visit the Spa Village at Pangkor Laut Resort. There, a traditional Chinese medicine doctor diagnoses guests and executes treatments — and teaches *tai chi* in the mornings.

QI GONG

According to ancient Chinese philosophy, *ch'i* or *qi* is the life energy that flows throughout the universe like an ancient river. It is regarded as a vital force that exists in every living thing, be it plant, animal or mineral. *Gong* translates as "work"—so the practice of *qi gong* is simply "working with *qi*."

Many different forms of *qi gong* have developed over time. Each stems from a different region and/or teacher, but the intention is the same. It is the flow of the *qi* in the body that determines how the exercises are performed and when the *qi* is fully charged, the exercises look and feel like a slow, graceful and powerful dance. Breathing is full, posture is composed and relaxation flows throughout the mind and body.

Through the practice of *qi gong* exercises, one is encouraged to fully charge the body and increase the reservoir of this healing energy. *Qi gong* increases vitality held in the body and therefore improves its ability to fight off disease and infection. Through various practices, exercises and movements, *qi gong* clears and enlivens the body and mind — and ultimately allows one personal mastery over one's life on earth.

MOXIBUSTION

Centuries-old texts from Tibet, China and India contain writings about healing where heat is applied to the body to stimulate the flow of *ch'i*. Originally performed with heated rocks, *moxa* wool made from artemisia, herbal packs or tree barks placed on acupuncture points, nowadays moxibustion is delivered with herb-saturated burning cones applied to different points on the body. It is most often prescribed to patients suffering excessive cool or dampness, fatigue and muscle and joint stiffness. Its purpose is to kickstart the flow of *ch'i* and increase the body's temperature.

As we know, many treatments across Asia were introduced into other cultures by early traders. At The Farm at San Benito in the Philippines, the *Moxa Ventoza* treatment is derived from ancient Chinese moxibustion and elements of *Yunani-Tibb* medicine (Greek-Persian medicine). Now practiced by Filipino traditional healers, it involves the application of warmed heat-resistent glasses upon the meridians on the upper and lower extremities of the back. They create a vacuum, thereby drawing out toxins and excess cold energy from the body.

Moxibustion may be recommended by a TCM physician as part of an acupuncture session. If this is the case, the *moxa* cones are attached to the end of inserted needles to further heat energy points.

CUPPING

Most acupuncture devotees will have experienced cupping from time to time, although it is not offered on many Asian spa menus —yet. Recommended for those in need of detoxification, it has been practiced in China, and reportedly even in Arabia, for centuries.

Opposite The beach at the Six Senses Spa at the Evason Hua Hin Resort is the perfect location to practice some of Asia's healing arts.

Below Cupping is a TCM treatment that uses heat to heal. It is on the menu at the Pangkor Laut Spa Village, Chiva-Som International Health Resort and selected Six Senses Spas to name but a few. At the Salus Per Aqua Spa at The Farm at San Benito in the Philippines, a unique version called the *Moxa Ventoza* is offered.

Originally it was performed with animal horns, but today the most common forms are with two types of jar made from either glass or bamboo. The Chinese name is *ba guan*, with *ba* translating as "pull" and *guan* as "container", thereby literally meaning "to pull (skin) with a container."

The purpose of cupping is to remove heat and wind in the body and encourage *ch'i* flow in the bloodstream and meridian system. By attaching the jars, with burning herbs within them, to the skin's surface, heat encourages flow of *ch'i*. The jars create a vacuum, thereby dispelling dampness and wind and offering relief from pain and respiratory problems. People suffering from lower back pain, sciatica, and muscular pain benefit enormously from cupping. It is also used to treat insomnia, headache and migraine, but is not recommended if you are pregnant, have a heart condition or suffer from heat sensitivity.

GU FANG XUN SHEN

Ancient Body Smoking is an old Chinese cultural practice that was often given in conjunction with a TCM treatment. As TCM modernized, it fell into disuse, as it was not considered "scientific." However, it has recently been rejuvenated at the

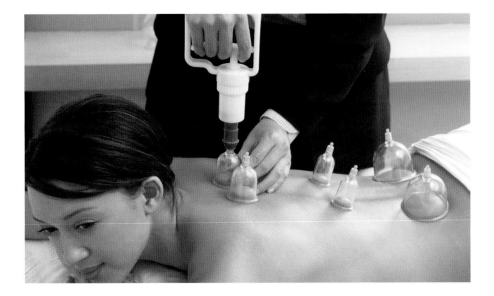

Pangkor Laut Spa Village and is offered to guests prior to a TCM therapy. The resort's traditional Chinese medicine consultant, Lee Jok Keng, feels that traditional healing should not be disregarded as many such practices have the ability to heal and have important cultural significance.

The purpose of the half-hour ritual is to expel negative energy that has built up in the body. This includes stress, worry and

excess heat. As you sit on a small stool with your eyes closed, the therapist heats a variety of cleansing herbs, primarily acorus root and mugwort, in a claypot on a charcoal burner. The smoke from this is then captured and swept over and around the body. All the while, the therapist recites ancient healing phrases.

The phrases:
"I honor the Eastern direction, the source of vitality." "I honor the Southern direction, the passion of life's manifestation." "I honor the Western direction, the keeper of silence." "I honor the Northern direction, the protector of the deep." "And finally, I honor your Being, the source of Creativity." "Through this clean body all goodness comes."

The significance of the phrases:
East = Wood (sprouting plant): beginning of rising energy. *South* = Fire: spark of life. *West* = Metal (deep inside but quiet): humility, precious but unknown to many. *North* = Water (sea): the deep sea upholds the land. *Center* = Earth: one's Being, one's ability to sense a higher force.

White Crane Silat is an Indonesian martial art and health system with its roots in the practices of ancient Chinese Shaolin monasteries. A well-balanced combination of movement forms, breathing practices and energy techniques, it is a synthesis of powerful martial movements and graceful ritual dance. It is effective for fitness, personal development and self-defense.

White Crane Silat teachers believe that there is a damaging conflict between a human being's natural need for balance, stability and rest and today's unnatural lifestyles. Many people are caught in cycles of pushing themselves too hard and then becoming drained. This lack of self-management and the resulting stress are a major cause of chronic tension, anxiety and illness. White Crane Silat techniques help people to break these cycles and return to being centered, grounded and at peace in the midst of daily activity. The major aim is to help cultivate balance.

WHITE CRANE SILAT FORMS

The White Crane Silat curriculum is vast. It comprises hundreds of forms including fitness exercises, short and long movements, specialized health and healing movements, and breathing and energy cultivation techniques. Partner interaction practices reveal the nature of active and passive (*yin/yang*) balance, while the self-defense training includes throwing techniques and free-form sparring.

This wide range of practices enables practitioners to utilize a variety of techniques to create a personal program that is realistic and effective. Both gentle, relaxing movements and vigorous, dynamic *kung fu* style forms develop flexibility, circulation and strength, promoting balance and vitality. Breathing techniques encourage relaxation, increase awareness and enhance energy.

Right top Movement series have evocative names such as "Sky, Earth and I are One."

Right below Interactive partner "feeling" movements combine gestures of assertiveness and receptivity to develop sensitivity to one's own and others' energetic expression. Here, a teacher instructs on correct palm positions.

Opposite top Movements like this one develop clear, confident and appropriate physical, mental and energetic expression.

Opposite middle White Crane Silat movements symbolize many principles including balance, flexibility, precision, gracefulness, tranquility and the integration of spirit and body.

Opposite bottom Embodying the principles of *yang* and *yin*, the Sky and Earth Breathing movement enables the absorption, circulation and return of energy.

MOVEMENT AS METAPHOR

White Crane Silat movements work with the "body-mind" in an integrated manner. A person's mental attention and energy and psychological-emotional dynamics are just as important as physical aspects. Key to this training is an emphasis on personal insight, self-management and transcending old lifestyle patterns.

The movements are used as metaphorical mirrors, exposing conditioned attitudes and personality patterns. The same movements can provide the medium for experimenting with alternatives. This provides practical experience, multi-dimensional feedback and a means for change.

For example, one can train with powerful and assertive gestures while also practicing sensitivity, moderation and containment. Developing openness and receptivity can be combined with maintaining proper boundaries. Such diversity encourages new forms of attunement, self-expression and a fuller realization of potential. This, in turn, enables one to live in the world with more confidence, acceptance, adaptability and peace. Such qualities can be crucial for personal health, harmonious relationships and more effective work practices.

LIVING THE MARTIAL ARTS WAY

The essence of a self-defense martial art is to know and master oneself. It enables one to learn to defend against one's own violence, thus recognizing and transforming conflict and self-destructive patterns in one's own

being. White Crane Silat training helps an individual recognize negative and destructive habits as the primary "opponent" in one's life. Balancing these patterns with positive alternatives is the personal practice of a martial artist. It is then possible for anyone to integrate such a practice into their life. This opportunity can be life transforming.

The White Crane Silat combination of awareness, empowerment and expanded self-expression fosters holistic balance and personal transformation. Like other Asian disciplines, it is a deep practice filled with wisdom and beauty that can improve mental and physical health, increase holistic wellbeing and foster fulfillment.

yoga

Yoga is one of the fastest growing health practices in the world and is often offered in Asian spas. The postures, meditation, breathing and relaxation techniques bring about a deep sense of inner peace. Practising yoga before a spa treatment relaxes the body and thereby enhances the healing experience.

Ashtanga. Viniyoga. Iyengar. Vinyasa. Tibetan yoga. Ki yoga. Sivanada and Kudalini yoga . . . the list of Hatha yoga styles continues to evolve as we do. With so many different styles to explore, it's reassuring to know that the basic aim of yoga—the union of body, mind, breath and spirit—has remained unchanged for over 5,000 years.

"The ultimate goal of yoga is to experience union and a sense of oneness with the self and all that is," says yoga instructor Jessie Chapman, who demonstrates the yoga postures on these pages. "Yoga gives us the tools to live a life rich with awareness, self-love and compassion. The various techniques and disciplines of yoga, its physical postures, regulated breathing techniques and meditation cultivate balance, strength, flexibility and presence on all levels of life. Physiologically we gain good health; mentally we find a balance between relaxation and action; emotionally we rest between life's highs and lows; and spiritually we get to know ourselves and experience inner peace."

A yoga practice does not need to be a structured one- or two-hour class. Rather, it is most beneficial when practiced with intention. Yoga cultivates the understand-

ing of quality as opposed to quantity. A balanced practice may be lying with the legs up the wall to rest after a stressful day, or some dynamic postures to motivate and inspire when feeling dull and lethargic.

Yoga postures were originally designed to help maintain a healthy body, mind and spirit. As we develop a deeper understanding of yoga and its effects on our physical and mental states, we can apply yoga postures, breathing techniques, meditation and other practices to heal ourselves as needed. Key to the practice of yoga is learning to breathe correctly. As we breathe more fully we increase oxygen supply to every cell and every part of our body.

Yoga is also a powerful anti-aging tool. The upside down postures stimulate circulation to the whole body, especially the brain, promoting a healthy body, a clear mind and toned glowing skin; the backward bending postures keep the spine young and supple and release built-up tension; the twisting postures massage deep into the internal and abdominal organs, cleansing and energizing; the forward bending postures calm the nervous system and help release stress; the standing postures give strength and stability; and *pranayama* or yoga's breathing techniques, brings fresh oxygen and life-force energy throughout our whole being.

Yoga helps to develop awareness. It promotes a deeper understanding of the self and of life itself, enabling practitioners to live a life of purpose. With increased awareness comes more energy, and actions and words also become more meaningful, as well as more powerful. Through yoga practice one learns that it does not matter what we do, but how well we do it.

If you're new to yoga, seek instruction from a qualified yoga teacher before practicing any of the postures on these pages. Do only what feels right for you and enjoy the benefits yoga brings.

YOGA IN THE ASIAN SPA
Many destination, resort and hotel spas offer yoga. The ayurvedic spas and centers dotted around India and Sri Lanka often include yoga in their detoxification and rejuvenation packages. Here one will get a taste of yoga at its best. Not only are classes delivered by expert masters, but they focus on breathing properly and cultivating the art of stillness. There is definitely a magic in experiencing yoga in these situations— but there are many other options too.

Today, most four- and five-star hotels offer yoga in extraordinary locations. Think of a traditional wooden yoga pavilion positioned elegantly overlooking the ocean or in a bamboo jungle in the rainforest, and be inspired to stretch your body to its full potential. Alila Ubud is home to a stunning open-aired yoga pavilion that looks out over emerald-colored rice fields, and at the Amanspa in Amanpuri in Phuket, yoga is practised in a generous sized wooden *sala* with glimpses of the surrounding forest and ocean. Naturally, at Six Senses Spas

where the focus is on the holistic, yoga is offered in a variety of forms.

Nowadays, yoga retreats at spas are incredibly popular. Como Shambhala Retreats in Bali, Bhutan, Bangkok and the Maldives are some of the region's most alluring. Como's Uma Ubud in Bali boasts one of the best yoga spaces on the island with yoga teachers and visiting masters to match. Nearby is the Como Shambhala Estate at Begawan Giri: it offers high quality yoga retreats complemented by visiting ayurvedic and naturopathic doctors and resident physiotherapists. All of the Como properties ensure that the whole experience is very "yogi-like" with fresh organic food and a spa menu of detoxifying and de-stressing therapies.

Alternatively, why not travel to Ananda in the Himalayas, close to the source of yoga's origination? The spiritual city of Rishikesh is blessed with some of the best yoga schools in the world, so expect nothing less from the teachers at the Ananda. Practicing yoga whilst overlooking this ancient city and the holy River Ganges is truly memorable.

So dedicated to wellness are the creators of the spa at the Landmark Mandarin Oriental in Hong Kong that they have employed highly qualified masters in the fields of yoga and Pilates to train and educate guests in this practice. Group Director of Spa, Ingo Schweder, believes his guests deserve nothing less. At most Mandarin Oriental Spas, the menu features a fabulous selection of yoga classes, with many offering classes twice daily. What's new is that they are now creating yoga platforms within some of their best accommodations, so guests can practice in the privacy of their own suites. Como hotels also have yoga mats in all their rooms.

YOGA AS TREATMENTS

It is interesting to see a new trend emerging: that of including yoga as part of an actual spa treatment. A yoga session is inserted into a two- to four-hour journey that may include a massage, a scrub, a steam and a bath. A fine example is the Shanti Shanti treatment at Four Seasons Spa in Langkawi, Malaysia. Here, a yoga session is integrated with *shirodhara*, an Indian herbal oil massage and a reiki session, with a traditional Indian *chai* as the finale. At the Per Aquum Spa at Huvafen Fushi in the Maldives, the Quintessential Aquum treatment starts with an hour of yoga and meditation followed by an Indian head massage and Thai and Maldivian massage. This is all conducted in an underwater room with views of marine life floating by.

Health-wise, it makes perfect sense to take deep full breathes and stretch your body prior to a massage or other spa treatment. Deep full breathing calms the nervous system, relaxes the body and returns one to equilibrium. It sets one up for the benefits to come.

Above, left to right These postures may be done separately or as a sequence to bring you back to balance: *supta virasana* or reclined hero pose; *supta baddha konasana* or reclined bound ankle pose; supported *urdhva dhanurasana* variation, a supported back bend; forward *konasana*; *kurmasana* variation; and *siddhasana* meditation, to finish.

Opposite *Kapotasana*, from the Sanskrit word for pigeon (*kapota*) is an advanced posture. Practice it visually, if you are not up to it physically!

Below, clockwise from top left *Ardha Matsyendrasana* (*Matsyendra* means "lord of the fishes"); *urdhava dhanurasana*, a full back bend; *ustrasana*, camel pose; *halasana* or plough pose.

meditation

Stillness. Mindfulness. Presence. With the words "meditation" and "medicine" deriving from the same root, it makes perfect sense that many Asian spas are beginning to offer this ancient Eastern practice. Whilst medicine heals the physical body, meditation focuses on spiritual healing. Naturally, the two are intertwined.

From a health perspective, meditation has been shown to reduce blood pressure, calm the nervous system and increase alpha wave patterns in the brain. Recent studies suggest that it dramatically improves the immune system by reducing anxiety, worry and stress. It is believed that regular meditation produces an increased number of antibodies and improves brain function as well. In the corporate world, meditation sessions are used as antidotes for stress, and meditation retreats for staff are gaining popularity.

Meditation can be described as an inward pilgrimage—a search inside to uncover the mysteries of life including one's own destiny. Regular meditation encourages us to find our own way and not to be influenced by what others consider right or wrong. It is the experience of breath, mind and body becoming one.

There are hundreds of varying styles of meditation. For some, meditation is sitting cross-legged in silence listening to the breath or focusing on the third eye and repeating a mantra over and over. Others, who like a bit more fire in their belly, use dance or Chinese disciplines like *qi gong* to bring them into presence. In Chinese Taoist lore, meditation is simply "sitting still, doing nothing." Then there are concentrating meditations where one focuses on breath, a point of reference like a candle or the ocean's waves. Mindful walking, chanting and yoga all integrate elements of meditation. In Japan, martial arts and the tea ceremony are considered meditative as they train the mind to be observant. Just being present in daily life is also considered an act of meditation.

Many resort and destination spas, realizing that treatments alone are not always sufficient, offer meditation classes to complement a retreat experience. Kirana Spa has an astounding environment in which to practice meditation: here you are invited to take time out pre- and post-treatment to experience the beauty of stillness.

In ayurvedic destinations across India and Sri Lanka, meditation classes are very much a part of the treatment journey. Ayurvedic doctors study meditation as part of their medical degree and are often meditation teachers too. Some of the notable spas in Kerala in India that offer meditation include the Jiva Spa and Taamra Spa at Taj hotels, as well as Coconut Lagoon and Somatheeram Ayurvedic Beach Resort.

Right In spas like Kirana Spa in Bali, the atmosphere is so still and rich it oftens feels as if every moment is a meditation. Here a guest takes some quiet time to appreciate stillness in the Zen Garden there.

At Ananda in the Himalayas, spiritual healers give discourses or *darshan* on meditation and spirituality in a memorable yoga pavilion overlooking the Himalayas. The therapists at Chiva-Som in Thailand have created an entire menu of Inner Peace therapies that are based on the traditional Vipassana/Anapanasati style of meditation. Another form, called Samadhi relaxation, is also offered. Based on traditional *yoga nidra* meditation, its aim is to encourage the nervous and endocrine systems to slow down and the body to really relax.

The breathtaking environments of many Aisan spas are highly conducive to quiet meditation. It's not that difficult to appreciate the present moment whilst overlooking gorgeous waterfall, jungle and ocean vistas!

BUDDHIST MEDITATION

Buddhist temples abound in Asia, and many monasteries offer meditation studies and courses. In Buddhist philosophy, "stillness" or "an empty mind" does not refer to stagnation. It more aptly describes the ability to remain calm and observe whilst clearing a busy mind of perceptions, emotions and judgments. In Thailand, a culture founded on strong Buddhist principles, there are many places to study this ancient art of stillness. In Japan, where the translation for meditation is Zen, meditation is considered "the study of the self."

TIBETAN MEDITATION

In Tibet, meditation is often practiced with prayer wheels, incense, chanting and prayer flags as well as through traditional Tibetan medicine. According to Ian Baker, who has written several books on Tibetan Buddhism, Tibetan forms of meditation typically begin with the recitation of sacred mantras while visualizing oneself as a Tantric deity. Ordinary thoughts are transformed into heightened consciousness and intention, with the aim being to connect both to one's self and the Buddha.

SOUND MEDITATION

Some meditation practices concentrate on sound as a method of clearing the mind. Sound is also believed to help restore, calm and equalize blood pressure. Tibetan "singing bowls," whereby the edge of a brass bowl is caressed to produce a melodious tone, are used in some rituals. This sound is believed to reflect the sound of the universe, so a sense of deep calm is induced throughout the body. Chanting is another form of sound meditation, and, at the end of a yoga practice, the singing of three deep *oms* is believed to give one the experience of being at one with the universe.

MEDITATION AT HOME

At home, be encouraged to take a few moments each day to learn the art of meditation. First, sit cross-legged or with your legs bent beneath you, straighten your back and close your eyes. Exhale slowly until the air in your body is completely let out. Next, take a breath deep into your stomach until it is filled fully and hold the breath for a few seconds. Then exhale two times more slowly than the inhalation. Repeat this breathing procedure five times, concentrating mostly on your exhalation. Observe over time and with regular practice, how your emotions seem calmer and your body more relaxed.

Author's acknowledgments

The author, Judy Chapman, would like to thank the staff and owners of Asia's spa industry—a global family whose distinctive spa sanctuaries are helping to transform the minds, bodies and souls of our time. It's an honor to be connected to you. It's a privilege to express your beautiful work to the world. I especially want to thank the publisher, Eric Oey for giving me this amazing opportunity to write this book and for his ongoing patience, integrity and support; Kim Inglis for her editing; Lora Krulak for styling many of the photos; Uab for make-up; the faces that grace these pages especially Joy, Tui and Melati; and the therapists, doctors and healers of Asia—the real essence of the ultimate spa experience.

Sincere gratitude to the following contributors: Carroll Dunham for the Himalayan recipes (www.wildearthnepal.com); Puan Sairani Mohd Sa'ad, Datin Sharifah Anisah and Chik Lai Ping for the Malay recipes; Adria Lake for her recipe contributions (www.awlakeonline.com); Dr Rajeev Mawaha and Dr Suchada Marwah for their contribution to ayurveda; Ian Baker, who was our Tibetan medical consultant (www.kamalaya.com); Lee Jok Keng, our TCM technical consultant; Dr Jaime Z. Galvez Tan MD, MPH, our Philippine healing medicine contributor; Jessie Chapman, for being our yoga contributor and model (www.radianceretreats.com); Lee Wai Ching for being our *watsu* adviser and model; Kent Watters, Susan Roziadi and Sendika, our Silat team; Derrik Gooch for his Tibetan reiki expertise; Anjali Nihalchand and Rosalind Freeman-Attwood from Aman Resorts; Shizuko Takayama of the Spa at Four Seasons Resorts & Spas; Kimberly Collier, Founder and CEO of Jamu Asian Spa Rituals (www.jamuspa.com); Praitma Raichur, ayurvedic beauty guru (www.pratimaskincare.com); Dr Reenita Malhotra, ayurveda clinician and creator of Ayoma (www.ayoma.com); and Mary Elizabeth Wakefield (www.chiakra.com)

A special credit must be given to our treatment editor Miriam Van Doorn. Her contribution in creating the recipes are a tribute to her knowledge. Miriam has been involved in the beauty, spa and wellness industry since 1988. She is responsible for creating one of Australia's first spas The Dome Retreat, as well as the spa at Ananda in the Himalayasand Spa Botanica in Singapore. She also held the prestigious position of Spa Manager for The Source at Begawan Giri in Bali. She is a qualified yoga teacher, wellness writer and runs her own holistic spa consultancy company, Babylon Enterprises (miriam@babylon-enterprises.com).

BALI Diah Permana from Bagus Jati-Health and Wellbeing Retreat; Tatsuki Nagao and Kadek Sumerjaya from Kirana Spa; Dr Martha Tilaar and Nuning S Barwa at Martha Tilaar Eastern Rejuvenating Center; Jeff Mathews, Trent Munday and Donna Wells at Mandara Spa at Alila Ubud; Jim Elliott and team at Prana Spa at The Villas; Michi Sonoda and Paul Czuba from The Ritz-Carlton, Bali Resort and Spa; John O' Sullivan and Putu Indrawati Yena Feliana from Four Seasons Resort Bali at Sayan and Jimbaran Bay; David Haughton and Feny Sri Sulistiawati from Jamu Jamu Traditional Eastern Spa Rituals (jamujamu@indosat.net.id). Also many thanks to John and Cynthia Hardy and Ardani from John Hardy Designs; Bee Hardy; Paul Ropp; Biasam, Bali; Selini Store in Bali; Asia Style, Bali; Victorias in Bali; and Jari Menari, Bali whose work added stylish elements to our photographs.

CHINA Mr Ho Kwon Ping, Ms Claire Chiang, Simone Chen, Mr Ravi Chandran and Ms Jeannie Sng from The Banyan Tree Hotels & Resorts.

INDIA Colin Hall and Dr Dinesh Thampi from Ananda in the Himalayas; Vrushali Londhe and Dr Sanjay Khanzode from Park Hyatt Goa Resort and Spa.

MALAYSIA Dr Li Hongke, Dr Chriamel Devassy Siby, Enola Kaneta, Sylvia Sepielli, Uzma Nawawi and Baldip Singh from The Spa Village at Pangkor Laut Resort; Luisa Anderson, Director of the spa at Four Seasons Resort Langkawi. You are all true spa beings.

MALDIVES Jane Quinn, Claire Branch and the team from Per Aquum Spa & Resorts (one of the most beautiful places on earth); Robert van der Maas and Juliana Ang the PR director from Four Seasons Resort Maldives.

NEPAL Sherba Barma and Tenzin Namdul.

PHILIPPINES Dr Eckard Remp and Jennifer Sanvictores at Salus Per Aqua Spa at The Farm at San Benito.

SINGAPORE Doris Sinnathurai and Lim Ee Jin from RafflesAmrita Spa; Dr Li Xing of Sanctuary Your Health; Sheila McCan of Spa Botanica; Sabrina Franzheim of Beach Lounge Spa, Singapore (www.beachloungespa.com); Arthur Lawrence, cosmetic chemist (www.arthurlawrence.com); Terry Liew, principal of The Shiatsu School, Singapore (www.shiatsuchool.com); Belinda Shepherd (www.spasavvy.com); and Liza Quddoos from Four Seasons Resorts.

SRI LANKA Dr Srikantha Arunachalea at the Siddhalepa Ayurveda Health Resort (www.ayurvedaresort.com) and Barberyn Ayurveda Resorts (www.barberynresorts.com).

THAILAND Chami Jotisalikorn of *Thai Spa Book* (www.Chami-J.com); Jens O. Reichert from Anantara Spa (MSpa International); Arlene Finch, Cathy Chon and Ian Brewis from CHI Spas; the team at Chiva-Som International Health Resort; Tisna Prapansiri, Anita Ting and Ingo Schweder from Mandarin Oriental Dhara Dhevi (We are fans!); Sonu and Eva Shivadasani and the gorgeous holistic tribe at Six Senses Resorts & Spas; Florence Jaffre of Ytsara (www.ytsara.com); Andrew Harrison, Maria Kuhn Marjorie Charlton and Andrew Harrison from Four Seasons Resort, Chiang Mai.

Above Treatments at Sejati Spa at Bagus Jati Wellbeing Resort in Bali make good use of local ingredients including lemongrass, cinnamon sticks, ginger and turmeric root.

Left Kirana Spa in Bali is like a temple to the living spirit with its water features, open-sided pavilions and beautiful gardens.

Right Outdoor meditation is popular at the spa at Mandarin Oriental Dhara Dhevi in Thailand.

Photographer's note

This book owes a lot to the women who appear in its pages. I have chosen these models not just for their looks, but because their commitment to creative endeavors make them stand apart from the usual pretty faces on the covers of glossy magazines. Dancer, fashion or jewellery designer, TV personality or movie star, healer or manager, they all give a face to that ideal of beauty that comes from within.

Born in countries as far apart as Bali, Sweden and Mauritius, almost all of them are of mixed parentage, and they give a glimpse of my ideal world of the future, where race and nationality will no longer exist.

Joy (Varaluk Vanichkul), Tui (Tui Sang) and Melati have contributed more than their faces to this project.

Thanks also to Cindy (Sirinya) Burbridge; Kanthima Buncherd; Rebecca Tan; Yana Odnopozof; Tomoka Yamamoto; Maria Nyquist; Shamita Singha; Carolyn Sivaram; Lovelyn (Maria Antonica) Bocus; Emi Stames; Camilla; Catharina Lee Azanza; Jessie Chapman; Simon Wright; Byron Bishop; Pop Areeya Chumsai; Lora Krulak and Lee Wai Ching.

The staff and the managers of the spas we visited have been very helpful in many ways. Special thanks to Tisna Prapansiri and Nan at Mandarin Oriental Dhara Dhevi, Michi at The Ritz-Carlton, Bali Resort & Spa, Frances Espino at The Farm at San Benito, and Perla Eckardt, who found a coffee for me in the most unlikely place.

Thanks also to Michaela MacDonnell of Bali Starz; Rai Von Bueren; Donald Siegel and Kim Inglis for advice and ideas.

Spa Directory

Amrita Spa
Swissôtel Merchant Court, 20 Merchant Court,
Singapore 058281, Tel: +65 6239 1780,
Fax: +65 6239 1781
Email: amrita.merchantcourt@swissotel.com
Website: www.amritaspas.com

Ananda In the Himalayas
The Palace Estate, Narendra Nagar, Tehri—Garhwal,
Uttaranchal 249175, India, Tel: +91 (1378) 227500,
Fax: +91 (1378) 227550
Email: sales@anandaspa.com
Website: www.anandaspa.com

Anantara Resort & Spa Hua Hin
43/1 Phetkasem Beach Road, Hua Hin 77110, Thailand,
Tel: +66 (32) 520 250, Fax: +66 (32) 520 259
Email: infothailand@minornet.com
Website: www.mspa-international.com

Banyan Tree Spa Ringha
Hong Po Village, Jian Tang Town, Shangri-La County,
Diqing Tibetan Autonomous Prefecture, Yunnan
Province, People's Republic of China 674400
Tel: +86 (887) 828 8822, Fax: +86 (887) 828 8911
Email: spa-ringha@banyantree.com,
reservations@banyantree.com
Website: www.banyantree.com

Chiva-Som International Health Resorts Co., Ltd.
73/4 Petchkasem Road, Hua Hin, Prachuabkirikhan
77110, Thailand, Tel: +66 (32) 536 536,
Fax: +66 (32) 511 154
Email: reservation@chivasom.com
Website: www.chivasom.com

Kirana Spa
Desa Kedewatan, Ubud 80571, Bali, Indonesia,
Tel: +62 (361) 976 333, Fax: +62 (361) 974 888
Email: info-english@kiranaspa.com
Website: www.kiranaspa.com

Mandara Spa at Alila Ubud
Desa Melinggih Kelod, Payangan, Giayar 80572, Bali,
Indonesia, Tel: +62 (361) 975 963   ext: 753,
Fax: +62 (361) 975 968
Email: infoasia@mandaraspa.com
Website: www.alilahotels.com;
www.mandaraspa.com

Martha Tilaar Eastern Rejuvenating Center
The Mansion, Private Estate & Spa, Jalan
Penestanan—Sayan, Ubud, Bali 80571, Indonesia
Tel: +62 (361) 972 616, Fax: +62 (361) 972 632
Email: home@the-mansionbali.com
Website: www.the-mansionbali.com

Prana Spa at The Villas
Jalan Kunti 118X, Seminyak, Bali, Indonesia,
Tel: +62 (361) 730 840, Fax: +62 (361) 733 751
Email: contact@thevillas.net
Website: www.thevillas.net

RafflesAmrita Spa
Raffles Hotel, 1 Beach Road, Singapore 189673,
Tel: +65 6337 1886, Fax: +65 6339 7650
Email: Ask-us.singapore-raffles@raffles.com
Website: www.singapore-raffles.raffles.com

Salus Per Aqua Spa
The Farm at San Benito, 119 Barangay Tipakan, Lipa
City, Batangas, Philippines, Tel: +63 (2) 696 3795,
Fax: +63 (2) 696 3175
Email: info@thefarm.com.ph
Website: www.thefarm.com.ph

Sejati Spa at Bagus Jati—Health & Wellbeing Retreat
Br. Jati, Desa Sebatu, Kecamatan Tegallalang,
P.O. Box 4—Ubud, Gianyar—Bali 80572, Indonesia,
Tel: +62 (361) 978 885, Fax: +62 (361) 974 666
Email: info@bagusjati.com
Website: www.bagusjati.com

Sereno Spa
Park Hyatt Goa Resort and Spa, Arossim Beach,
Cansaulim, South Goa 403 712, India,
Tel: +91 (832) 272 1234, Fax: +91 (832) 272 1235
Email: spa.phgoa@hyattintl.com;
parkhyattgoa@hyattintl.com
Website: www.goa.park.hyatt.com

Six Senses Spa
Evason Hua Hin Resort, 9 Moo 3 Paknampran Beach,
Pranburi, Prachuap Khiri Khan 77220, Thailand,
Tel: +66 (32) 632 111, Fax: +66 (32) 632 112
Email: reservations-huahin@evasonresorts.com
Website: www.sixsenses.com/evason-huahin

Spa Botanica
The Sentosa Resort and Spa, 2 Bukit Manis Road,
Sentosa, Singapore 099891
Tel: +65 6371 1318, Fax: +65 6371 1278
Email: info@thesentosa.com
Website: www.spabotanica.com

Spa Village
Pangkor Laut Resort, Pangkor Laut Island, 32200
Lumut, Perak, Malaysia,
Tel: +60 (5) 699 1100 ext: 580
Fax: +60 (5) 699 1025
Email: spavillageplr@ytlhotels.com.my
Website: www.pangkorlautresort.com/spa.html

The Island Spa
Four Seasons Resort Maldives at Kuda Huraa, North
Male Atoll, Republic of Maldives,
Tel: +960 66 44 888, Fax: +960 66 44 800
Email: spa.mal@fourseasons.com
Website: www.fourseasons.com/maldiveskh

The Ritz-Carlton, Bali Thalasso & Spa
The Ritz-Carlton, Bali Resort & Spa,
JL. Karang Mas Sejahtera Jimbaran, Bali 80364,
Indonesia, Tel: +62 (361) 702 222,
Fax: +62 (361) 705 084
Email: spa.reservation@ritzcarlton-bali.com
Website: www.ritzcarlton.com,
www.ritzcarlton-bali.jp

The Spa at Four Seasons Resort Jimbaran Bay
Jimbaran, Denpasar 80361, Bali, Indonesia,
Tel: +62 (361) 701010, Fax: +62 (361) 701020
Email: fsrb.jimbaran@fourseasons.com
Website: www.fourseasons.com/jimbaranbay

The Spa at Four Seasons Resort Sayan
Ubud, Gianyar 80571, Bali, Indonesia,
Tel: +62 (361) 977577, Fax: +62 (361) 977588
Email: sayan.fsrb@fourseasons.com
Website: www.fourseasons.com/sayan

The Spa at Four Seasons Resort Chiang Mai
Mae Rim-Samoeng Old Road, Mae Rim, Chiang Mai
50180, Thailand, Tel: +66 (53) 298 181,
Fax: +66 (53) 298 190
Email: spa.chiangmai@fourseasons.com
Website: www.fourseasons.com/chiangmai

The Spa at Mandarin Oriental Dhara Dhevi
51/4 Chiang Mai-Sankampaeng Road, Moo 1,
T. Tasala, A. Muang, Chiang Mai 50000, Thailand
Tel: +66 (53) 888 888, Fax: +66 (53) 888 999
Email: mocnx-enquiry@mohg.com
Website: www.mandarinoriental.com

The Spa at The Lalu
Sun Moon Lake, 142 Jungshing Road, Yuchr Shiang,
Nantou, Taiwan 555, R.O.C.
Tel: +886 (49) 285 6888, Fax: +886 (49) 285 5688
Email: reservations@thelalu.com.tw
Website: www.thelalu.com.tw

Above The spirit of ayurveda is invoked in this
face as artwork.

Overleaf A beautiful Balinese Kamasan-style
painting at Kirana Spa depicts the rituals of
bathing, showering, massage and relaxation,
all of which are part of the Kirana Spa story.